PENGUIN BOOKS

RUSSIAN PHRASE BOOK

THE PENGUIN PHRASE BOOKS

RUSSIAN
PHRASE BOOK

THIRD EDITION

JILL NORMAN
PAMELA DAVIDSON

PENGUIN BOOKS

PENGUIN BOOKS

Published by the Penguin Group
Penguin Books Ltd, 27 Wrights Lane, London W8 5TZ, England
Penguin Books USA Inc., 375 Hudson Street, New York, New York 10014, USA
Penguin Books Australia Ltd, Ringwood, Victoria, Australia
Penguin Books Canada Ltd, 10 Alcorn Avenue, Toronto, Ontario, Canada M4V 3B2
Penguin Books (NZ) Ltd, 182–190 Wairau Road, Auckland 10, New Zealand

Penguin Books Ltd, Registered Offices: Harmondsworth, Middlesex, England

First published 1969 with text by
Victor Gregory and Jill Norman
Second edition 1980
Third edition 1989
5 7 9 10 8 6 4

Printed in England by Clays Ltd, St Ives plc
Filmset in Lasercomp Ehrhardt

CONTENTS

INTRODUCTION

In this series of phrase books only those words and phrases that are essential to the traveller have been included. For easy reference the phrases are divided into several sections, each one dealing with a different situation. Some of the Russian phrases are marked with an asterisk* – these attempt to give an indication of the kind of reply you may get to your questions, or of questions you may be asked. Capital letters are used to indicate street signs and other notices that you should be aware of.

A transcript which incorporates a pronunciation guide is provided for each phrase, and for each word in the extensive vocabulary list at the end of the book. In addition there is an explanation of Russian pronunciation at the beginning of the book and a brief survey of the essential points of grammar on page 245. It would be advisable to read these sections before starting to use the book.

ALPHABET & PRONUNCIATION

There are thirty-three letters in the Russian alphabet. The first column shows the printed letters, capital and small. The second column shows the letters as they are written, capital and small. The third column gives the symbols which have been adopted throughout the phrase book to represent Russian letters in a system of transliteration. Finally, in the fourth column, an approximate guide to the pronunciation of each Russian letter or equivalent symbol is given.

The pronunciation guide is intended for people with no knowledge of Russian. As far as possible the system is based on English pronunciation. Each phrase and each word in the vocabulary is transliterated in roman characters in accordance with this pronunciation guide. As a result complete accuracy may sometimes be lost for the sake of simplicity, but if the reader learns the Russian alphabet and the pronunciation of the letters he should be able to understand some Russian and make himself understood.

Printed	*Written*	*Symbol*	*Approximate pronunciation*	
А а	*А а*	a	a	in car *when stressed*
			a	in aloud *when unstressed*
Б б	*Б б*	b	b	in book
В в	*В в*	v	v	in vice
Г г	*Г г*	g	g	in get

Printed	*Written*	*Symbol*	*Approximate pronunciation*	
Д д	*Д д*	d	d	in day
Е е[1]	*Е е*	yé	ye	in yes
Ё ё	*Ё ё*	yo	yo	in yonder
Ж ж[2]	*Ж ж*	zh	s	in pleasure
З з	*З з*	z	z	in zone
И и	*И и*	ee	ee	in meet
Й й[3]	*Й й*	y	y	in boy
К к	*К к*	k	k	in kind
Л л[4]	*Л л*	l	l	in lamp
М м	*М м*	m	m	in man
Н н	*Н н*	n	n	in nut
О о	*О о*	o	o	in pot *when stressed*
		a	a	in aloud *when unstressed*
П п	*П п*	p	p	in pen
Р р[5]	*Р р*	r	r	in rose
С с	*С с*	s	s	in sea
Т т	*Т т Т т*	t	t	in top
У у	*У у*	oo	oo	in boot
Ф ф	*Ф ф*	f	f	in fat
Х х[6]	*Х х*	h	h	in hard
Ц ц	*Ц ц*	ts	ts	in lots
Ч ч	*Ч ч*	ch	ch	in chair
Ш ш	*Ш ш*	sh	sh	in ship *hard sound*
Щ щ[7]	*Щ щ*	sh	sh	in shoe *soft sound*
Ъ ъ	*ъ*	none		not pronounced, but suggests a slight separation from the next letter
Ы ы	*ы*	i	i	in ill
Ь ь[8]	*ь*	'		softens the preceding consonant
Э э	*Э э*	e	e	in met
Ю ю	*Ю ю*	yoo	u	in use
Я я	*Я я*	ya	ya	in yard

NOTES

1. The letter **e** is represented by the symbol yé with an accent in order to remind readers to pronounce syllables like pyé to rhyme with the French word pied rather than with the English word pie.
2. The letter **ж** is the same as the French j in bonjour.
3. The letter **й** is a semi-vowel, and is always used together with a full vowel to form a diphthong. It has the effect of adding a y sound to the end of a vowel. The Russian pronunciation of the preceding vowel should always be retained. For example the Russian word **рай** (paradise) is transliterated ray; the a in this word should be pronounced like the a in car, and the sound of the whole word should be closer to the sound of the English word rye than to the sound of the English word ray.
4. The letter **л** (l) is normally pronounced like the l in lamp. When followed by a soft sign, **ь** (represented in transliteration by the symbol '), it is softened and pronounced like the l in million.
5. The letter **р** (r) has no exact equivalent in English. It is always rolled, and is closer to a French **r** in sound.
6. The letter **х** (h) has no exact equivalent in English. It is like the ch in the Scottish word loch or in the German word Buch. In the transliteration system it is represented by the letter h which should be strongly aspirated.
7. The letter **щ** is often transliterated as shch, pronounced as one sound. However, since in practice the sound щ is often indistinguishable from the sound ш, it has been rendered by the same symbol in this phrase book for the sake of greater simplicity and ease of reading.
8. The soft sign **ь** is not pronounced as a separate sound, but has the effect of softening the pronunciation of the consonant which precedes it. This letter, the letter **ы**, and the hard sign **ъ** can never begin a word.

Stress

It is important to stress Russian words correctly. The stressed syllable should be pronounced with much greater emphasis than the unstressed syllables. This will automatically weaken, and in some cases change the sound, of the unstressed vowels. A stressed a sounds like the a in father, and a stressed o sounds like the o in pot; however, when unstressed, both vowels sound more like the a in aloud. In the Russian script, the stress is indicated by an accent mark over the vowel in the syllable which is stressed (ко́мната). In the English transliteration, the stressed syllable is printed in **bold** type (**kom**-na-ta). The stress is not marked on words of one syllable, or on the letter ё, since these are both always stressed.

ESSENTIALS

FIRST THINGS

Yes	Да	da
No	Нет	nyét
Please	Пожáлуйста	pa-zha-loo-sta
Thank you	Спасúбо	spa-see-ba

LANGUAGE PROBLEMS

I'm British/ I'm American	Я из Великобритáнии/ я из Амéрики	ya eez vyé-lee-ka-bree-ta-nee-ee/ya eez-a-myé-ree-kee
Do you speak English?	Вы говорúте по-англúйски?	vi ga-va-ree-tyé pa-an-gleey-skee

Does anybody here speak English?	Здесь кто-нибу́дь говори́т по-англи́йски?	zdyés' kto-nee-**boot** ga-va-**reet** pa-an-**gleey**-skee
I don't speak Russian	Я не говорю́ по-ру́сски	ya nyé ga-va-**ryoo** pa-**rooss**-kee
I speak a little Russian	Я немно́го говорю́ по-ру́сски	ya nyé-**mno**-ga ga-va-**ryoo** pa-**rooss**-kee
I don't understand	Я не понима́ю	ya nyé pa-nee-**ma**-yoo
I understand	Я понима́ю	ya pa-nee-**ma**-yoo
Do you understand me?	Вы меня́ понима́ете?	vi me-**nya** pa-nee-**ma**-yé-tyé
What does that mean?	Что э́то зна́чит?	shto **é**-ta **zna**-cheet
What is this called in Russian?	Как э́то называ́ется по-ру́сски?	kak **é**-ta na-zi-**va**-yét-sa pa-**rooss**-kee
Can you translate this for me?	Переведи́те мне э́то, пожа́луйста	pyé-ryé-vyé-**dee**-tyé mnyé **e**-ta, pa-**zha**-loo-sta
Could you please repeat that?	Повтори́те, пожа́луйста	paf-ta-**ree**-tyé, pa-**zha**-loo-sta
Please speak slowly	Говори́те, пожа́луйста, ме́дленнее	ga-va-**ree**-tyé, pa-**zha**-loo-sta, **myé**-dlyén-nyé-yé
Please write it down	Запиши́те, пожа́луйста	za-pee-**shi**-tyé, pa-**zha**-loo-sta
Please show me the word in the book	Пожа́луйста, покажи́те э́то сло́во в кни́ге	pa-**zha**-loo-sta, pa-ka-**zhi**-tyé **e**-ta **slo**-va fknee-**gyé**

I'll look in my phrase book	Я посмотрю́ в разгово́рнике	ya pa-sma-tryoo fraz-ga-vor-nee-kyé

QUESTIONS

Where is the women's toilet?	Где же́нский туале́т?	gdyé zhen-skeey too-a-lyét
Where is the men's toilet?	Где мужско́й туале́т?	gdyé moozh-skoy too-a-lyét
Where is/are ... ?	Где ... ?	gdyé ...
When ... ?	Когда́ ... ?	kag-da ...
Why?	Почему́?	pa-chyé-moo
How ... ?	Как ... ?	kak ...
What ... ?	Что ... ?	shto ...
Which ... ?	Како́й ... ?	ka-koy ...
What is it?	Что э́то?	shto e-ta
Who ... ?	Кто ... ?	kto ...
Who is that?	Кто э́то?	kto é-ta
Is there/are there ... ?	Есть ли ... ?	yést'-lee ...
Do you have ... ?	У вас есть ... ? (+ nom.)	oo-vas yést' ...
How much/many ... ?	Ско́лько ... ? (+ gen.)	skol'-ka ...
How much is ... ?	Ско́лько сто́ит ... ?	skol'-ka sto-eet ...
How long?	Как до́лго?	kak dol-ga

May I/we ...?	Мóжно ...? (+inf.)	mozh-na ...
What's the matter?	В чём дéло?	fchyom dyé-la
What should I do?	Что мне дéлать?	shto mnyé dyé-lat'
Where can I find ...?	Где мóжно найтú ...? (+acc.)	gdyé mozh-na nay-tee ...
What do you want?	Что вы хотúте?	shto vi ha-tee-tyé
Have you seen ...?	Вы вúдели ...? (+ acc.)	vi vee-dyé-lee ...

REQUESTS

Could I please have ...?	Дáйте мне, пожáлуйста ... (+ acc.)	day-tyé mnyé, pa-zha-loo-sta ...
Please bring ...	Принесúте, пожáлуйста ... (+ acc.)	pree-nyé-see-tyé, pa-zha-loo-sta ...
Please show that to me	Покажúте мне, пожáлуйста, э́то	pa-ka-zhi-tyé mnyé, pa-zha-loo-sta, e-ta
Please let me pass	Разрешúте мне пройтú	raz-ryé-shi-tyé mnyé pray-tee
Come here, please	*Подойдúте сюдá, пожáлуйста	pa-day-dee-tyé syoo-da, pa-zha-loo-sta
May I come in?	Мóжно войтú?	mozh-na vay-tee
Come in	*Войдúте	vay-dee-tyé
Just a moment	*Минýточку	mee-noo-tach-koo

Please wait	*Подождите, пожалуйста	pa-dazh-dee-tyé, pa-zha-loo-sta
Hurry up/quickly	Скорée	ska-ryé-yé

USEFUL STATEMENTS

It is/it does ...	Э́то ... (+ adj./+ verb)	é-ta ...
It isn't/it doesn't ...	Э́то не ... (+ adj./+ verb)	é-ta nyé ...
I am not/I don't ...	Я не ... (+ adj./+ verb)	ya nyé ...
There isn't any/aren't any ...	Нет ... (+ gen.)	nyét ...
I have ...	У меня́ ... (+ nom.)	oo-me-nya ...
I don't have ...	У меня́ нет ... (+ gen.)	oo-me-nya nyét ...
He has ...	У него́ ... (+ nom.)	oo-nyé-vo ...
She hasn't ...	У неё нет ... (+ gen.)	oo-nyé-yo nyét ...
I want ...	Я хочу́ ... (+ acc.)	ya ha-choo ...
I don't want ...	Я не хочу́ ... (+ gen.)	ya nyé ha-choo ...
I like it	Мне э́то нра́вится	mnyé e-ta nra-veet-sa
I don't like it	Мне э́то не нра́вится	mnyé é-ta nyé nra-veet-sa
I don't know	Я не зна́ю	ya nyé zna-yoo

I didn't know	Я не знал/зна́ла *f*	ya nyé znal/zna-la
I need to ...	Мне ну́жно ... (+ inf.)	mnyé noozh-na ...
I'm looking for ...	Я ищу́ ... (+ acc.)	ya ee-shoo ...
Here it is	Вот	vot
There they are	Вот они	vot a-nee
I'm hungry	Я голо́ден/голо́дна *f*	ya ga-lo-dyén/ga-lod-na
I'm thirsty	Я хочу́ пить	ya ha-choo peet'
I'm in a hurry	Я спешу́	ya spyé-shoo
I'm tired	Я уста́л/уста́ла *f*	ya oo-stal/oo-sta-la
I want to have a rest	Я хочу́ отдохну́ть	ya ha-choo at-dah-noot'
I'm lost	Я заблуди́лся/заблуди́лась *f*	ya za-bloo-deel-sa/za-bloo-dee-las'
I'm ready	Я гото́в/гото́ва *f*	ya ga-tof/ga-to-va
It's not my fault	Я не винова́т/винова́та *f*	ya nyé vee-na-vat/vee-na-va-ta
You are mistaken	Вы оши́блись	vi a-shi-blees'
You're right/you're wrong	Вы пра́вы/вы непра́вы	vi pra-vi/vi nyé-pra-vi
Good/that's fine	Хорошо́	ha-ra-sho
It's annoying	Э́то доса́дно	é-ta da-sad-na
It's pretty/beautiful	Э́то краси́во	é-ta kra-see-va
It's very important	Э́то о́чень ва́жно	é-ta o-chyén' vazh-na
It's urgent	Э́то сро́чно	é-ta sroch-na

GREETINGS

Hello	Здра́вствуйте	zdrast-vooy-tyé
How are you?	Как дела́?	kak dyé-la
Fine, thank you	Спаси́бо, хорошо́	spa-see-ba, ha-ra-sho
Good morning	До́брое утро	do-bra-yé oo-tra
Good day	До́брый день	do-briy dyén'
Good evening	До́брый ве́чер	do-briy vyé-chyér
Good night	Споко́йной но́чи	spa-koy-noy no-chee
Goodbye	До свида́ния	da-svee-da-nya
See you soon *most informal*	Пока́	pa-ka
Bon voyage!	Счастли́вого пути́!	shas-lee-va-va poo-tee

POLITE PHRASES

Could you please tell me ...[1]	Скажи́те, пожа́луйста ...	ska-zhi-tyé, pa-zha-loo-sta ...
Would you be so kind ...	Бу́дьте добры́ ...	bood'-tyé da-bri ...
Excuse me (please) ...	Извини́те (пожа́луйста) ...	eez-vee-nee-tyé (pa-zha-loo-sta) ...

1. The first three phrases in this section are all useful expressions for attracting someone's attention before asking a question.

Sorry	Прости́те	**pra-stee-tyé**
That's all right *in reply to sorry*	Ничего́	**nee-chyé-vo**
You're welcome *in reply to thanks*	Пожа́луйста	**pa-zha-loo-sta**
I would be very grateful ...	Я вас о́чень прошу́ ...	ya vas o-**chyén'** pra-**shoo** ...
Don't worry	Не беспоко́йтесь	nyé byés-pa-**koy**-tyés'
With pleasure	С удово́льствием	soo-da-**vol'**-stvee-yém
Am I disturbing you?	Я вам не меша́ю?	ya vam nyé myé-**sha**-yoo
Excuse me, what did you say?	Извини́те, что вы сказа́ли?	eez-vee-**nee**-tyé, shto vi ska-**za**-lee

SIGNS & PUBLIC NOTICES

In this section you will find an alphabetical list of the main signs and public notices which you are likely to come across in the Soviet Union. The list does not include large signs displayed on buildings and kiosks, identifying shops and public places – these signs are grouped together at the beginning of the shopping section (page 104). Signs which you will only come across in specific situations are given in the sections which deal with these situations: travel (page 19), the metro (page 38), the hotel (page 58), going to a restaurant (page 77), in the post office (page 145), telephoning (page 152), museums (page 162), entertainment (page 166), on the beach (page 177), driving (page 184) and at the doctor's (page 213).

Street signs are given in the 'Directions' section (page 50).

БЕЗ СТУКА НЕ ВХОДИТЬ	Knock before entering
БЕРЕГИСЬ	Caution
БЕРЕГИСЬ АВТОМОБИЛЯ	Beware of vehicles
ВХОД	Entrance
ВХОДА НЕТ	No entry
ВХОД ВОСПРЕЩЁН	No admission
ВЫХОД	Exit
ВЫХОДА НЕТ	No exit

Ж/ЖЕНСКАЯ КОМНАТА/ ЖЕНСКИЙ ТУАЛЕТ	Women's toilet
ЗАКРЫТО (НА РЕМОНТ)	Closed (for repairs)
ЗАНЯТО	Engaged/Occupied/Reserved
ЗАПАСНОЙ ВЫХОД	Emergency exit
КАССА/КАССЫ	Ticket-office/Cash desk
К СЕБЕ	Pull
КУРИТЕЛЬНАЯ КОМНАТА	Smoking room
КУРИТЬ ВОСПРЕЩАЕТСЯ	No smoking
ЛИФТ	Lift
М	Metro
МЕСТА ЕСТЬ	Places available
МЕСТ НЕТ	Full up
МЕТРО	Metro
М/МУЖСКАЯ КОМНАТА/ МУЖСКОЙ ТУАЛЕТ	Men's toilet
НЕ ДЛЯ ПИТЬЯ	Not for drinking
НЕ КУРИТЬ	No smoking
НЕ РАБОТАЕТ	Out of order
НЕТ МЕСТ	Full up
НЕ ТРОГАТЬ	Do not touch
ОКРАШЕНО	Wet paint
ОПАСНО ДЛЯ ЖИЗНИ	Danger
ОСТОРОЖНО	Caution
ОТКРЫТО	Open
ОТ СЕБЯ	Push
ПЕРЕВОДЧИК	Translator
ПЕРЕХОД	Pedestrian crossing
ПИТЬЕВАЯ ВОДА	Drinking water
ПО ГАЗОНАМ НЕ ХОДИТЬ	Please keep off the grass

ПОСТОРОННИМ ВХОД ВОСПРЕЩЁН	Private/No admittance
ПРОСЬБА НЕ КУРИТЬ	No smoking
РЕМОНТ	Under repair
РУКАМИ НЕ ТРОГАТЬ	Do not touch
СВОБОДНО	Vacant/Unoccupied
СЛУЖЕБНОЕ ПОМЕЩЕНИЕ	Staff only
СЛУЖЕБНЫЙ ВХОД	Staff entrance
СПРАВКИ	Information
СПРАВОЧНОЕ БЮРО	Information bureau
СТОП	Stop
СТОЯНКА ТАКСИ	Taxi rank
ТЕЛЕФОН (НЕ РАБОТАЕТ)	Telephone (out of order)
ТУАЛЕТ	Toilet
УБОРНАЯ	Toilet
У НАС НЕ КУРЯТ	No smoking

ABBREVIATIONS[1]

Abbreviations are widely used in the Soviet Union. Here is a list of some of the most common abbreviations which you are likely to meet, their meaning, and their pronunciation in cases where the abbreviation is used as a word in its own right.

АЗС (a-zé-és)	автозаправочная станция	petrol station
АН	Академия наук	Academy of Sciences

1. See also p. 54 for Russian addresses.

АПН (a-pé-én)	Агентство Печати Новости	Novosti Press Agency
АССР (a-és-és-ér)	автономная советская социалистическая республика	Autonomous Soviet Socialist Republic
в.	век	century
в	вольт	volts
вв.	века	centuries
ВДНХ (vé-dé-én-ha)	Выставка достижений народного хозяйства СССР	U.S.S.R. Economic Achievements Exhibition
ВЛКСМ (vé-él-ka-és-ém)	Всесоюзный Ленинский Коммунистический Союз Молодёжи	the 'Komsomol' Young Communist League
вт	ватт	watts
ВУЗ (vooz)	высшее учебное заведение	higher educational institution
г.	год	year
г./гор.	город	town
г	грамм	gram
ГАИ (ga-ee)	Государственная автомобильная инспекция	State Traffic Police

гг.	годы	years
гл.	глава	chapter
гр.	гражданин/ гражданка	citizen *m/f*
ГУМ (goom)	Государственный универсальный магазин	State Department Store
д./дер.	деревня	village
ДК (dé-ka)	Дворец культуры	Palace of Culture
до н.э.	до нашей эры	B.C.
ж.д.	железная дорога	railway
к.	комната	room
к.	копейка	kopeck
кг	килограмм	kilogram
КГБ (ka-gé-bé)	Комитет государственной безопасности	KGB – Committee for State Security
кл.	класс	class
км	километр	kilometre
коп.	копейка	kopeck
КПСС (ka-pé-és-és)	Коммунистическая партия Советского Союза	Communist Party of the Soviet Union
л	литр	litre

м	метр	metre
МГУ (ém-gé-oo)	Московский государственный университет	Moscow State University
млн.	миллион	million
мм	миллиметр	millimetre
МХАТ (mhat)	Московский Художественный академический театр	Moscow Art Theatre
н.	номер	number
нач.	начальник	director
н.э.	нашей зры	A.D.
о.	остров	island
обл.	область	region
ОВИР (o-veer)	отдел виз и регистрации иностранцев	department for visas and registration of foreigners
оз.	озеро	lake
ок.	около	near/about
пос.	посёлок	village
р.	река	river
р.	рубль	rouble

РСФСР (ér-és-éf-és-ér)	Российская Советская Федеративная Социалистическая Республика	Russian Soviet Federal Socialist Republic
с.	ссло	village
СА (és-a)	Советская Армия	Soviet Army
сб.	сборник	collection
св.	святой	saint
с.г.	сего года	of this year
сек.	секунда	second
см	сантиметр	centimetre
СССР (és-és-és-ér)	Союз Советских Социалистических Республик	Union of Soviet Socialist Republics
ст.	станция	station
ст.	старший	the elder
стр.	страница	page
США (s-sha)	Соединённые Штаты Америки	United States of America
т.	товарищ	comrade
ТАСС (tass)	Телеграфное агенство Советского Союза	TASS – Soviet News Agency

т.д.	так далее	etc.
т.е.	то есть	i.e.
тел.	телефон	telephone
тов.	товарищ	comrade
тыс.	тысяча	thousand
ул./у.	улица	street
ЦК (tsé-ka)	Центральный Комитет	Central Committee
ЦУМ (tsoom)	Центральный универмаг	Central Department Store
ч.	час	hour
ч.	часть	part
шт.	штука	article/item

MONEY

All foreign currency brought into the U.S.S.R. must be registered with customs on arrival, and can only be changed into roubles at branches and exchange offices of the U.S.S.R. State Bank and of the U.S.S.R. Foreign Trade Bank at the official rate of exchange set by the bank. Any other foreign-currency transactions are illegal. Official exchange offices are at air, sea, road, and rail entry points, and at Intourist hotels. You will probably find it most convenient to change money in your hotel. When foreign currency and traveller's cheques are exchanged for roubles on the basis of the customs certificate, the tourist receives a bank receipt which enables him to change any unused roubles back into foreign currency. This can only be done on departure from the U.S.S.R. before passing through customs and passport control. It is illegal to import or export roubles.

Foreign currency is only accepted in foreign-currency shops and some bars, and as payment for Intourist services. The foreign-currency shops ('Beryozka') will also accept major international credit cards such as Access, Visa, American Express, but not Eurocheques.

Soviet national currency: The basic unit of money is the rouble, which consists of 100 kopecks. There are notes for 1, 3, 5, 10, 25, 50, and 100 roubles. Each note has a distinctive colour: 1-rouble notes are yellow, 3-rouble notes are green, 5-rouble notes are blue, 10-rouble notes are red, and

25-rouble notes are purple. There are copper coins for 1, 2, 3, and 5 kopecks, and silver coins for 10, 15, 20, and 50 kopecks, and for 1 rouble.

Where can I change some money?	Где мóжно обменя́ть дéньги?	gdyé mozh-na ab-myé-nyat' dyén'-gee
I want to change some	Я хочу́ обменя́ть	ya ha-choo ab-myé-nyat'
pounds/dollars	фу́нты/дóллары	foon-ti/dol-la-ri
traveller's cheques	дорóжные чéки	da-rozh-ni-yé chyé-kee
What is the exchange rate for pounds/dollars?	Какóй курс фу́нта/дóллара?	ka-koy koors foon-ta/dol-la-ra
How many roubles will I get	Скóлько рублéй я получу́	skol'-ka roo-blyéy ya pa-loo-choo
for ... pounds?	за ... фу́нтов	za ... foon-taf?
for ... dollars?	за ... дóлларов?	za ... dol-la-raf
Please give me your customs declaration form	*Дáйте вáшу тамóженную декларáцию	day-tyé va-shoo ta-mo-zhén-noo-yoo dyé-kla-ra-tsi-yoo
Please sign	*Подпиши́те, пожáлуйста	pad-pee-shi-tyé, pa-zha-loo-sta
Where should I sign?	Где мне подписáть?	gdyé mnyé pad-pee-sat'
Can you give me some small change?	Дáйте мне мéлочь, пожáлуйста	day-tyé mnyé myé-lach', pa-zha-loo-sta
Will you take a credit card?	Вы принимáете креди́тные кáрточки?	vi pree-nee-ma-yé-tyé kryé-deet-ni-yé kar-tach-kee

TRAVEL

ARRIVAL AND CUSTOMS

When entering the Soviet Union foreign tourists must complete a customs declaration form; this must be presented again on departure, together with a newly completed customs form. All currency and valuables which you are bringing into the U.S.S.R. must be registered on this form, which enables you to change foreign currency into roubles at official exchange offices, and to re-export your currency and valuables at the end of your visit.

Customs inspection of luggage is conducted in the presence of the owner at entry and exit points. It is illegal to import or export firearms and drugs; fresh fruit and vegetables must be submitted for inspection on entry. It is also illegal to import publications which may be construed as harmful to the U.S.S.R., and to export antiques and works of art (unless you have an export permit, issued by the Ministry of Culture on payment of a special tax).

Your passport, please	*Ваш па́спорт, пожа́луйста	**vash pas-part, pa-zha-loo-sta**

I need a customs declaration form in English	Мне ну́жен бланк деклара́ции по-англи́йски	mnyé noo-zhén blank dyé-kla-ra-tsi-ee pa-an-gleey-skee
Where is your customs declaration form?	*Где ва́ша тамо́женная деклара́ция?	gdyé va-sha ta-mo-zhén-na-ya dyé-kla-ra-tsi-ya
I have come	Я прие́хал/прие́хала *f* . . .	ya pree-yé-hal/pree-yé-ha-la
from England/from America	из А́нглии/из Аме́рики	eez-an-glee-ee/ eez-a-myé-ree-kee
with a group of tourists	с туристи́ческой гру́ппой	stoo-rees-tee-chyés-koy groop-poy
on a private invitation	по ча́стному приглаше́нию	pa-chas-na-moo pree-gla-shé-nee-yo
on business	по дела́м	pa-dyé-lam
We are together	Мы вме́сте	mi vmyé-styé
Where is your luggage?	*Где ваш бага́ж?	gdyé vash ba-gazh
This is my luggage	Э́то мой бага́ж	é-ta moy ba-gazh
That isn't my suitcase	Э́то не мой чемода́н	é-ta nyé moy chyé-ma-dan
Where is my luggage?	Где мой бага́ж?	gdyé moy ba-gazh
Open your suitcase	*Откро́йте чемода́н	at-kroy-tyé chyé-ma-dan
Do you have any books?	*У вас есть кни́ги?	oo-vas yést' knee-gee

have only my personal things in it	Здесь то́лько мой ли́чные ве́щи	zdyés' tol'-ka ma-ee leech-ni-yé vyé-shee
t is a present	Э́то пода́рок	e-ta pa-da-rak
You will have to pay duty on this	*Вы должны́ плати́ть по́шлину за э́то	vi dalzh-ni pla-teet' posh-li-noo za e-ta
May I shut my case?	Мо́жно мне закры́ть чемода́н?	mozh-na mnyé za-krit' chyé-ma-dan
May I go through?	Могу́ ли я идти́?	ma-goo-lee ya eet-tee
You may go now	*Вы мо́жете идти́	vi mo-zhé-tyé eet-tee

MOVING ON

Where is the Intourist representative?	Где представи́тель Интури́ста?	gdyé pryéd-sta-vee-tyél' een-too-rees-ta
My luggage has not arrived	Мой бага́ж ещё не при́был	moy ba-gazh yé-sho nyé pree-bil
My luggage is damaged	Мой бага́ж повреждён	moy ba-gazh pa-vryézh-dyon
One suitcase is missing	Недостаёт одного́ чемода́на	nyé-da-sta-yot ad-na-vo chyé-ma-da-na
Are there any luggage trolleys?	Здесь есть теле́жки для багажа́?	zdyés' yést' tyé-lyézh-kee dlya ba-ga-zha
Is there a bus/train into the town?	Есть ли авто́бус/по́езд, кото́рый идёт в го́род?	yést' lee af-to-boos/po-yézd, ka-to-riy ee-dyot fgo-rat

How can I get to ...?	Как мне добра́ться до ...? (+ gen.)	kak mnyé da-**brat'**-sa do ...
Porter, take my luggage to the taxi rank please	Носи́льщик, к такси́, пожа́луйста	na-**seel'**-sheek, ktak-**see**, pa-**zha**-loo-sta

ВЫХОД В ГОРОД	To the city
В ГОРОД	To the city
К ТАКСИ	To the taxi rank
К МЕТРО	To the metro

BY TRAIN

If you are travelling in the Soviet Union, it is likely that you will either have booked the tickets in advance through Intourist, or that you will buy tickets through the service bureau of your hotel. It is not possible for a foreigner simply to buy a ticket at a station or booking office in the usual way, since he must first have the authorization to travel.

INQUIRIES AND TIMETABLES

There are large timetables on display at stations, as well as information bureaux and various automatic push-button devices for consulting information stored on cards. Timetables for main-line trains and for suburban-line trains are often in different places; main-line trains are usually numbered.

СПРАВОЧНОЕ БЮРО	Information bureau
СПРАВКИ	Information
РАСПИСАНИЕ	Timetable
РАСПИСАНИЕ ПОЕЗДОВ	Train timetable
РАСПИСАНИЕ ДВИЖЕНИЯ ПОЕЗДОВ	Train timetable

РАСПИСАНИЕ ПОЕЗДОВ ДАЛЬНЕГО СЛЕДОВАНИЯ	Main-line trains timetable
РАСПИСАНИЕ ПРИГОРОДНЫХ ПОЕЗДОВ	Suburban-line trains timetable
ПРИГОРОДНЫЕ ПОЕЗДА	Suburban lines
ПРИБЫТИЕ	Arrivals
ОТПРАВЛЕНИЕ	Departures
ПЛАТФОРМА № ...	Platform No ...
ИЗ ...	From ...
№ ПОЕЗДА ...	Train No ...
ВРЕМЯ ОТПРАВЛЕНИЯ	Departure time
ПРИБЫТИЕ В ...	Arrival time at ...

Where is the train timetable?	Где расписа́ние поездо́в?	gdyé ras-pee-sa-nee-yé pa-yéz-dof
Where is the suburban train timetable?	Где расписа́ние при́городных поездо́в?	gdyé ras-pee-sa-nee-yé pree-ga-rad-nih pa-yéz-dof
Where is the information bureau?	Где спра́вочное бюро́?	gdyé spra-vach-na-yé byoo-ro
How often do the trains to ... run?[1]	Как ча́сто хо́дят поезда́ в ... ? (+ acc.)	kak chas-ta ho-dyat pa-yéz-da v ...
When does the next train for ... leave?[2]	Когда́ отхо́дит сле́дующий по́езд в ... ? (+ acc.)	kag-da at-ho-deet slyé-doo-sheey po-yézt v ...

1. See the list 'Towns in the Soviet Union' (p. 47).
2. See 'Times and Dates' (p. 228).

Is there a train earlier/later?	Есть ли по́езд ра́ньше/по́зже?	**yést'-lee po-yézt ran'-shé/po-zhé**
How long does the train to ... take?	Ско́лько вре́мени идёт по́езд до ...? (+ gen.)	**skol'-ka vryé-myé-nee ee-dyot po-yézt da ...**
Do I need to change trains?	Мне на́до сде́лать переса́дку?	**mnyé na-da zdyé-lat' pyé-ryé-sat-koo**
Where should I change trains?	Где мне на́до сде́лать переса́дку?	**gdyé mnyé na-da zdyé-lat' pyé-ryé-sat-koo**

BUYING A TICKET

There are different ticket offices for main-line and suburban-line services. You are most likely to use this section when making a journey into the suburbs or outlying countryside by **e-lyék-treech-ka** (ЭЛЕКТРИ́ЧКА). This is a slow, stopping train which runs on electricity. Tickets for these trains are obtainable at suburban-line ticket offices or from automatic ticket-dispensing machines. For this you must first establish the number of the zone (ЗО́НА – **zona**) in which the station you want to travel to is located; there is usually a large map on display which shows the different zones into which an area is divided. To use the ticket-machine, insert the correct number of coins, and press a button to show which zone you are travelling to, and whether you want a single or return ticket. If you do not have the right change for the machine, you can get it from a window in the ticket office.

КАССА	Tickets
БИЛЕТНЫЕ КАССЫ	Tickets
ЗАЛ ПРОДАЖИ БИЛЕТОВ	Ticket office
КАССА ПРЕДВАРИТЕЛЬНОЙ ПРОДАЖИ БИЛЕТОВ	Booking office

ПОЕЗДА ДАЛЬНЕГО СЛЕДОВАНИЯ	Main lines
ПРОДАЖА БИЛЕТОВ НА ПОЕЗДА ДАЛЬНЕГО СЛЕДОВАНИЯ	Tickets for main-line trains
ПРИГОРОДНЫЕ ПОЕЗДА	Suburban lines
КАССЫ ПРИГОРОДНЫХ ПОЕЗДОВ	Tickets for suburban-line trains
ПРОДАЖА БИЛЕТОВ НА ПРИГОРОДНЫЕ ПОЕЗДА	Tickets for suburban-line trains

Where is the ticket office?	Где ка́ссы?	**gdyé kas-si**
Where is the advance booking office?	Где ка́ссы предвари́тельной прода́жи биле́тов?	**gdyé kas-si pryéd-va-ree-tyél'-noy pra-da-zhi bee-lyé-taf**
Where is the suburban ticket office?	Где ка́ссы при́городных поездо́в?	**gdyé kas-si pree-ga-rad-nih pa-yéz-dof**
One ticket to ...[1]	Оди́н биле́т до ... (+ gen.)	**a-deen bee-lyét da ...**
A return ticket?	*Туда и обратно?[2]	**too-da ee a-brat-na**
A return ticket to ...	Оди́н биле́т до ... (+ gen.), туда́ и обра́тно	**a-deen bee-lyét da ..., too-da ee a-brat-na**

1. See the list 'Towns in the Soviet Union' (p. 47).
2. The literal meaning of this expression is 'there and back'.

Two/three return tickets to ...	Два/три билéта до ... (+ gen.), тудá и обрáтно	dva/tree bee-lyé-ta da ... , too-da ee a-brat-na
on the fast train[1]	на скóрый пóезд	na sko-riy po-yézt
on the commuters' train[2]	на пассажи́рский пóезд	na pas-sa-zhir-skeey po-yézt
in a first-class two-berth sleeping compartment	в междунарóдном вагóне	fmyézh-doo-na-rod-nam va-go-nyé
in a first-class four-berth sleeping compartment	в мя́гком вагóне	fmyag-kam va-go-nyé
in a second-class four-berth sleeping compartment	в купéйном вагóне	fkoo-pyéy-nam va-go-nyé
Please give me	Дáйте мне, пожáлуйста	day-tyé mnyé, pa-zha-loo-sta
a lower berth	ни́жнюю пóлку	neezh-nyoo-yoo pol-koo
an upper berth	вéрхнюю пóлку	vyérh-nyoo-yoo pol-koo

1. A long-distance train, stopping only at main stations.
2. An inter-city train stopping frequently but not at all stations.

AT THE STATION

Where is the	Где	gdyé
waiting room?	ЗАЛ ОЖИДА́НИЯ?[1]	zal a-zhi-da-nee-ya
left-luggage room?[2]	КА́МЕРА ХРАНЕ́НИЯ?	ka-myé-ra hra-nyé-nee-ya
lost-property office?	БЮРО́ НАХО́ДОК?	byoo-ro na-ho-dak
mothers' and children's room?	КО́МНАТА МА́ТЕРИ И РЕБЁНКА?	kom-na-ta ma-tyé-ree ee ryé-byon-ka
snack bar/ restaurant?[3]	БУФЕ́Т/ РЕСТОРА́Н?	boo-fyét/ryés-ta-ran

DEPARTURE

Various signs which you may need to know in order to find your train are given in this section, including the information which you will find on your ticket. Porters charge 30 kopecks per piece of luggage.

At the station

К ПОЕЗДАМ ДАЛЬНЕГО СЛЕДОВАНИЯ	To main-line trains
ВЫХОД К ПРИГОРОДНЫМ ПОЕЗДАМ	To suburban-line trains

1. The use of capitals indicates that a word also appears on signs.
2. Left-luggage rooms usually have combination-lock individual lockers which you can operate yourself, using a 15-kopeck coin.
3. See 'Going to a Restaurant' (p. 77).

НА МОСКВУ	To Moscow
НА ЛЕНИНГРАД	To Leningrad

On the platform

ОТПРАВЛЕНИЕ ...	Departure ...
ПОЕЗД ...	Train ...
ПЛАТФОРМА ...	Platform ...
ПУТЬ ...	Line ...

On your ticket

... ВОКЗАЛ	... station
ПОЕЗД ...	Train ...
ВАГОН ...	Carriage ...
МЕСТО ...	Seat/berth ...
ОТПРАВЛЕНИЕ	Departure

Where can I find a porter?	Где здесь носи́льщик?	gdyé zdyés' na-**seel'**-sheek
Please take my luggage to train number ...	Доста́вьте, пожа́луйста, мой багаж в по́езд но́мер ...	da-**staf**-tyé, pa-**zha**-loo-sta, moy ba-**gazh** fpo-yézt **no**-myér ...
carriage number ...	ваго́н но́мер ...	va-**gon** **no**-myér ...
Put it up there please	Положи́те наве́рх, пожа́луйста	pa-la-**zhi**-tyé na-**vyérh**, pa-**zha**-loo-sta
Where is train number ... ?[1]	Где по́езд но́мер ... ?	gdyé **po**-yézt **no**-myér ...

1. See 'Numbers' (p. 235).

Where is the train to ... ?[1]	Где пóезд в ... ? (+ acc.)	gdyé po-yézt v ...
What platform does the train for ... leave from?	С какóй платфóрмы отхóдит пóезд в ... ? (+ acc.)	ska-koy plat-for-mi at-ho-deet po-yézt v ...
Where is platform number ... ?[2]	Где платфóрма нóмер ... ?	gdyé plat-foor-ma no-myér ...
Does this train go to ... ?[3]	Э́тот пóезд идёт в ... ? (+ acc.)	é-tat po-yézt ee-dyot v ...
There will be a delay of ...	*Отхóд пóезда задéрживается на ... (+ acc.)	at-khod pó-yéz-da za-dyér-zhi-va-yét-sa na ...

ON THE TRAIN

On long-distance trains with sleeping compartments, there is an attendant in charge of every carriage. His duties include making up the beds and serving tea.

Men and women are often allocated to the same sleeping compartment, but the attendant is usually able to change this arrangement if it does not suit you.

Your ticket please	*Ваш билéт	vash bee-lyét
Where is the attendant?	Где проводни́к?	gdyé pra-vad-neek
Where is my compartment?	Где моё купé?	gdyé ma-yo koo-pé
Where is my place?	Где моё мéсто?	gdyé ma-yo myés-ta

1. See the list 'Towns in the Soviet Union' (p. 47).
2. See 'Numbers' (p. 235).
3. See the list 'Towns in the Soviet Union' (p. 47).

Is this seat free?	Здесь свобóдно?	zdyés' sva-bod-na
This seat is taken	Здесь зáнято	zdyés' za-nya-ta
Where is the lavatory?	Где туалéт?	gdyé too-a-lyét
Could you unlock the lavatory?	Вы мóжете откры́ть туалéт?	vi mo-zhe-tyé at-krit' too-a-lyét
Where is the restaurant car?	Где вагóн-ресторáн?	gdyé va-gon ryés-ta-ran
When is the buffet car open?	Когдá вагóн-ресторáн откры́т?	kag-da va-gon ryés-ta-ran at-krit
When will we arrive at ...?[1]	Когдá мы прибу́дем в ...? (+ acc.)	kag-da mi pree-boo-dyém v ...
Which is the next station?	Какáя слéдующая стáнция?	ka-ka-ya slyé-doo-sha-ya stan-tsi-ya
What town is this?	Какой э́то гóрод?	ka-koy é-ta go-rat
How long does the train stop for here/at ...?	Скóлько врéмени пóезд стоúт здесь/в ...? (+ loc.)	skol'-ka vryé-myé-nee po-yézt sto-eet zdyés/v ...
Do I have time to leave the train?	Я успéю вы́йти из пóезда?	ya oo-spyé-yoo viy-tee eez po-yéz-da
Will you be having tea?	*Вы бу́дете пить чай?	vi boo-dyé-tyé peet' chay
A glass of tea please	Стакáн чáю, пожáлуйста	sta-kan cha-yoo, pa-zha-loo-sta
without sugar	без сáхара	byéz sa-ha-ra

1. See the list 'Towns in the Soviet Union' (p. 47) and 'Times and Dates' (p. 228).

How much do I owe you for the tea?	Ско́лько я вам до́лжен/должна́ *f* за чай?	skol'-ka ya vam dol-zhén/dalzh-na za-chay
May I make the beds up?	*Мо́жно постели́ть?	mozh-na pa-styé-leet'
Please bring me	Да́йте мне, пожа́луйста,	day-tyé mnyé, pa-zha-loo-sta
a blanket/a pillow	одея́ло/поду́шку	a-dyé-ya-la/ pa-doosh-koo
some bed-linen	бельё	byé-lyo
a glass	стака́н	sta-kan
Please open the window	Откро́йте, пожа́луйста, окно́	at-kroy-tyé, pa-zha-loo-sta, ak-no
Please shut the window	Закро́йте, пожа́луйста, окно́	za-kroy-tyé, pa-zha-loo-sta, ak-no
It's too hot/cold here	Здесь сли́шком жа́рко/хо́лодно	zdyés' sleesh-kam zhar-ka/ho-lad-na
Please wake me at ... o'clock[1]	Разбуди́те меня́, пожа́луйста, в ... часо́в	raz-boo-dee-tyé me-nya, pa-zho-loo-sta, f ... cha-sof
May I turn on the radio?	Мо́жно включи́ть ра́дио?	mozh-na fklyoo-cheet' ra-dee-o
May I turn off the radio?	Мо́жно вы́ключить ра́дио?	mozh-na vi-klyoo-cheet' ra-dee-o
May I turn out the light?	Мо́жно вы́ключить свет?	mozh-na vi-klyoo-cheet' svyét

1. See 'Times and Dates' (p. 228).

Do you mind if I smoke?	Мóжно закурúть?	mozh-na za-koo-reet'
Where are you going?	Кудá вы éдете?	koo-da vi yé-dyé-tyé
I am going to ...	Я éду в . . . (+ acc.)	ya yé-doo v ...

BY AIR

RESERVATIONS AND INQUIRIES

If you are travelling on a package tour with a group, all ticket reservations for international flights and Aeroflot flights within the Soviet Union will have been made in advance, and Intourist will take care of the confirmations. If you are travelling independently, or if there is a need to change the plan, you may need to use some of the phrases given below.

In Moscow, the Aeroflot offices are in the Metropole hotel on Sverdlov Square; the British Airways office is on Krasnopresnenskaya Naberezhnaya 12, Floor 19 (tel. 253–24–81).

КАССЫ АЭРОФЛОТА	Aeroflot booking office
СПРАВОЧНОЕ БЮРО	Information bureau

Where is the Aeroflot office?	Где кассы́ Аэрофлóта?	gdyé kas-si a-é-ra-flo-ta
I would like to book ...	Я хочý заказáть ...	ya ha-choo za-ka-zat' ...

I would like to buy two/three tickets	Я хочу́ купи́ть два/три биле́та	ya ha-choo koo-peet' dva/tree bee-lyé-ta
for the flight to ...[1]	на самолёт до ... (+ gen.)	na-sa-ma-lyot da ...
How much is a ticket to ... ?	Ско́лько сто́ит биле́т до ... ? (+ gen.)	skol'-ka sto-eet bee-lyét da ...
I want to cancel my reservation on the flight to ...	Я хочу́ отмени́ть зака́з на рейс в ... (+ acc.)	ya ha-choo at-myé-neet' za-kaz na-réys v ...
I want to change my reservation to ...	Я хочу́ перенести́ зака́з на ...	ya ha-choo pyé-ryé-nyés-tee za-kaz na ...
Will it cost more?	Бу́дет ли э́то сто́ить доро́же?	boo-dyét lee e-ta sto-eet' da-ro-zhe
Is there a flight to ... ?[1]	Есть ли самолёт в ... ? (+ acc.)	yést'-lee sa-ma-lyot v ...
When are the flights to ... ?[2]	Когда́ самолёт вылета́ет в ... ? (+ acc.)	kag-da sa-ma-lyot vi-lyé-ta-yét v ...
When is the next plane to ... ?	Когда́ сле́дующий самолёт в ... ? (+ acc.)	kag-da slyé-doo-sheey sa-ma-lyot v ...
When does the plane leave/arrive?	Когда́ самолёт вылета́ет/прилета́ет?	kag-da sa-ma-lyot vi-lyé-ta-yét/pree-lyé-ta-yét

1. See the list 'Towns in the Soviet Union' (p. 47).
2. See 'Times and Dates' (p. 228).

How long is the flight?	Ско́лько дли́тся полёт?	**skol'-ka dleet-sa pa-lyot**
When must I check in?	Когда́ мне ну́жно быть в аэропорту́?	**kag-da mnyé noozh-na bit' va-é-ra-par-too**
Is there a bus	Хо́дит ли авто́бус	**ho-deet-lee af-to-boos**
to the airport/to the town?	до аэропо́рта/ в го́род?	**da-a-é-ra-por-ta/fgo-rat**
How long does it take?	Ско́лько он идёт?	**skol'-ka on ee-dyot**

THE FLIGHT[1]

РЕЙС И°	Flight No. ...
РЕГИСТРАЦИЯ БИЛЕТОВ И БАГАЖА	Registration of tickets and luggage
ВЫХОД НА ПОСАДКУ	Boarding gate
ПРИБЫТИЕ	Arrivals
ПОСАДКА	Boarding
ОТЛЁТ	Departures
ИНТУРИСТ	Intourist
ВЫДАЧА БАГАЖА	Luggage collection point
ЗАСТЕГНУТЬ РЕМНИ	Fasten seat-belts
НЕ КУРИТЬ	No smoking
ЗАПАСНЫЙ ВЫХОД	Emergency exit

What is the number of the flight to ... ?[2]	Како́й но́мер ре́йса в ... ? (+ acc.)	**ka-koy no-myér réy-sa v ...**

1. See also the list 'Towns in the Soviet Union' (p. 47).
2. See 'Numbers' (p. 235).

Where do I check in for flight number ...[1] to ...	Где регистрáция на рейс ... в ... ? (+ acc.)	gdyé ryé-gee-stra-tsi-ya na réys ... v ...
What is the charge for excess baggage?	Скóлько стóит лúшний вес?	skol'-ka sto-eet leesh-neey vyés
When will flight number ... be boarding?	Когдá бýдет посáдка на рейс ... ?	kag-da boo-dyét pa-sat-ka na réys ...
Is the flight to ... leaving on time?	Самолёт в ... (+ acc.) отлетáет по расписáнию?	sa-ma-lyot v ... at-lyé-ta-yét pa-ras-pee-sa-nee-yoo
How long is the flight to ... delayed for?	На скóлько задéрживается самолёт в ... ? (+ acc.)	na skol'-ka za-dyér-zhi-va-yét-sa sa-ma-lyot v ...
Fasten your seat-belts	*Застегнúте рéмни	za-styég-nee-tyé ryém-nee
I feel sick	Меня́ тошнúт	me-nya tash-neet
Please bring me	Принесúте, пожáлуйста	pree-nyé-see-tyé, pa-zha-loo-sta
a (sick) bag/a glass of water	мешóчек/ стакáн воды́	myé-sho-chyék/ sta-kan va-di
a blanket/a pillow	одея́ло/подýшку	a-dyé-ya-la/ pa-doosh-koo

1. See 'Numbers' (p. 235).

BY SHIP

You can travel to and from the Soviet Union by ship (there are services between Tilbury and Leningrad, and Marseille and Odessa, for instance). You can also go on a cruise along the Volga from Kazan to Rostov-on-Don. Or you may want to go on hydrofoil or steamer trips; you can visit Petrodvorets near Leningrad by hydrofoil, or explore the Crimean coast by steamer.

The word for motor-ship is ТЕПЛОХО́Д (tyé-pla-hot) and has been used throughout this section. If necessary, you should substitute the words for steamer or hydrofoil – a steamer is a ПАРОХО́Д (pa-ra-hot) and a hydrofoil is colloquially known as a РАКЕ́ТА (ra-kyé-ta).

Is there a ship to ... ?[1]	Хо́дит ли теплохо́д до ... ? (+ gen.)	**ho-deet-lee tyé-pla-hot da....**
How often do ships go to ... ?	Как ча́сто теплохо́ды хо́дят в ... ? (+ acc.)	**kak chas-ta tyé-pla-ho-di ho-dyat v ...**
When does the ship for ... leave?[2]	Когда́ теплохо́д отхо́дит в ... ? (+ acc.)	**kag-da tyé-pla-hot at-ho-deet v ...**
When does the ship arrive at ... ?	Когда́ теплохо́д прихо́дит в ... ? (+ acc.)	**kag-da tyé-pla-hot pree-ho-deet v ...**
How long does the ship take to reach ... ?	Ско́лько вре́мени теплохо́д идёт до ... ? (+ gen.)	**skol'-ka vryé-myé-nee tyé-pla-hot ee-dyot da ...**

1. See the list 'Towns in the Soviet Union' (p. 47).
2. See 'Times and Dates' (p. 228).

How much is a ticket to . . . ?	Ско́лько сто́ит билет до . . . ? (+ gen.)	skol'-ka sto-eet bee-lyét da . . .
One ticket to . . .	Оди́н биле́т до . . . (+ gen.)	a-deen bee-lyét da . . .
One return ticket to . . .	Оди́н биле́т до . . . (+ gen.) туда́ и обра́тно	a-deen bee-lyét da . . . too-da ee a-brat-na
I would like a cabin	Я хочу́ каю́ту	ya ha-choo ka-yoo-too
with 1 berth/2 berths	на одного́/на двои́х	na-ad-na-vo/ na-dva-eeh
with 3 berths/4 berths	на трои́х/на четверы́х	na-tra-eeh/na-chet-vyé-rih
first class/second class	пе́рвого кла́сса/ второ́го кла́сса	pyér-va-va klas-sa/ fta-ro-va klas-sa
I would like a berth in a cabin	Я хочу́ ме́сто в каю́те	ya ha-choo myés-ta fka-yoo-tyé
Where is	Где	gdyé
the lounge/the dining-room?	сало́н/столо́вая	sa-lon/sta-lo-va-ya
the snack bar/the lavatory?	буфе́т/туале́т?	boo-fyét/too-a-lyét
cabin number . . . ?[1]	каю́та но́мер . . . ?	ka-yoo-ta no-myér . . .

1. See 'Numbers' (p. 235).

How can I get out on deck?	Как вы́йти на па́лубу?	kak viy-tee na-pa-loo-boo
Where can I get a deck-chair?	Где мо́жно получи́ть складно́е кре́сло?	gdyé mozh-na pa-loo-cheet' sklad-no-yé kryés-la
How long will the ship be here for?	Ско́лько теплохо́д здесь сто́ит?	skol'-ka tyé-pla-hot zdyés' sta-eet
Lifebelt	Спаса́тельный круг	spa-sa-tyél'-niy krook
Lifeboat	Спаса́тельная шлю́пка	spa-sa-tyél'-na-ya shlyoop-ka

BY METRO

The entrance to metro stations is marked by a large red M which is illuminated when it is dark. The trains run at extremely frequent intervals from 6 a.m. to 1 a.m. The Moscow metro consists of a circle line crossed by five radial lines, each of which has a distinctive colour. There is a clear map of the metro at the entrance to every station, and maps are also on sale at newspaper kiosks.

To use the metro, you must have a 5-kopeck coin or a ticket. There are change machines at the entrance to every metro station. The word РАЗМЕН (Change) appears on these machines, followed by the number 10, 15, or 20, indicating the denomination of coin which the machine will accept. Insert the correct coin into the slot, and the machine will disgorge the equivalent sum of money in 5-kopeck pieces. If you do not have any suitable coins for using the change machine, you can get change at the ticket office (КАССА). You can also buy a book of ten metro tickets for 50 kopecks (these can be used instead of coins), or a yédeeniy bee-lyét (see page 24) valid for one month's travel on all forms of public transport. Once you have obtained your 5-kopeck coin or ticket, you can enter the metro system.

You can travel as far as you like for 5 kopecks. There are arrow-shaped signs on the outer walls of both sides of the platform; these show the direction in which the train on that side of the platform is travelling, and list all the stations on that line before the terminus. Stations at which one can change over to other lines are marked with the characteristic colour of that line. There are automatic announcements on the trains (see page 22) which tell you which station you are arriving at, and, as you draw out, the name of the following station. The name of each station is written clearly on the outside walls, so you should have no problem identifying your stop. Signs for changing over to another line or for the exit to the street are also clearly marked.

М	Metro
МЕТРО	Metro
ВХОД (В МЕТРО)	Entrance (to the metro)
ВХОДА НЕТ	No entry
КАССА/КАССЫ	Ticket office/Cash desk
РАЗМЕН	Change machine
К ПОЕЗДАМ	To the trains
ДЕРЖИТЕСЬ ПРАВОЙ СТОРОНЫ	Keep to the right
ДЕРЖИТЕСЬ ЛЕВОЙ СТОРОНЫ	Keep to the left
НА ПЕРЕСАДКУ	To connection (with other metro lines)
ПЕРЕХОД	To connection (with other metro lines)
ВЫХОД	Exit
ВЫХОД В ГОРОД	Way out to street

ВЫХОДА НЕТ	No exit
МЕСТА ДЛЯ ПАССАЖИРОВ С ДЕТЬМИ И ДЛЯ ИНВАЛИДОВ	Seats for passengers with children and for invalids
НЕ ПРИСЛОНЯТЬСЯ	Do not lean (against the doors)

Where is the nearest metro station?	Где ближáйшее метрó?	gdyé blee-zhay-shé mé-tro
How can I get to the metro?	Как добрáться до метрó?	kak da-brat'-sa da-mé-tro
Is this train going to the centre?	Э́тот пóезд идёт в центр?	é-tat po-yézt ee-dyot ftsentr
Which line goes to ...?	Какáя лúния идёт в ...? (+ acc.)	ka-ka-ya lee-nee-ya ee-dyot v ...
How many stops are there till ...? *name of station*	Скóлько останóвок до ...?	skol'-ka a-sta-no-vak da ...
Which station is this?	Какáя э́то стáнция?	ka-ka-ya é-ta stan-tsi-ya
Is the next station ...? *name of station*	Слéдующая стáнция ...?	slyé-doo-sha-ya stan-tsi-ya
Which is the next station?	Какáя слéдующая стáнция?	ka-ka-ya slyé-doo-sha-ya stan-tsi-ya
Where should I change for ...? *name of station*	Где нáдо сдéлать пересáдку, чтóбы попáсть на ...?	gdyé na-da zdyé-lat' pyé-ryé-sat-koo shto-bi pa-past' na ...
Where is the way out?	Где вы́ход?	gdyé vi-had

METRO TRAIN ANNOUNCEMENTS

Please be careful, the doors are closing. The next station will be ...	*Осторóжно, двéри закрывáются. Слéдующая стáнция ...	a-sta-rozh-na, dvyé-ree za-kri-va-yoot-sa, slyé-doo-sha-ya stan-tsi ya ...
... station	*Стáнция ...	stan-tsi-ya ...
Change for ... station	*Перехóд на стáнцию ...	pyé-ryé-hot na-stan-tsi-yoo ...
The train is not going any further. All change	*Пóезд дáльше не пойдёт. Просьба освободи́ть вагóны.	po-yézt dal'-shé nyé pay-dyot. pros'-ba a-sva-ba-deet' va-go-ni
The train is going as far as ... station	*Пóезд слéдует до стáнции ...	po-yézt slyé-doo-yét da-stan-tsi-ee ...

BY BUS, TROLLEYBUS AND TRAM

Buses, trolleybuses, and trams run at frequent intervals from about 6 a.m. till 1 a.m. The signs for buses and trolleybuses are usually on a post or attached to a building by the side of the road, sometimes near a shelter. The bus-stop sign is yellow, and has a large A on it (for aftoboos, a bus), and the trolleybus sign is white and has a large T for trallyéyboos on it. Tram-stop signs are suspended above the tram tracks and display a large T for tramvay (tram). The number of the route and the name of the stop are also written on the sign. Each stop has a name, usually referring to a nearby street or shop; these names are sometimes announced by the drivers, and serve as a useful method of identification. There is a plaque on the side of the bus or tram near the rear entrance which gives the names of the most important stops on the route. It is normal practice to enter a bus or tram through the rear or central doors, and to leave through the front or central doors. Elderly people or passengers with children are allowed to jump the queue, and to board at the front.

There are no conductors, and passengers are expected to get their own tickets as soon as they board the bus. The buses are patrolled by plain-clothes inspectors who will fine you 1 rouble if they catch you travelling without a ticket. There is a flat-rate fare of 5 kopecks. To buy a ticket you must first find the ticket-machine (the **kassa**), usually located at the back and front of the vehicle. Drop the money into the box, roll off the required number of tickets and tear them off. Some ticket-machines require the money for each ticket to be dropped through a slot; the tickets are released one at a time, after the money has been fed in, by pressing a lever. If you carry a large suitcase, you must pay an additional fare. It is also possible to buy a book of ten tickets from the driver when he is waiting at a bus stop. In Moscow and Leningrad you can also buy a special card called a **yédeeniy bee-lyét** for 6 roubles at metro stations. This card enables you to travel on all forms of public transport at no further cost. It is valid for a month, and is extremely convenient.

Smoking is not allowed on buses or trams.

FINDING OUT WHICH BUS OR COACH TO TAKE

Where is the bus station?	Где автóбусная стáнция?	**gdyé af-to-boos-na-ya stan-tsi-ya**
Where is the timetable?	Где расписáние?	**gdyé ras-pee-sa-nee-yé**
Is there a bus to ...?	Хóдит ли автóбус до ...? (+ gen.)	**ho-deet-lee af-to-boos da ...**
How can I get to ...?	Как мне доéхать до ...? (+ gen.)	**kak mnyé da-yé-hat' da ...**

Which number goes to	Какóй нóмер идёт до (+ gen.)	ka-koy no-myér ee-dyot da
the ... hotel/ ... museum?	гости́ницы .. музéя ... ?	ga-stee-nee-tsi ... / moo-zyé-ya ...
the centre/metro?	цéнтра/метрó?	tsen-tra/mé-tro
Take bus/trolleybus number ...[1]	*Сади́тесь на автóбус/ троллéйбус нóмер ...	sa-dee-tyés' na af-to-boos/tral-lyéy-boos no-myér ...
Go as far as ...	*Доéдете до ...	da-yé-dyé-tyé da ...
Then change to ...	*Затéм переся́дете на ...	za-tyém pyé-ryé-sya-dyé-tyé na ...
Please write down the number of the bus	Напиши́те, пожáлуйста, нóмер автóбуса	na-pee-shi-tyé, pa-zha-loo-sta, no-myér af-to-boo-sa
Where is the nearest bus stop?	Где ближáйшая останóвка автóбуса?	gdyé blee-zhay-sha-ya a-sta-nof-ka af-to-boo-sa
Where is the stop of trolleybus/tram number ... ?	Где здесь останóвка троллéйбуса/ трамвáя нóмер ...?	gdyé zdyés' a-sta-nof-ka tral-lyéy-boo-sa/ tram-va-ya no-myér ...

AT THE BUS OR COACH STATION

Does it go to ... ?	Он идёт до ... ? (+ gen.)	on ee-dyot da ...

1. See 'Numbers' (p. 235).

When does the bus to ... leave?[1]	Когда́ отхо́дит авто́бус в ... ? (+ acc.)	kag-da at-ho-deet af-to-boos v ...
When does the bus arrive at ... ?	Когда́ прихо́дит авто́бус в ... ? (+ acc.)	kag-da pree-ho-deet af-to-boos v ...
How often do the buses run to ... ?	Как ча́сто хо́дят авто́бусы в ... ? (+ acc.)	kak chas-ta ho-dyat af-to-boo-si v ...
How long does the journey take?	Ско́лько дли́тся пое́здка?	skol'-ka dleet-sa pa-yézd-ka

IN THE BUS

Please pass along ... (*money for a ticket*)	Переда́йте, пожа́луйста ...	pyé-ryé-day-tyé, pa-zha-loo-sta
There aren't any tickets	*Биле́тов нет	bee-lyé-taf nyét
One book of tickets, please	Одну́ кни́жечку, пожа́луйста	ad-noo knee-zhech-koo, pa-zha-loo-sta
Your ticket, please	*Ваш биле́т, пожа́луйста	vash bee-lyét, pa-zha-loo-sta
Which is the right stop for ... ?	Где мне вы́йти, что́бы попа́сть в ... ? (+ acc.)	gdyé mnyé viy-tee, shto-bi pa-past' v ...

1. See the list 'Towns in the Soviet Union' (p. 47) and 'Times and Dates' (p. 228).

You must get off	*Вам выходи́ть	vam vi-ha-deet'
at the next stop	на сле́дующей остано́вке	na-slyé-doo-shéy a-sta-nof-kyé
at ... street	на у́лице ...	na-oo-lee-tsé ...
Which is the next stop?	Кака́я сле́дующая остано́вка?	ka-ka-ya slyé-doo-sha-ya a-sta-nof-ka
Is this the right stop for ...?	Я попаду́ отсю́да в ...? (+ acc.)	ya pa-pa-doo at-syoo-da v ...
Will you tell me when I ought to get off?	Вы мне ска́жете, когда́ мне ну́жно выходи́ть?	vi mnyé ska-zhé-tyé, kag-da mnyé noozh-na vi-ha-deet'
Please let me pass	Разреши́те пройти́	raz-ryé-shi-tyé pray-tee

BY TAXI

Taxis are easily recognizable; they are pale green, and have a chequered band on both sides. When the green light in the top right-hand corner of the windscreen is on, the taxi is free, and can be hailed or picked up at a taxi rank. Taxi ranks can be identified by a sign with a large T on it. It is also possible to order a taxi by telephone. The fare is 20 kopecks a kilometre plus 20 kopecks service charge and is registered on the meter (р. or руб. stand for roubles and к. or коп. for kopecks). It is customary, but not necessary, to give a small tip.

The time when the driver finishes work is displayed on a sign at the front of the taxi on the windscreen. When a taxi-driver is finishing work, he may put up an additional sign В ПАРК (v park – to the taxi-park), and, although the green light will be on, he will only take passengers who are going in his direction.

It is always useful to have the address you are going to written down on a piece of paper to show the driver.

There are also fixed-route taxis (marsh**root**nayé tak**see**). These are minibuses, usually red, which follow a set route, often running along main roads or linking metro stations with bus stops. They are faster than buses, and cheaper than individual taxis. They have definite stops along their routes (you must inform the driver when you want to get off), but if they are not full, they will stop at any point to pick up extra passengers. The fare is a flat rate of 15 kopecks per person.

Where is the nearest taxi rank?	Где здесь стоя́нка такси́?	gdyé zdyés' sta-**yan**-ka tak-**see**
Are you free?	Вы свобо́дны?	vi sva-**bod**-ni
Where do you want to go?	*Куда́ е́хать?	koo-**da** **yé**-hat'
Please take me to	Пожа́луйста,	pa-**zha**-loo-sta,
the ... hotel/museum	гости́ница/музе́й ...	gas-**tee**-nee-tsa/moo-**zyéy** ...
this address/... street	вот а́дрес/у́лица ...	vot **a**-dryés/**oo**-lee-tsa ...
I'm in a hurry, could you go faster?	Я спешу́, мо́жно скоре́е?	ya spyé-**shoo**, **mozh**-na ska-**ryé**-yé
Please stop here	Останови́тесь здесь, пожа́луйста	as-ta-na-**vee**-tyés' zdyés', pa-**zha**-loo-sta
Please wait for me	Подожди́те меня́, пожа́луйста	pa-dazh-**dee**-tyé me-**nya**, pa-**zha**-loo-sta
Please write down how much I owe you	Пожа́луйста, напиши́те ско́лько э́то сто́ит	pa-**zha**-loo-sta, na-pee-**shi**-tyé **skol'**-ka **é**-ta **sto**-eet

TOWNS IN THE SOVIET UNION

A list of the principal towns in the Soviet Union which are open to foreign tourists is given below so as to enable you to recognize the name of your destination when it is written down or spoken in Russian.

Moscow	МОСКВА́	mask-va
Leningrad	ЛЕНИНГРА́Д	lyé-neen-grat
Abakan	АБАКА́Н	a-ba-kan
Alma-Ata	АЛМА-АТА́	al-ma-a-ta
Ashkhabad	АШХАБА́Д	ash-ha-bat
Baku	БАКУ́	ba-koo
Batumi	БАТУ́МИ	ba-too-mee
Beltsy	БЕ́ЛЬЦЫ	byél'-tsi
Bratsk	БРАТСК	bratsk
Brest	БРЕСТ	bryést
Bukhara	БУХАРА́	boo-ha-ra
Cherkassy	ЧЕРКА́ССЫ	chyér-kas-si
Chernovtsy	ЧЕРНОВЦЫ́	chyér-naf-tsi
Donetsk	ДОНЕ́ЦК	da-nyétsk
Druskininkai	ДРУСКИ́НИНКАЙ	droos-kee-neen-kay
Dushanbe	ДУШАНБЕ́	doo-shan-bé
Erevan	ЕРЕВА́Н	ye-re-van
Fergana	ФЕРГАНА́	fyér-ga-na
Frunze	ФРУ́НЗЕ	froon-zé
Gelendzhik	ГЕЛЕНДЖИ́К	ge-lyénd-zhik
Gori	ГО́РИ	go-ree
Irkutsk	ИРКУ́ТСК	eer-kootsk

Ivanovo	ИВА́НОВО	ee-va-na-va
Kalinin	КАЛИ́НИН	ka-lee-neen
Kazan	КАЗА́НЬ	ka-zan'
Khabarovsk	ХАБА́РОВСК	ha-ba-rafsk
Kharkov	ХА́РЬКОВ	har'-kaf
Kherson	ХЕРСО́Н	hyér-son
Kiev	КИ́ЕВ	kee-yéf
Kishinev	КИШИНЁВ	kee-shee-nyof
Kislovodsk	КИСЛОВО́ДСК	kees-la-vodsk
Krasnodar	КРАСНОДА́Р	kras-na-dar
Kursk	КУРСК	koorsk
Kutaisi	КУТАИСИ	koo-ta-ee-see
Lvov	ЛЬВОВ	l'vof
Minsk	МИНСК	meensk
Murmansk	МУ́РМАНСК	moor-mansk
Novgorod	НО́ВГОРОД	nov-ga-rat
Novosibirsk	НОВОСИБИ́РСК	na-va-see-beersk
Odessa	ОДЕ́ССА	a-dyés-sa
Ordzhonikidze	ОРДЖОНИКИ́ДЗЕ	ar-dzha-nee-keed-zé
Orel	ОРЁЛ	a-ryol
Pasanauri	ПАСАНАУ́РИ	pa-sa-na-oo-ree
Petrozavodsk	ПЕТРОЗАВО́ДСК	pyé-tra-za-vodsk
Pitsunda	ПИЦУ́НДА	pee-tsoon-da
Poltava	ПОЛТА́ВА	pal-ta-va
Pskov	ПСКОВ	pskof
Pyatigorsk	ПЯТИГО́РСК	pya-tee-gorsk
Riga	РИ́ГА	ree-ga
Rostov-on-Don	РОСТО́В-НА-ДОНУ́	ra-stof-ha-da-noo

Rovno	РО́ВНО	rov-na
Samarkand	САМАРКА́НД	sa-mar-kand
Simferopol	СИМФЕРО́ПОЛЬ	seem-fyé-ro-pal’
Smolensk	СМОЛЕ́НСК	sma-lyensk
Sochi	СО́ЧИ	so-chee
Stavropol	СТА́ВРОПОЛЬ	sta-vra-pal’
Sukhumi	СУХУ́МИ	soo-hoo-mee
Suzdal	СУ́ЗДАЛЬ	sooz-dal’
Tallinn	ТА́ЛЛИН	tal-leen
Tashkent	ТАШКЕ́НТ	tash-kyént
Tbilisi	ТБИЛИ́СИ	tbee-lee-see
Ternopol	ТЕРНО́ПОЛЬ	tyér-no-pal’
Ulyanovsk	УЛЬЯ́НОВСК	oo-lya-nofsk
Urgench	УРГЕ́НЧ	oor-gyénch
Uzhgorod	У́ЖГОРОД	oozh-ga-rat
Vilnius	ВИ́ЛЬНЮС	veel’ nyoos
Vinnitsa	ВИ́ННИЦА	veen-nee-tsa
Vladimir	ВЛАДИ́МИР	vla-dee-meer
Volgograd	ВОЛГОГРА́Д	val-ga-grat
Yalta	Я́ЛТА	yal-ta
Yaroslavl	ЯРОСЛА́ВЛЬ	ya-ra-slavl’
Zagorsk	ЗАГО́РСК	za-gorsk
Zaporozhie	ЗАПОРО́ЖЬЕ	za-pa-ro-zhyé

DIRECTIONS

RULES FOR PEDESTRIANS

It is against the law to cross a main road anywhere except at officially authorized crossing points. These are marked by two types of signs – either a yellow arrow with ПЕРЕХО́Д (Pyéryéhot – Crossing) written on it, or a square sign with a picture of a man crossing a zebra crossing (a black and white triangle inset against a blue background). It is important to realize that zebra crossings only indicate *where* the pedestrian is allowed to cross a road; they do not give him any right of way, and cars will not stop for him. If you cross a main road at the wrong place, you risk being caught by a militiaman or by a droozhineek (a voluntary keeper of public order) wearing a red arm-band. They will ask you to pay a fine (shtraf) of 3 roubles.

ПЕРЕХОД	Crossing
ПЕРЕХОДА НЕТ	No crossing
ПОДЗЕМНЫЙ ПЕРЕХОД	Underground crossing
СТОЙТЕ	Wait

ДИТЕ	Cross
СТОП	Stop
ОСТОРОЖНО	Careful
ОДНОСТОРОННЕЕ ДВИЖЕНИЕ	One-way traffic
БЕРЕГИСЬ АВТОМОБИЛЯ	Watch out for cars

ASKING THE WAY

The Russian language distinguishes between the idea of going somewhere on foot and the idea of going by vehicle, and uses different verbs for each case. Eettee is the basic verb for going somewhere on foot, and yéhat' for going somewhere by vehicle. Start your inquiries by asking how you can get somewhere (either by foot or by vehicle, using an all-purpose verb to get – papast'). If you are told that you must go by bus or metro, turn to the relevant sections in 'Travel' (page 19). If you are travelling by car, see 'Driving' (page 184). If you can get to your destination on foot, use the phrases in this section. The most common directions which you are likely to be given are listed below; if you have difficulty in understanding them, you can use the phrases yourself as questions and find out the correct way to go by a process of elimination. It is always useful to have the name or the address of the place you are trying to find written down in Russian to show to people when asking for directions. Maps are sold at news-stands (see page 117), but they are usually schematic and insufficiently detailed.

Try to get a clear set of directions from your guide or from the hotel service bureau before setting out to walk somewhere. A militiaman is a good person to approach for directions; otherwise, try using the services of an information bureau – these are little kiosks on the street, often near metro stations, where, in exchange for a minimal sum of money, directions will be written out for you on a scrap of paper.

СПРАВКИ	Information	
Please help me	Помоги́те мне, пожа́луйста	pa-ma-gee-tyé mnyé, pa-zha-loo-sta
I'm lost	Я заблуди́лся/ заблуди́лась *f*	ya za-bloo-deel-sa/ za-bloo-dee-las'
Where am I?	Где я нахожу́сь?	gdyé ya na-ha-zhoos'
Where is ...?	Где ...?	gdyé ...
Please show me on the map	Покажи́те мне на ка́рте, пожа́луйста	pa-ka-zhi-tyé mnyé na kar-tyé, pa-zha-loo-sta
Could you please tell me ...	Скажи́те, пожа́луйста ...	ska-zhi-tyé, pa-zha-loo-sta ...
How can I get	Как мне попа́сть	kak mnyé pa-past'
to the centre?	в центр?	ftsentr
to the ... hotel?	в гости́ницу ...?	fga-stee-nee-tsoo ...
to the ... museum?	в музе́й ...?	fmoo-zyéy ...
to ... street?	на у́лицу ...?	na-oo-lee-tsoo ...
to this address?	по э́тому а́дресу?	pa-e-ta-moo a-dryé-soo
I want to walk there	Я хочу́ идти́ пешко́м	ya ha-choo eet-tee pyésh-kom
Can I walk there?	Мо́жно дойти́ туда́ пешко́м?	mozh-na day-tee too-da pyésh-kom
Yes, you can	*Да, мо́жно	da, mozh-na

No, you must go by bus/by metro	*Нет, вам нáдо éхать на автóбусе/на метрó	nyét, vam na-da yé-hat' na-af-to-boo-syé/ na-mé-tro
Should I go ... ?	Нáдо идти́ ... ?	na-da eet-tee ...
Go	*Иди́те/вам нáдо идти́	ee-dee-tyé/vam na-da eet-tee
straight ahead	пря́мо/вперёд	prya-ma/fpyé-ryot
back	назáд/обрáтно	na-zat/a-brat-na
that way	в ту стóрону	ftoo sto-ra-noo
as far as the corner	до углá	da-oo-gla
as far as the end of the street	до концá ýлицы	da-kan-tsa oo-lee-tsi
Turn left/right	*Поверни́те налéво/ напрáво	pa-vyér-nee-tyé na-lyé-va/ na-pra-va
Cross the street	*Перейдёте ýлицу	pyé-ryéy-dyo-tyé oo-lee-tsoo
Sorry – should I go straight on, right or left?	Прости́те – идти́ пря́мо, напрáво или́ налéво?	pra-stee-tyé – eet-tee prya-ma, na-pra-va ee-lee na-lyé-va?
Could you draw me a map of how to get there?	Нарисýйте, пожáлуйста, как пройти́	na-ree-sooy-tyé, pa-zha-loo-sta, kak pray-tee
Am I going the right way for ... ?	Я прáвильно идý к ... ? (+ dat.)	ya pra-veel'-na ee-doo k ...
Is it far?	Э́то далекó?	é-ta da-lyé-ko?

It's	*Э́то	é-ta
far away	далеко́	da-lyé-ko
not far from here	недалеко́ отсю́да	nyé-da-lyé-ko at-syoo-da
over there	там	tam
around the corner	за угло́м	za-oo-glom
Can you give me a lift to ... ?	Вы не подвезёте меня́ до ... ? (+ gen.)	vi nyé pad-vyé-zyo-tyé me-nya do ...
Is there a short cut?	Есть ли путь покоро́че?	yést' lee poot' pa-ka-ro-chyé
Where is the crossing?	Где перехо́д?	gdyé pyé-ryé-hot
I'm sorry, I don't know	*Извини́те, я не зна́ю	eez-vee-nee-tyé, ya nyé zna-yoo
Where is the nearest information bureau?	Где ближа́йшее спра́вочное бюро́?	gdyé blee-zhay-shé spra-vach-na-yé byoo-ro

RUSSIAN ADDRESSES

Russian addresses are written back to front – that is to say, in the opposite order to that used in Britain and America. They go from the general to the particular, starting with the country or region, continuing with the name of the town (often followed by a postcode), the street, the house or building number, the flat number, and finally, in the case of a letter, the name of the erson to whom the letter is addressed. Abbreviations are widely used in ddresses. Here is a list of the most common ones, given in the order in vhich they would appear in a Russian address.

бл.	óбласть o-blast'	region
./гор.	гóрод go-rat	town, city
л./у.	ýлица oo-lee-tsa	street, road
р./пр-т	проспéкт pra-spyékt	avenue
р.	проéзд pra-yézd	passage
ул.	бульвáр bool'-var	boulevard
ер.	переýлок pyé-ryé-oo-lak	lane
аб.	нáбережная na-byé-ryézh-na-ya	embankment
ш.	шоссé shas-syé	highway
л.	плóщадь plo-shat'	square
д.	дом dom	house, block of flats
./корп.	кóрпус kor-poos	building
в.	квартира kvar-tee-ra	flat

There are three main types of names for streets and squares – either an adjective, followed by the noun for street, lane, square etc., as in Ле́нинский проспе́кт (**Lyéneenskeey Praspyékt** – Lenin Avenue), or the noun for street, lane, square, etc., followed by another noun or by the name of a person in the genitive case, as in У́лица Го́рького (**Ooleetsa Gor'kava** – Gorky Street, literally 'the street of Gorky'), Проспе́кт Ма́ркса (**Praspyékt Marksa** – Marx Avenue), Пло́щадь Свердло́ва (**Ploshat' Svyérdlova** – Sverdlov Square). The third type of name is a single word, usually with historical connotations, such as the names of the famous streets in Moscow and Leningrad, the Арба́т (**Arbat**) and the Фонта́нка (**Fontanka**).

When you have found the street, the next thing to do is to locate the house or block of flats. A '**dom**' can either be a single building, or it can refer to a group of buildings, each of which is called a '**korpoos**'. If there is a '**korpoos**' number on the address which you are looking for, you must be careful to check that you have found the right building within the complex. This system can be confusing, particularly in 'micro-regions' – the new housing areas built on the outskirts of large towns; these often lack street names, and consist of large numbers of '**korpoos**' buildings, many of which are grouped under the same '**dom**' number.

Once you have located the right building, you must find the right entrance. The entrances are often numbered (each is called a '**padyézd**'), and are not on the street, but at the back of the building in the yard (the '**dvor**'). If you do not know which is the number of the entrance, ask where the flat is, and you will be directed to the right entrance. It helps to know what floor the flat you are looking for is on, since there is not usually any indication of this in the lift.

Here is an example of a typical address, as written in Russian, with an English translation:

г. Москва 117571, Ленинский пр., д.152, к.8а, кв.462	(city) Moscow 117571, Lenin Avenue, House 152, Building 8a, Flat 462

Where is	Где	gdyé
... street?	у́лица ...?	oo-lee-tsa ...
house/building ...?[1]	дом/ко́рпус ...?	dom/kor-poos ...
entrance/flat ...?[1]	подъе́зд/кварти́ра ...?	pad-yézd/kvar-tee-ra ...

1. See 'Numbers' (cardinal), p. 235.

HOTEL

ARRIVAL AND CHOICE OF ROOM

Tourists travelling to the Soviet Union must make all arrangements for accommodation in advance; the situation of simply turning up at a hotel and booking a room on the spot does not therefore normally arise. However, something may go wrong with the arrangements, or you may not be satisfied with your room; the phrases in this section are designed to help you cope with any such difficulties. You should speak to the hotel manager on duty in the reception area – the **ad-mee-nee-stra-tar** (АДМИНИСТРА́ТОР).

Where is the manager?	Где администра́тор?	**gdyé ad-mee-nee-stra-tar?**
Your passport please	*Ваш па́спорт, пожа́луйста	**vash pas-part, pa-zha-loo-sta**
My name is ...	Меня́ зову́т ...	**me-nya za-voot ...**
I booked a room ...	Я заказа́л/заказа́ла *f* но́мер ...	**ya za-ka-zal/za-ka-za-la no-myér ...**

I would like a room	Я хочу́ но́мер	ya ha-choo no-myér
for one person	на одного́	na-ad-na-vo
for two people	на двои́х	na-dva-eeh
with twin beds	с дву́мя крова́тями	sdvoo-mya kra-va-tya-mee
with a double bed	с двуспа́льной крова́тью	sdvoo-spal'-noy kra-va-tyoo
with an extra bed	с допольни́тельной крова́тью	sda-pal'-nee-tyél'-noy kra-va-tyoo
with a private toilet	с отде́льным туале́том	sat-dyél'-nim too-a-lyé-tam
with a bathroom	с ва́нной	svan-noy
with a shower	с ду́шем	sdoo-shém
with a telephone	с телефо́ном	stýe-lyé-fo-nam
with a television	с телеви́зором	styé-lyé-vee-za-ram
with an air conditioner	с кондиционе́ром	skan-dee-tsi-a-nyé-ram
which is larger	побо́льше	pa-bol'-shé
with a view of the sea	с ви́дом на мо́ре	svee-dam na-mo-ryé
with a balcony	с балко́ном	sbal-ko-nam
How much is the room per night?	Ско́лько сто́ит но́мер в су́тки?	skol'-ka sto-eet no-myér fsoot-kee

Do you have anything cheaper?	У вас есть что-нибудь дешёвле?	oo-vas yést' shto-nee-boot dyé-shev-lyé
I shall be here for ... days[1]	Я здесь пробу́ду ... дня	ya zdyés' pra-boo-doo ... dnya
What is the number of my room?	Како́й но́мер моéй ко́мнаты?	ka-koy no-myér ma-yéy kom-na-ti
What floor is my room on?	На како́м этажé мой но́мер?	na-ka-kom e-ta-zhé moy no-myér
I am staying in room number ...[1]	Я живу́ в но́мере ...	ya zhi-voo fno-myé-ryé ...
Please have my luggage taken up to my room	Доста́вьте, пожа́луйста, мой бага́ж в но́мер	da-staf-tyé, pa-zha-loo-sta, moy ba-gazh fno-myér
Where is my luggage?	Где мой бага́ж?	gdyé moy ba-gazh

INQUIRIES IN THE HOTEL

Intourist hotels offer a variety of facilities for the foreign tourist; the most important of these is the service bureau where English-speaking staff can provide you with information about museums and shopping, as well as with directions on how to get to places of interest. The service bureau also deals with all travel arrangements, including car hire, and arranges excursions. There is always a poster on display giving details of what is on in the way of entertainment, and you can book tickets for the theatre, opera or ballet, as well as make reservations for restaurants.

1. See 'Numbers' (p. 235).

If you are travelling with a group, you will be served set meals at fixed times in the hotel restaurant; if you do not wish to attend all the meals, which can be time-consuming, there are snack bars on most floors of the hotel which usually stay open till 10 p.m.

There is also a news-stand (where foreign newspapers can sometimes be purchased), a post office, a hairdresser, and a currency exchange office. Phrases used in these places are dealt with elsewhere in the corresponding sections of the phrase book. In Moscow, unlike other towns in the Soviet Union, hotels remain open all night.

Where is	Где	gdyé
the restaurant	РЕСТОРА́Н[1]	ryés-ta-ran
the café?	КАФЕ́?	ka-fé
the snack bar	БУФЕ́Т	boo-fyét
the bar?	бар?	bar
the news-stand?	ГАЗЕ́ТНЫЙ КИО́СК?	ga-zyét-niy kee-osk
the post office?	ПО́ЧТА?	poch-ta
the hairdresser?	ПАРИКМА́ХЕР-СКАЯ?	pa-reek-ma-hyér-ska-ya
the service bureau?	БЮРО́ ОБСЛУ́-ЖИВАНИЯ?	byoo-ro ab-sloo-zhi-va-nee-ya
the store room for luggage?	КА́МЕРА ХРАНЕ́НИЯ?	ka-myé-ra hra-nyé-nee-ya
the lift?	лифт?	leeft
the toilet?	туалéт?	too-a-lyét

1. The use of capitals indicates that a word also appears on signs.

When is	Когда́	kag-da
breakfast?	за́втрак?	zav-trak
dinner?	обе́д?	a-byét
supper?	у́жин?	oo-zhin
Can I eat later/earlier?	Мо́жно пое́сть попо́зже/пора́ньше?	mozh-na pa-yést' pa-po-zhé/pa-ran'-shé
Is the hotel open all night?	Гости́ница откры́та всю ночь?	ga-stee-nee-tsa at-kri-ta fsyoo noch'
What time does it close?	В кото́ром часу́ она́ закрыва́ется?	fka-to-ram cha-soo a-na za-kri-va-yét-sa
May I deposit something for safe-keeping?	Мо́жно сдать ве́щи на хране́ние?	mozh-na sdat' vyé-shee na hra-nyé-nee-yé
Porter	Швейца́р	shvyéy-tsar
Telephonist	Телефони́ст	tyé-lyé-fa-neest
Please post this	Отпра́вьте э́то, пожа́луйста, по по́чте	at-praf-tyé e-ta, pa-zha-loo-sta, pa-poch-tyé
Is there a telex?	У вас есть те́лекс?	oo-vas yést' tyé-lyéks
Can I dial direct to England/America?	Мо́жно ли набра́тъ но́мер в А́нглию/в Аме́рику?	mozh-na lee na-brat' no-myér van-glee-yoo/va-myé-ree-koo
Where can I park the car?	Где я могу́ поста́вить маши́ну?	gdyé ya ma-goo pa-sta-veet' ma-shi-noo

SERVICES ON YOUR FLOOR

Each floor of the hotel is supervised twenty-four hours a day by a woman on duty known as the **dyézhoornaya** (дежу́рная). The duties of the dyezhóornaya are manifold; she hands out the room keys, and you are expected to leave your key with her whenever you go out (although in some hotels the practice is different, and keys are left downstairs in the hotel lobby). She will also take messages, wake you up in the morning, order taxis, and dispense tea and mineral water. It is not usual to have breakfast in your room, unless you are ill, and room service is not common, since there is a snack bar on most floors of the hotel. If you want to have any laundry done, ask the dyézhoornaya or the maid, the **gorneechnaya** (го́рничная). It is usually possible to use the hotel ironing room on your floor.

Tipping is not customary in Soviet hotels.

Where is the floor attendant?	Где дежу́рная?	**gdyé dyé-zhoor-na-ya?**
The key to room number ..., please[1]	Но́мер ..., пожа́луйста	**no-myér ..., pa-zha-loo-sta**
I have lost the key to my room	Я потеря́л/потеря́ла *f* ключ от но́мера	**ya pa-tyé-ryal/pa-tyé-rya-la klyooch at-no-myé-ra**
My room-mate has taken the key away, I cannot get into my room	Мой сосе́д унёс ключ, я не могу́ попа́сть в но́мер	**moy sa-syéd oo-nyos klyooch, ya nyé ma-goo pa-past' fno-myér**

1. See 'Numbers' (p. 235).

Where is room number ...?[1]	Где но́мер ...?	gdyé no-myér ...
Is there a message for me?	Есть ли для меня́ запи́ска?	yést'-lee dlya me-nya za-pees-ka
Please wake me at ...[2]	Пожа́луйста, разбуди́те меня́ в ... часо́в ... мину́т	pa-zha-loo-sta, raz-boo-dee-tyé me-nya f ... cha-sof ... mee-noot
I would like to order a taxi for ...[2]	Я хочу́ заказа́ть такси́ на ... часо́в ... мину́т	ya ha-choo za-ka-zat' tak-see na ... cha-sof ... mee-noot
Could I please have some tea/a bottle of mineral water	Да́йте, пожа́луйста, ча́ю/буты́лку минера́льной воды́	day-tyé, pa-zha-loo-sta cha-yoo/boo-til-koo mee-nyé-ral'-noy va-di
I'd like some ice cubes	Я хочу́ немно́го льда	ya ha-choo nyé-mno-ga l'da
I would like to have breakfast in my room	Я хочу́ за́втракать в но́мере	ya ha-choo zav-tra-kat' fno-myé-ryé
Where is the bathroom?	Где ва́нная?	gdyé van-na-ya
Where is the maid?	Где го́рничная?	gdyé gor-neech-na-ya

1. See 'Numbers' (p. 235).
2. See 'Times and Dates' (p. 228).

Please send the chambermaid	Пришли́те, пожа́луйста, го́рничную	pree-shlee-tyé, pa-zha-loo-sta, gor-neech-noo-yoo
Come in	Войди́те	vay-dee-tyé
Just a moment	Одну́ мину́ту	ad-noo mee-noo-too
Could you please clean my room now?	Вы мо́жете сейча́с убра́ть мой но́мер?	vi mo-zhé-tyé seey-chas oo-brat' moy no-myér
Please come back and clean later	Пожа́луйста, приди́те и убери́те попо́зже	pa-zha-loo-sta, pree-dee-tyé ee oo-byé-ree-tyé pa-po-zhé
Could you change the sheets?	Вы мо́жете смени́ть посте́льное бельё?	vi mo-zhé-tyé smyé-neet' pos-tyél-no-yé byé-lyo
Do you have a laundry service?	Мо́жно отда́ть ве́щи в сти́рку?	mozh-na at-dat' vyé-shee fsteer-koo
I need to have this	Мне ну́жно э́то	mnyé noozh-na e-ta
washed/cleaned	постира́ть/ почи́стить	pa-stee-rat'/ pa-chees-teet'
ironed/mended	погла́дить/ почини́ть	pa-gla-deet'/ pa-chee-neet'
When will it be ready?	Когда́ э́то бу́дет гото́во?	kag-da e-ta boo-dyét ga-to-va
Where can I iron?	Где мо́жно погла́дить?	gdyé mozh-na pa-gla-deet'
Do you have a needle and thread?	У вас есть иго́лка с ни́ткой?	oo-vas yést' ee-gol-ka sneet-koy

REQUIREMENTS IN YOUR ROOM

The standard voltage in the Soviet Union is the same as in Britain. There are no special sockets for electric shavers; normal sockets are used, and these require a Continental-type plug (with longer prongs, spaced further apart) or an adaptor. If the hotel is unable to provide you with a spare plug, try a Soviet electrical shop, **ma-ga-zeen** e-lyék-tra-ta-va-raf, usually designated by the sign ЭЛЕКТРОТОВАРЫ (see page 140).

It is a wise precaution to take a rubber plug with you to the Soviet Union, since there are often no plugs in hotel basins.

Could I please have	Да́йте мне, пожа́луйста	day-tyé mnyé, pa-zha-loo-sta
an ashtray	пе́пельницу	pyé-pyél'-nee-tsoo
a blanket/a glass	одея́ло/стака́н	a-dyé-ya-la/sta-kan
some hangers/a pillow	ве́шалки/поду́шку	vyé-shal-kee/ pa-doosh-koo
a plug/some soap	про́бку для ра́ковины/мы́ло	prop-koo dlya ra-ka-vee-ni/mi-la
some toilet paper/a towel	туале́тную бума́гу/ полоте́нце	too-a-lyét-noo-yoo boo-ma-goo/ pa-la-tyén-tsé
Could you put an extra bed in the room?	Вы могли́ бы поста́вить ещё одну́ крова́ть?	vi ma-glee bi pa-sta-veet' yé-sho ad-noo kra-vat'
I need an electric plug	Мне нужна́ ште́псельная ви́лка	mnyé noozh-na shtép-syél'-na-ya veel-ka

How can I switch the air conditioning on?	Как включи́ть кондиционе́р?	kak fklyoo-cheet' kan-dee-tsi-a-nyér
Please open the window	Откро́йте, пожа́луйста, окно́	at-kroy-tyé, pa-zha-loo-sta, ak-no

DIFFICULTIES AND COMPLAINTS

In my room	У меня́ в но́мере	oo-me-nya fno-myé-ryé
it is too hot	сли́шком жа́рко	sleesh-kam zhar-ka
it is too cold	сли́шком хо́лодно	sleesh-kam ho-lad-na
it is too noisy	сли́шком шу́мно	sleesh-kam shoom-na
a bulb has gone	ла́мпочка перегоре́ла	lam-pach-ka pyé-ryé-ga-ryé-la
the light isn't working	нет све́та	nyét svyé-ta
there is no hot water	нет горя́чей воды́	nyét ga-rya-chyéy va-di
there are bed-bugs/cockroaches	клопы́/тарака́ны	kla-pi/ta-ra-ka-ni
When will there be some hot water?	Когда́ бу́дет горя́чая вода́?	kag-da boo-dyét ga-rya-cha-ya va-da
The shower isn't working	Душ не рабо́тает	doosh nyé ra-bo-ta-yét

The toilet won't flush	Сливно́й бачо́к испо́ртился	sleev-noy ba-chok ees-por-teel-sa
My room hasn't been cleaned	Моя́ ко́мната не у́брана	ma-ya kom-na-ta nyé oo-bra-na
The bathroom is dirty	В ва́нной гря́зно	vvan-noy gryaz-na
The blind is stuck	Што́ры застря́ли	shto-ri za-strya-lee
The curtains won't close	За́навески не закрыва́ются	za-na-vyés-kee nyé za-kri-va-yoot-sa

DEPARTURE

Rooms must be vacated by noon on the day of departure. Your luggage will be taken down to the hotel store-room, where it will be held for you until you leave the hotel.

I am leaving today/tomorrow	Я уезжа́ю сего́дня/за́втра	ya oo-yéz-zha-yoo syé-vod-nya/zav-tra
Please prepare my bill	Пригото́вьте счёт, пожа́луйста	pree-ga-tof-tyé shyot, pa-zha-loo-sta
There is a mistake on the bill	В э́том счёте оши́бка	vé-tam sho-tyé a-shib-ka
Please store the luggage, we will be back at ...[1]	Пожа́луйста, подержи́те бага́ж, мы вернёмся в ...	pa-zha-loo-sta, pa-dyer-zhi-tyé ba-gazh, mi vyér-nyom-sa v ...

1. See 'Times and Dates' (p. 228).

Could you have my luggage brought down?	Попросите, пожалуйста, снести мой багаж вниз	pa-pra-see-tyé, pa-zha-loo-sta, snyés-tee moy ba-gazh vneez
Thank you for a pleasant stay	Спасибо, здесь было очень приятно	spa-see-ba, zdyés' bi-la o-chyén' pree-yat-na

MEETING PEOPLE

INTRODUCTIONS[1]

A Russian has three names: a first name, a patronymic, and a surname. For example, Chekhov's full name is 'Anton Pavlovich Chekhov'.

In informal situations, you may be introduced to someone just by their first name, or even by a diminutive form of their first name. Diminutives are very commonly used in Russia – Aleksandr becomes Sasha, Edooard becomes Edik, Ivan becomes Vanya, or even Vanechka or Vanyoosha.

In more formal situations a person will be introduced by his or her first name and patronymic, and this is the form of address which you should use. Patronymics are never used without a first name, and should not be confused with surnames. They are formed from the first name of the father, and express the idea of 'son of ...' or 'daughter of ...'. For example, if Ivan's father is called 'Boris', Ivan's patronymic will be 'Borisovich', and the polite way to address him will be 'Ivan Borisovich'. A woman called Anna, whose father's name is 'Ivan', will be addressed as 'Anna Ivanovna'. To form a patronymic, you add a suffix to the father's name: '-ovich',

1. See also 'Greetings' (p. 7).

'-yevich', or '-ich' in the case of men, and '-ovna', '-yevna', or '-ichna' in the case of women.

Russian surnames have a masculine form (Ivanov, Petrov) and a feminine form (Ivanova, Petrova). There is no equivalent in Russian to the English forms of address, Mr, Mrs, Miss and Ms. When introducing yourself or Western friends, just use a first name and surname, and when addressing a Russian, use his first name and patronymic (unless you know him very well and have been invited to call him by his first name).

This is my husband	Э́то мой муж	é-ta moy moozh
This is my wife	Э́то моя́ жена́	é-ta ma-ya zhé-na
This is my friend *male*	Э́то мой друг	é-ta moy drook
This is my friend *female*	Э́то моя́ подру́га	é-ta ma-ya pa-droo-ga
Hello/how do you do	Здра́вствуйте!	zdrast-vooy-tyé
Pleased to meet you	О́чень прия́тно	o-chyén' pree-yat-na
My name is ...	Меня́ зову́т ...	me-nya za-voot ...
What's your name?	Как вас зову́т?	kak vas za-voot
May I introduce ... ?	Позво́льте мне предста́вить ... (+ acc.)	paz-vol'-tyé mnyé pryéd-sta-veet' ...

MAKING FRIENDS

Where do you come from?	Вы отку́да?	vi at-koo-da

I'm from	Я из	ya eez
Britain/America	Великобритáнии/ Амéрики	vyé-lee-ka-bree-ta-nee-ee/a-myé-ree-kee
Canada/Australia	Канáды/Австрáлии	ka-na-di/af-stra-lee-e
Do you travel a lot?	Вы мнóго éздите?	vi mno-ga yéz-dee-tyé
We've been here a week	Мы здесь ужé недéлю	mi zdyés' oo-zhe nyé-dyé-lyoo
I am with	Я	ya
my husband/wife	с мýжем/с женóй	smoo-zhem/szhe-noy
my parents	с родúтелями	sra-dee-tyé-lya-mee
my family	с семьёй	ssyé-myoy
a friend	с дрýгом/ с подрýгой *f*	sdroo-gam/ spa-droo-goy
I am travelling alone	Я путешéствую одúн/однá *f*	ya poo-tyé-shest-voo-yo a-deen/ad-na
Are you married?	Вы женáты/ зáмужем *f*?	vi zhe-na-ti/za-moo-zhem
Do you have children?	У вас есть дéти?	oo-vas yést' dyé-tee
Have you been to Britain/America?	Вы бы́ли в Великобритáнии/ в Амéрике?	vi-bi-lee v-vyé-lee-ka-bree-ta-nee-ee/va-myé-ree-kyé
What do you do? *profession, etc.*	Чем вы занимáетесь?	chyém vi za-nee-ma-yé-tyés'
I'm a businessman/ businesswoman	Я бизнесмéн	ya beez-nés-myén

I'm a housewife	Я домохозяйка	ya da-ma-ha-zyay-ka
I'm a student	Я студéнт/студéитка *f*	ya stoo-dyént/stoo-dyént-ka
I'm a worker	Я рабóчий/рабóчая *f*	ya ra-bo-cheey/ra-bo-cha-ya
I work in an office	Я слýжащий/слýжащая *f*	ya sloo-zha-sheey/sloo-zha-sha-ya
I work at ...	Я рабóтаю в ... (+ loc.)	ya ra-bo-ta-yoo v ...
How do you like it here?	Как вам здесь нрáвится?	kak vam zdyés' nra-veet-sa
Are you here on your own?	Вы здесь оди́н/однá *f*?	vi zdyés' a-deen/ad-na
Are you free tomorrow?	Вы свобóдны зáвтра?	vi sva-bod-ni zav-tra
Shall we go for a walk?	Пойдёмте погуля́ем	pay-dyom-tyé pa-goo-lya-yém
Shall we go to a café?	Пойдёмте в кафé	pay-dyom-tyé fka-fé
I like it here very much	Мне здесь óчень нрáвится	mnyé zdyés' o-chyén' nra-veet-sa
What is your address/telephone number?	Какóй ваш áдрес/телефóн?	ka-koy vash a-dryés/tyé-lyé-fon
I hope to see you again	Я надéюсь, что мы опя́ть уви́димся	ya na-dyé-yoos', shto mi a-pyat' oo-vee-deem-sa
Come and see us	*Приходи́те к нам	pree-ha-dee-tyé knam

Would you like to have lunch tomorrow?	Вы хоти́те за́втра вме́сте обе́дать?	vi ha-tee-tyé zav-tra fmyé-styé a-byé-dat'
I'd love to come	Я бы о́чень хоте́л/хоте́ла *f* прийти́	ya bi o-chyén' ha-tyél/ha-tyé-la pree-tee
I'm sorry, I can't come	К сожале́нию я не могу́ прийти́	ksa-zhe-lyé-nee-yoo ya nyé ma-goo pree-tee
May I bring a friend?	Могу́ ли я привести́ дру́га/подру́гу *f*?	ma-goo lee ya pree-vyés-tee droo-ga/pa-droo-goo

VISITING FRIENDS

This section contains a few phrases which you may find useful if invited to visit a Russian friend's house.[1] When arriving at a Russian household it is sometimes a necessary politeness to change out of one's boots or shoes into slippers offered by the host. Russians are tremendously hospitable, and will ply you with food and drink, whatever the time of day. Drinks are never served before the meal, but always with the meal, particularly with the substantial hors-d'œuvres or zakooskee with which every proper Russian meal starts. Toasts are proposed, and it is usual to clink glasses with everybody round the table before drinking.

Come in	*Проходи́те	pra-ha-dee-tyé
Please take your coat off	*Раздева́йтесь	raz-dyé-vay-tyés'

1. For finding the house of a Russian friend, see 'Russian Addresses' (p. 54).

Please sit down	*Сади́тесь	sa-dee-tyés'
I'm sorry I'm late	Прости́те, я опозда́л/опозда́ла *f*	pra-stee-tyé, ya a-paz-dal/a-paz-da-la
What would you like to drink?	*Что вы бу́дете пить?	shto vi boo-dyé-tyé peet'
Your health!	За ва́ше здоро́вье!	za va-shé zda-ro-vyé
Help yourself	*Угоща́йтесь/Бери́те са́ми	oo-ga-shay-tyés'/byé-ree-tyé sa-mee
A little more, please	Ещё немно́жко, пожа́луйста	ye-sho nyé-mnozh-ka, pa-zha-loo-sta
Thank you, I'm afraid I'm full	Спаси́бо, бо́льше не могу́	spa-see-ba, bol'-shé nyé ma-goo
What is this dish called?	Как называ́ется э́то блю́до?	kak na-zi-va-yét-sa é-ta blyoo-da
It's delicious	Э́то о́чень вку́сно	é-ta o-chyén' fkoos-na
You are very kind	Вы о́чень добры́	vi o-chyén' da-bri
Do you mind if I smoke?	Вы не возража́ете, е́сли я покурю́?	vi nyé voz-ra-zha-yé-tyé yés-lee ya pa-koo-ryoo
Do you smoke?	Вы ку́рите?	vi koo-ree-tyé
Could I have a match?	Мо́жно спи́чки?	mozh-na speech-kee
It's time for us to go	Нам пора́ идти́	nam pa-ra eet-tee
Thank you for a lovely time	Спаси́бо, бы́ло о́чень прия́тно	spa-see-ba, bi-la o-chyén' pree-yat-na

DIFFICULTIES

Sorry, I'm in a hurry	Извини́те, я о́чень тороплю́сь	eez-vee-nee-tyé, ya o-chyén' ta-ra plyoos
Who are you?	Кто вы?	kto-vi
I don't want to talk to you	Я не хочу́ с ва́ми разгова́ривать	ya nyé ha-choo sva-mee raz-ga-va-ree-vat'
Go away	Уходи́те	oo-ha-dee-tyé
Leave me alone	Оста́вьте меня́	a-staf-tyé me-nya

GOING TO A RESTAURANT

WHERE TO EAT

If you are travelling with a group on a package tour, you will be served set meals at fixed times in the hotel restaurant. These meals are often time-consuming, and you may prefer to try eating out in establishments frequented by Russians. There is a great variety of places to eat where you can have anything from a full meal to a light snack. The main types of eating establishments are described below. First, there is the restaurant (PECTOPÁH – ryéstaran). This is the most expensive type of eating-place. Russians go to restaurants for a whole evening's entertainment, rather than just for a meal – they spin out the evening by drinking numerous toasts and dancing between courses; there is often a band which plays loud music. Nobody expects the service to be quick. In Moscow there are many excellent restaurants which specialize in the cuisine of the various Soviet republics.

The Aragvi (Georgian food), the Uzbekistan and the Baku (Eastern food) are amongst the most famous restaurants in Moscow. National Russian cuisine can also be sampled at the Slavyansky Bazar or at the Tsentralniy, or at the Skazka or Russkaya Izba restaurants just outside Moscow. In Leningrad it is well worth eating at the Sadko restaurant, or at the Astoria hotel which has a mirrored restaurant decorated in an extravagant Art Nouvea style.

Next there is the café (КАФÉ – kafé). These vary considerably – som are almost as smart as the restaurants, others are considerably cheape There are no cafés where you can just sit and have a drink; you ar expected to eat a full meal. There are, however, two particular types of café the КАФÉ-КОНДИ́ТЕРСКАЯ (kafé-kandeetyérskaya) which serve cakes and coffee, and the КАФЕ-МОРОЖЕНОЕ (kafé-marozhénayé which serves various kinds of ice-cream with cakes and drinks (champagn or cocktails). There is a good ice-cream parlour in Moscow on Gorky Stree opposite the Intourist hotel. The newest developments are cooperative café or restaurants – РЕСТОРА́НЫ КООПЕРАТИ́ВЫ such as 36 Kropot kinskaya, Moscow.

There are also cafeterias or canteens (СТОЛОВАЯ – stalovaya). Thes are both public establishments and canteens attached to libraries and insti tutions. The system is self-service; a limited range of dishes is available, an the prices are very low. No alcoholic drinks are served. There are som 'dietetic cafeterias' (ДИЕТИ́ЧЕСКАЯ СТОЛО́ВАЯ – deeyéteechyés kaya stalovaya) where health foods are served.

A whole range of smaller eating establishments specializes in particula types of foods. A ЗАКУ́СОЧНАЯ (zakoosachnaya) serves zakooskee – snacks. A ПИРОЖКО́ВАЯ (peerazhkovaya) serves peerazhkee – smal pies or pasties with a savoury stuffing, usually of meat, onion, or cabbage These are usually eaten with a meat broth. They are also sold on th street by pie-vendors. A ПЕЛЬМЕ́ННАЯ (pyel'myénnaya) serve pyél'myénee, Siberian meat dumplings, somewhat similar to ravioli, serve with a touch of vinegar or sour cream. A ШАШЛЫ́ЧНАЯ (shashlichnaya) serves shashlik – a Caucasian speciality rather like kebabs Some other Central Asian specialities, such as spicy meatballs, are als served. A БЛИ́ННАЯ (bleennaya) offers bleeni – Russian pancakes served hot with sour cream, butter, jam, curd cheese or honey, and tea. A ПИВНО́Й БАР (peevnoy bar) serves beer (peeva) by the tankar (kroozhka). Russians enjoy chewing a piece of salted fish while they drin beer. Sometimes these establishments are no more than a kiosk on the street. Recently, pizzerias have also appeared (ПИЦЦЕ́РИЯ).

Where is the nearest restaurant/café?	Где здесь поблúзости ресторáн/кафé	gdyé zdyés' pa-**blee**-za-stee ryés-ta-**ran**/ka-**fé**
Which restaurant would you recommend?	Какóй ресторáн вы мóжете порекомендовáть?	ka-**koy** ryés-ta-**ran** vi **mo**-zhé-tyé pa-ryé-ka-myén-da-**vat'**
Where can we have a meal near here?	Где здесь мóжно пообéдать?	gdyé zdyés' **mozh**-na pa-a-**byé**-dat'
Where can we get a snack near here?	Где здесь мóжно перекусúть?	gdyé zdyés' **mozh**-na pyé-ryé-koo-**seet'**

The most popular restaurants are usually guarded by a doorman, and almost invariably display a sign at the entrance saying 'Full up'. This should not, however, be taken as the literal truth; it is always worth making a determined effort to get into the restaurant, and the most effective method of doing so is simply by explaining you are a foreigner. Otherwise, it is possible to make an advance reservation, either through the service bureau of your hotel, or independently. Once in the restaurant you leave your coat in the cloakroom before proceeding to your table.

НЕТ МЕСТ	Full up
ЗАКАЗАНО	Reserved
СТОЛ ЗАКАЗАН	Table reserved

Where is the cloakroom?	Где гардерóб?	gdyé gar-dyé-**rop**
May I leave a bag with you?	Мóжно у вас остáвить сýмку?	**mozh**-na oo-vas a-**sta**-veet' **soom**-koo

Do you have a table for three/for four?	У вас есть сто́лик на трои́х/на четверы́х?	oo-vas yést' sto-leek na-tra-eeh/na-chét-vyé-rih
Is this table/seat free?	Здесь свобо́дно?	zdyés' sva-bod-na
Can we sit over there?	Мо́жно сесть там?	mozh-na syést' tam
How long will we have to wait?	Ско́лько нам придётся ждать?	skol'-ka nam pree-dyot-sa zhdat'
I have reserved a table. My name is ...	Я заказа́л/заказа́ла *f* сто́лик. Меня́ зову́т ...	ya za-ka-zal/za-ka-za-la sto-leek. me-nya za-voot ...
I would like to book a table	Я хочу́ заказа́ть сто́лик	ya ha-choo za-ka-zat' sto-leek
for today/for tomorrow	на сего́дня/на за́втра	na-syé-vod-nya/ na-zav-tra
for Monday	на понеде́льник	na-pa-nyé-dyel'-neek
for eight o'clock	на во́семь часо́в	na-vo-syém' cha-sof
Can I have this dance?[1]	Мо́жно вас пригласи́ть на та́нец?	mozh-na vas pree-gla-seet' na-ta-nyéts
Where is the toilet?	Где туалéт?	gdyé too-a-lyét

1. In a restaurant with a band where people are dancing, both men and women may ask a stranger of the opposite sex to dance.

THE MENU

This menu includes typical dishes which you will find in cafeterias, as well as in smarter eating establishments. The menu is divided into sections which correspond to the order of a Russian meal (first course, soup, main course, dessert, and hot or cold drink). Within each section the dishes are listed in alphabetical order.

Many restaurants and some cafés have standard menus which are printed with an English translation. The dishes are only available if the price is typed in opposite the entry.

Could we have the menu, please?	Да́йте, пожа́луйста, меню́	day-tyé, pa-zha-loo-sta, myé-nyoo

МЕНЮ́ — myé-nyoo — MENU

ХОЛО́ДНЫЕ ЗАКУ́СКИ — ha-lot-ni-yé za-koos-kee — COLD HORS D'OEUVRES

Ассорти́ мясно́е	as-sar-tee myas-no-yé	assorted cold meats
Ассорти́ ры́бное	as-sar-tee rib-na-yé	assorted fish
Бужени́на с гарни́ром	boo-zhé-nee-na sgar-nee-ram	cold boiled pork with vegetable garnish
Ветчина́ с гарни́ром	vyét-chee-na sgar-nee-ram	ham with vegetable garnish
Винегре́т	vee-nyé-gryét	Russian salad – mixed finely chopped vegetables, meat or fish
Грибы́ – марино́ванные/солёные	gree-bi – ma-ree-no-van-ni-yé/sa-lyo-ni-yé	mushrooms – pickled/salted

Закýска сбóрная мяснáя	za-koos-ka sbor-na-ya myas-na-ya	mixed hors-d'œuvres of cold meats
Ивасú по купéчески	ee-va-see pa-koo-pyé-chyés-kee	tinned herring
Икрá баклажáнная	ee-kra ba-kla-zhan-na-ya	aubergine purée
Икрá	ee-kra	caviare
зернúстая	zyér-nees-ta-ya	type of black caviare
крáсная/чёрная	kras-na-ya/ chyor-na-ya	red/black
Кúльки	keel'-kee	sprats (tinned)
Колбасá копчёная	kal-ba-sa kap-chyo-na-ya	smoked sausage
Маслúны	mas-lee-ni	olives
Мáсло	mas-la	butter
Осетрúна	a-syé-tree-na	sturgeon
заливнáя/под майонéзом	za-leev-na-ya/pad ma-yo-né-zam	in aspic/with mayonnaise
с гарнúром	sgar-nee-ram	with vegetable garnish
Рóстбиф с гарнúром	rost-beef sgar-nee-ram	cold roast beef with vegetable garnish
Салáт	sa-lat	salad
из огурцóв	eez a-goor-tsof	cucumber salad
из помидóров	eez pa-mee-do-raf	tomato salad
из редúски	eez ryé-dees-kee	radish salad

столи́чный	sta-leech-niy	salad of chopped meat and vegetable
Сарди́ны с лимо́ном	sar-dee-ni slee-mo-nam	sardines with lemon
Севрю́га отварна́я с гарни́ром	syé-vryoo-ga at-var-na-ya sgar-nee-ram	cold poached sturgeon, served with a vegetable garnish
Сельдь	syél'd'	herring
Сёмга	syom-ga	salmon
Спи́нка осетра́	speen-ka a-syé-tra	pieces of sturgeon, cut from the back
Сыр	sir	cheese
Тёша	tyo-sha	smoked belly of sturgeon or white fish
Шпро́ты	shpro-ti	sprats (tinned)
Язы́к с гарниром	ya-zik sgar-nee-ram	tongue with vegetable garnish
Яйцо́ под майонéзом	yay-tso pad ma-yo-né-zam	egg mayonnaise
ПÉРВЫЕ БЛЮ́ДА	**pyér-vi-yé blyoo-da**	**SOUPS**
Борщ	borsh	borsch – soup of beetroot, and other vegetables
со свини́ной	sa-svee-nee-noy	borsch with pork
украи́нский	oo-kra-een-skeey	Ukrainian borsch

Бульóн	boo-lyon	consommé
с пирожкáми	spee-razh-ka-mee	served with small meat pies
с фрикадéльками	sfree-ka-dél'-ka-mee	with meat balls
с яйцóм	syay-tsom	with a hard-boiled egg
Окрóшка мяснáя	a-krosh-ka myas-na-ya	cold soup of kvas,[1] chopped egg, meat, spring onion, and cucumber
Рассóльник	ras-sol'-neek	soup made with kidneys and pickled cucumbers
Свекóльник	svyé-kol'-neek	beetroot soup, usually served cold with sour cream
Соля́нка	sa-lyan-ka	salyanka – soup with pickled cucumbers and olives
мяснáя/ры́бная	myas-na-ya/rib-na-ya	meat salyanka/fish salyanka
сбóрная	sbor-na-ya	mixed meat salyanka
Суп горóховый	soop ga-ro-ha-viy	pea soup
Суп из фасóли	soop eez fa-so-lee	bean soup
Суп-лапшá молóчный	soop lap-sha ma-loch-niy	milk soup with noodles

1. See p. 96.

Суп моло́чный вермише́левый	soop ma-loch-niy vyér-mee-shé-lyé-viy	milk soup with fine noodles
Уха́	oo-ha	fish soup
Харчо́	har-cho	spicy Caucasian mutton soup
Щи (ки́слые/све́жие)	shee (kees-li-yé/svyé-zhi-yé)	cabbage soup (made with sauerkraut/fresh cabbage)

ВТОРЫ́Е БЛЮ́ДА — fta-ri-yé blyoo-da — MAIN DISHES

МЯСНЫ́Е БЛЮ́ДА[1] — myas-ni-yé blyoo-da — MEAT AND POULTRY DISHES

Азу́ из говя́дины	a-zoo eez ga-vya-dee-ni	beef stew
Антреко́т	an-tryé-kot	entrecote steak
Бара́нина	ba-ra-nee-na	mutton
Бефстро́ганов	byéf-stro-ga-nof	beef stroganoff
Бито́чки	bee-toch-kee	meatballs
Бифште́кс	beef-shtéks	steak
натура́льный/с лу́ком	na-too-ral'-niy/sloo-kam	plain/with onion
с яйцо́м	syay-tsom	with a fried egg
Бли́нчики с мя́сом	bleen-chee-kee smya-sam	pancakes with a meat filling

1. See p. 89 for cooking methods.

Говя́дина	ga-vya-dee-na	beef
Гуля́ш	goo-lyash	stew
Гусь, жа́реный с я́блоками	goos', zha-rye-niy sya-bla-ka-mee	goose, roasted with apples
Инде́йка	een-dyéy-ka	turkey
Котле́ты	kat-lyé-ti	meat or chicken rissoles
Котле́ты кури́ные	kat-lyé-ti koo-ree-ni-yé	chicken rissoles
Котле́ты по-ки́евски	kat-lyé-ti pa-kee-yéf-skee	chicken kiev – chicken breast stuffed with butter
Кро́лик	kro-leek	rabbit
Купа́ты	koo-pa-ti	spicy Caucasian pork sausage with garlic
Ку́рица отварна́я с ри́сом	koo-ree-tsa at-var-na-ya sree-sam	boiled chicken with rice
Куропа́тка	koo-ra-pat-ka	partridge
Ланге́т	lan-gyét	fillet (of meat)
Люля́-keба́б	lyoo-lya ke-bap	spicy Caucasian meatballs
Мя́со тушёное	mya-sa too-sho-na-yé	stewed meat
Пе́чень говя́жья	pyé-chyén' ga-vyazh'-ya	calf's liver
Плов	plof	pilaf
Поджа́рка	pad-zhar-ka	roast meat (usually pork)

Поросёнок с гре́чневой ка́шей	pa-ra-syo-nak sgryéch-nyé-voy ka-shéy	roasted suckling pig stuffed with buckwheat
Рагу́	ra-goo	stew
Ромште́кс	rom-shtéks	rump steak
Ря́бчик	ryap-cheek	hazel-grouse
Свина́я отбивна́я	svee-na-ya at-beef-na-ya	slice of pork fillet, beaten until flat
Свини́на	svee-nee-na	pork
Соси́ски	sa-sees-kee	frankfurters
с гарни́ром/ с капу́стой	sgar-nee-ram ska-poos-toy	with vegetable garnish with cabbage
Теля́тина	tyé-lya-tee-na	veal
Тефте́ли	tyéf-tyé-lee	meat or chicken rissoles
У́тка, жа́реная с я́блоками	oot-ka, zha-ryé-na-ya sya-bla-ka-mee	duck, roasted with apples
Цаци́ви	tsa-tsee-vee	young chicken served with a Caucasian nut sauce
Цыплёнок табака́	tsi-plyo-nak ta-ba-ka	Caucasian dish of chicken, pressed flat under a weight, and fried
Чахохби́ли из кур	cha-hah-bee-lee eez koor	Caucasian chicken casserole

Шашлы́к по-кавка́зски	shash-lik pa-kaf-kaz-skee	Caucasian kebabs of lamb, beef, or pork
Шашлы́к по-ка́рски	shash-lik pa-kar-skee	kebabs of lamb, beef or pork, and kidneys
Шни́цель	shnee-tsél'	fillet of pork or veal
Шни́цель ру́бленый	shnee-tsél' roo-blyé-niy	minced meat rissole
Эскало́п	é-ska-lop	escalope

РЫ́БНЫЕ БЛЮ́ДА[1]	rib-ni-yé blyoo-da	FISH DISHES
Ка́мбала	kam-ba-la	plaice/flounder
Карп	karp	carp
Ке́та	kyé-ta	Siberian salmon
Котле́ты ры́бные	kat-lyé-ti rib-ni-yé	fish cakes
Лещ	lyésh	bream
Лососи́на	la-sa-see-na	salmon
Нали́м	na-leem	burbot
О́кунь	o-koon'	perch
Осетри́на	a-syé-tree-na	sturgeon
Па́лтус	pal-toos	halibut
Ры́ба фарширо́ванная	ri-ba far-shee-ro-van-na-ya	gefilte fish – fish cakes or a stuffed fish

1. See opposite page for cooking methods.

Севрю́га	syé-vryoo-ga	sevruga (a kind of sturgeon)
Сёмга	syom-ga	salmon
Сиг	seek	similar to salmon
Ску́мбрия	skoom-bree-ya	mackerel
Сом	som	sheat-fish
Стéрлядь	styér-lyat'	sterlet
Суда́к	soo-dak	pike-perch
Треска́	tryés-ka	cod
Филé трески́	fee-lyé tryés-kee	fillet of cod
Форéль	fa-ryél'	trout
Щу́ка	shoo-ka	pike

COOKING METHODS

варёный/варёная[1]	va-ryo-niy/va-ryo-na-ya	boiled
в горшо́чке	fgar-shoch-kyé	baked in a pot
в смета́не	fsmyé-ta-nyé	in a sour cream sauce
в тома́те	fta-ma-tyé	in a tomato sauce
жа́реный/жа́реная	zha-ryé-niy/zha-ryé-na-ya	fried, roasted or grilled
запечённый/запечённая	za-pyé-chyon-niy/za-pyé-chyon-na-ya	baked

1. Adjectives are given in both masculine and feminine forms.

на вéртеле	na vyér-tyé-lyé	grilled on a skewer
отварнóй/отварнáя	at-var-noy/ at-var-na-ya	boiled
паровóй/паровáя	pa-ra-voy/pa-ra-va-ya	steamed
печёный/печёная	pyé-chyo-niy/pyé-chyo-na-ya	baked
со сметáной	sa-smyé-ta-noy	with sour cream
тушёный/тушёная	too-sho-niy/too-sho-na-ya	stewed or braised
фарширóванный/ фарширóванная	far-shee-ro-van-niy/ far-shee-ro-van-na-ya	stuffed
фри	free	fried

OTHER MAIN DISHES, MADE WITH CEREALS, MILK, FLOUR OR EGGS[1]

Блúнчики сварéньем	bleen-chee-kee sva-ryén'-yém	pancakes with jam
Блúнчики с твóрогом	bleen-chee-kee stvo-ra-gam	pancakes filled with curd cheese
Блины́ с мáслом и сметáной	blee-ni smas-lam ee smyé-ta-noy	pancakes with butter and sour cream
Запекáнка рúсовая	za-pyé-kan-ka ree-sa-va-ya	baked rice pudding

1. These dishes are usually eaten as a main course at dinner or for breakfast.

Запека́нка тво́рожная со смета́ной	za-pyé-kan-ka tvo-razh-na-ya sa smyé-ta-noy	baked curd cheese cake with raisins and sour cream
Ка́ша ма́нная	ka-sha man-na-ya	semolina pudding
Ка́ша ри́совая	ka-sha ri-sa-va-ya	rice pudding
Ола́дьи	a-lad'-ee	thick pancakes
Омле́т	am-lyét	omelette
Сы́рники со смета́ной	sir-nee-kee sa smyé-ta-noy	fried curd cheese cakes with sour cream
Яи́чница	ya-eech-nee-tsa	fried eggs
СЛА́ДКИЕ БЛЮ́ДА	slat-kee-yé blyoo-da	**DESSERTS**
Моро́женое	ma-ro-zhé-na-yé	ice-cream
Пиро́жное	pee-rozh-na-yé	cake (small)
Сли́вки взби́тые с са́харом	sleef-kee vzbee-ti-yé ssa-ha-ram	whipped cream with sugar
Торт	tort	cake
МОЛО́ЧНЫЕ ПРОДУ́КТЫ[1]	ma-loch-ni-yé pra-dook-ti	**MILK PRODUCTS**
Кефи́р с са́харом	ke-feer ssa-ha-ram	kefir – a type of yoghurt – with sugar
Молоко́	ma-la-ko	milk
Смета́на	smyé-ta-na	sour cream

1. The first three items are served in glasses in cafeterias.

Твóрог	tvo-rag	curd cheese
ХОЛÓДНЫЕ НАПИТКИ	ha-lot-ni-yé na-peet-kee	**COLD DRINKS**
Кисéль	kee-syel'	a starchy drink flavoured with fruit juice or milk
Компóт	kam-pot	*compote* – made from fresh or dried fruit, with a lot of liquid added
Кóфе гляссé	ko-fyé glyas-syé	iced coffee
Сок я́блочный	sok ya-blach-niy	apple juice
ГОРЯ́ЧИЕ НАПИТКИ	ga-rya-chee-yé na-peet-kee	**HOT DRINKS**
Какáо	ka-ka-o	cocoa
Кóфе с молокóм	ko-fyé sma-la-kom	coffee with milk
Кóфе чёрный (с лимóном)	ko-fyé chyor-niy (slee-mo-nam)	black coffee (with lemon)
Чай с лимóном	chay slee-mo-nam	tea with lemon
Чай с сáхаром	chay ssa-ha-ram	tea with sugar

ORDERING

A full Russian meal starts with '**zakooskee**' – hors-d'œuvres. These are often quite extensive, and are accompanied by drinks – spirits as well as wines. The next stage of the meal is the soup – this is known as the 'first course' ('**pyérvayé blyooda**'); it is followed by the 'second course' ('ftaroyé **blyooda**') or main dish, which consists of a piece of meat, chicken, or fish, served with a set garnish of vegetables. The dessert is referred to as 'the sweet' ('**slatkayé**') or as the 'third course' ('**tryétyé blyooda**') and is usually served with tea or coffee. The Russian idea of a dessert is something very light, like ice-cream. Anything heavier, like a pudding or a cheesecake, is regarded as a main course.

Excuse me, please ...[1]	Извини́те, пожа́луйста ...	eez-vee-**nee**-tyé, pa-**zha**-loo-sta ...
Where is our waiter?	Где наш официа́нт?	gdyé nash a-fee-tsi-**ant**
Please take our order	Прими́те, пожа́луйста, зака́з	pree-**mee**-tyé, pa-**zha**-loo-sta, za-**kaz**
What can you recommend?	Что вы посове́туете?	shto vi pa-sa-**vyé**-too-yé-tyé
What are your specialities?	Каки́е у вас фи́рменные блю́да?	ka-**kee**-yé oo-vas **feer**-myén-ni-yé **blyoo**-da
What is this dish, please?	Что э́то за блю́до?	shto **é**-ta za-**blyoo**-da
What kind of meat is it made with?	Из како́го мя́са э́то пригото́влено?	eez ka-**ko**-va **mya**-sa **é**-ta pree-ga-**tov**-lyé-na
I'll have this	Я возьму́ э́то	ya vaz'-**moo** **é**-ta
Could you please bring us	Принеси́те, пожа́луйста	pree-nyé-**see**-tyé, pa-**zha**-loo-sta
one helping/two helpings	одну́ по́рцию/две по́рции	ad-**noo** **por**-tsi-yoo/dvyé **por**-tsi-ee

1. This is the best phrase to use for attracting the waiter's attention.

Do you have	У вас есть	oo-vas yést'
something for children?	что-нибу́дь для дете́й?	shto-nee-boot dlya dyé-tyéy
half-portions?[1]	пол-по́рции?	pal-por-tsi-ee?
I'm a vegetarian. What dishes do you have without	Я вегетериа́нец. Каки́е у вас есть блю́да без	ya vyé-gyé-tyé-ree-a-nyéts. ka-kee-yé oo-vas yést' blyoo-da byéz
meat?	мя́са?	mya-sa
fish?	ры́бы?	ri-bi
eggs?	яи́ц?	ya-eets
I don't like	Я не люблю́	ya nyé lyoo-blyoo
onion	лук	look
fat foods	жи́рную пи́щу	zhir-noo-yoo pee-shoo
fried foods	жа́реное	zha-ryé-na-yé
Could I have some more?	Мо́жно ещё?	mozh-na yé-sho
Could you please bring us a(n)/some	Принеси́те, пожа́луйста	pree-nyé-see-tyé, pa-zha-loo-sta
ashtray	пе́пельницу	pyé-pyél'-nee-tsoo
bread	хлеб	hlyép
butter	ма́сло	mas-la
chair	стул	stool

1. Normally only half-portions of soup are served.

cigarettes	сигаре́ты	see-ga-ryé-ti
fork	ви́лку	veel-koo
fruit	фру́кты	frook-ti
glass	стака́н	sta-kan
ice-cream	моро́женое	ma-ro-zhé-na-yé
jam	варе́нье	va-ryé-nyé
knife	нож	nosh
matches	спи́чки	speech-kee
mayonnaise	майоне́з	ma-yo-néz
milk	молоко́	ma-la-ko
mustard	горчи́цу	gar-chee-tsoo
napkins	салфе́тки	sal-fyét-kee
pepper	пе́рец	pyé-ryéts
plate	гаре́лку	ta-ryél-koo
salt	соль	sol'
spoon	ло́жку	losh-koo
sugar/water	са́хар/воды́	sa-har/va-di
wine glass	рю́мку	ryoom-koo

DRINKS

Only the smartest restaurants have a separate wine list. Drinks are usually listed on the menu. Georgian wines, Crimean port and Armenian cognac are all excellent; Soviet champagne is different from French champagne, but well worth trying. The famous Russian drink 'kvas' is made from black bread or a mixture of flours fermented with yeast. It is not alcoholic, and the lactic acid which it contains is reputed to have beneficial effects on the digestive system. You can order it by the bottle in a restaurant, or sample it in the street from a roadside tanker.

Russian fruit juices are delicious, and can be sampled at kiosks in the metro or at special juice and mineral-water bars in town (СО́КИ-ВО́ДЫ – sokee-vodi: 'Juices – mineral waters'). Kiosks usually have one or two of the following varieties: apple, peach, cherry, pear, mandarin, grape, apricot, plum and tomato. Most of the mineral waters come from natural springs in the Caucasus; the most well known are НАРЗА́Н (narzan) and БОРЖО́МИ (barzhomee).

You can also order the Russian version of Coca Cola – БАИКАЛ (baykal) – or the drink known as leemanad which is not really like lemonade, but more like a fizzy flavoured drink.

Could I please have	Да́йте, пожа́луйста	**day-tyé, pa-zha-loo-sta**
a bottle	буты́лку	**boo-til-koo**
50/100 grams[1]	пятьдеся́т/сто грамм	**pyat'-dyé-syat/sto gramm**
150 grams	сто пятьдеся́т грамм	**sto pyat'-dyé-syat gramm**
200/300 grams	две́сти/три́ста грамм	**dvyé-stee/tree-sta gramm**

1. Wines and spirits can be ordered by the bottle or by the weight. The normal capacity of a bottle is three-quarters of a litre for wines, and half a litre for spirits (vodka and cognac). If you want to order the equivalent of half a bottle of wine, you must ask for 350 grams of wine. Fifty grams is the equivalent of a small single measure of cognac or vodka; 150 grams is the equivalent of a generous wineglassful.

of red/white wine	кра́сного/ бе́лого вина́	kras-na-va/ byé-la-va vee-na
of Georgian wine	грузи́нского вина́	groo-zeen-ska-va vee-na
of dry/sweet wine	сухо́го/сла́дкого вина́	soo-ho-va/slat-ka-va vee-na
of Soviet champagne	сове́тского шампа́нского	sa-vyét-ska-va sham-pan-ska-va
of cognac/of vodka	коньяка́/во́дки	kon'-ya-ka/vot-kee
of beer/kvas	пи́ва/ква́са	pee-va/kva-sa
of lemonade	лимона́да	lee-ma-na-da
of fruit juice	фрукто́вого со́ка	frook-to-va-va so-ka
of mineral water	минера́льной воды́	mee-nyé-ral'-noy va-di
Which wine would you recommend?	Како́е вино́ вы мо́жете нам порекомендова́ть?	ka-ko-yé vee-no vi mo-zhé-tyé nam pa-ryé-ka-myén-da-vat'
Could you chill this wine?	Мо́жно охлади́ть э́то вино́?	mozh-na a-hla-deet' é-ta vee-no
How much does a bottle of ... cost?	Ско́лько сто́ит буты́лка ...? (+ gen.)	skol'-ka sto-eet boo-til-ka ...
Do you serve cocktails?	У вас есть кокте́йлы	oo-vas yést' kak-tyéy-lee

Could you bring us	Принеси́те, пожа́луйста	pree-nyé-see-tyé, pa-zha-loo-sta
three coffees/one tea	три ко́фе/оди́н чай	tree ko-fyé/a-deen chay
with milk/without milk	с молоко́м/без молока́	sma-la-kom/byéz ma-la-ka
with lemon	с лимо́иом	slee-mo-nam
Soft drinks	Безалкого́льные напи́тки	byéz-al-ka-gol'-ni-yé na-peet-kee
I'd like	Я хочу́	ya ha-choo
apple juice	я́блочный сок	ya-blach-niy sok
grape juice	виногра́дный сок	vee-na-grad-niy sok
orange juice	апельси́новый сок	a-pyel'-see-na-viy sok
a fruit juice	фрукто́вый сок	frook-to-viy sok
tomato juice	тома́тный сок	to-mat-niy sok
a milk shake	моло́чный кокте́йль	ma-loch-niy kak-tyéyl'
cocoa	кака́о	ka-ka-o
beer	пи́во	pee-va
dark	тёмное	tyom-na-yé
light	све́тлое	svyét-la-yé
bottled	в буты́лке	fboo-til-kyé
in a can	в ба́нке	fban-kyé
draught	из бо́чки	eez boch-kee

COMPLAINTS

Could you bring my order, please?	Принеси́те, пожа́луйста, мой зака́з	pree-nyé-**see**-tyé, pa-**zha**-loo-sta, moy za-**kaz**
Excuse me, could you speed up the service, we're in a hurry	Извини́те, мо́жно поскоре́е, мы спеши́м	eez-vee-**nee**-tyé, **mozh**-na pa-ska-**ryé**-yé, mi spyé-**shim**
I have been waiting for a long time	Я уже́ давно́ жду	ya oo-**zhé** dav-**no** zhdoo
This isn't what I ordered	Э́то не то, что я зака́зывал/ зака́зывала *f*	**é**-ta nyé to shto ya za-**ka**-zi-val/za-**ka**-zi-va-la
I asked for . . .	Я проси́л/проси́ла *f* . . .	ya pra-**seel**/pra-**see**-la . . .
This bread is stale	Э́тот хлеб чёрствый	**é**-tat hlyep **chyorst**-viy
This isn't fresh	Э́то несве́жее	**é**-ta nyé-**svyé**-zhé-yé
This isn't cooked	Э́то недожа́рено	**é**-ta nyé-da-**zha**-ryé-na
This is cold	Э́то осты́ло	**é**-ta a-**sti**-la
Could you heat this up?	Мо́жете ли вы э́то разогре́ть?	**mo**-zhé-tyé-lee-vi **é**-ta ra-za-**gryét'**
This is dirty	Э́то гря́зное	**é**-ta **gryaz**-na-yé
I don't like this	Мне э́то не нра́вится	mnyé **é**-ta nyé **nra**-veet-sa

Could you please call the manager	Позови́те, пожа́луйста, заве́дующего	pa-za-vee-tyé, pa-zha-loo-sta, za-vyé-doo-yoo-shé-va

PAYING

In restaurants and cafés, the waiter or waitress will bring you a bill at the end of the meal. Some self-service establishments operate a canteen type of system – you take a tray, help yourself to the dishes you want (hot dishes must usually be asked for) and pay at a cash desk before eating. In other places, there is a menu pinned up by the cash desk; you must first pay for your meal, listing the names or the prices of the dishes which you would like to the cashier, and then hand the receipt or chyék in at the food counter, where you are issued with the food you have paid for.

Service is always included in the bill.

May we have the bill please?	Счёт, пожа́луйста	shyot, pa-zha-loo-sta
Please give us separate bills	Посчита́йте нам отде́льно, пожа́луйста	pa-shee-tay-tyé nam at-dyél'-na pa-zha-loo-sta
Please check the bill	Прове́рьте, пожа́луйста, счёт	pra-vyér-tyé, pa-zha-loo-sta, shyot
It was very good	Бы́ло о́чень вку́сно	bi-la o-chyén' fkoos-na
We enjoyed it, thank you	Нам о́чень понра́вилось, спаси́бо	nam o-chyén' pa-nra-vee-las', spa-see-ba

SNACK BAR

The boofyét, a snack bar or refreshment room, is found in hotels, theatres, cinemas, museums, and stations. The menu varies from establishment to establishment – you might find champagne and caviare in the refreshment room of thc Bolshoi Theatre, but would not expect to come across it in the snack bar of a museum. There is no written menu, but the food which is available is usually all displayed in a glass stand or on a table. In hotel snack bars, it is sometimes possible to ask for an omelette or fried eggs to be cooked.

Where is the snack bar?	Где здесь буфе́т?	gdyé zdyés' boo-fyét
Could I please have	Да́йте, пожа́луйста	**day**-tyé, pa-**zha**-loo-sta
that/another one	э́то/ещё оди́н	**é**-ta/yé-**sho** a-**deen**
A bottle/a glass	Буты́лка/стака́н	boo-**til**-ka/sta-**kan**
of juice/of lemonade	со́ка/лимона́да	**so**-ka/lee-mo-**na**-da
of beer/of champagne	пи́ва/ шампа́нского	**pee**-va/ sham-**pan**-ska-va
of kefir[1]/of ryazhenka[2]	кефи́ра/ря́женки	ké-**fee**-ra/ **rya**-zhén-kee
One (two) coffee(s)	Оди́н (два) ко́фе	a-**deen** (dva) **ko**-fyé
One tea (two teas) with lemon	Оди́н чай (два ча́я) с лимо́ном	a-**deen** chay (dva **cha**-ya) slee-**mo**-nam

1. Similar to yoghurt, sold by the bottle or by the glass.
2. A delicious milk product, made from fermented boiled milk.

A sandwich	Оди́н бутербро́д	a-deen boo-tér-brot
with cheese/with ham	с сы́ром/с ветчино́й	ssi-ram/svyét-chee-noy
with sausage	с колбасо́й	skal-ba-soy
with fish/with caviare	с ры́бой/с икро́й	sri-boy/see-kroy
A piece of black/white bread	Кусо́чек чёрного/ бе́лого хле́ба	koo-so-chyék chyor-na-va/byé-la-va hlyé-ba
Cheese	Сыр	sir
Frankfurters	Соси́ски	sa-sees-kee
Ham	Ветчина́	vyét-chee-na
Pancake	Бли́нчик	bleen-cheek
Roll	Бу́лочка	boo-lach-ka
A small pie	Пирожо́к	pee-ra-zhok
A hard-boiled egg	Круто́е яйцо́	kroo-to-yé yay-tso
A soft-boiled egg	Яйцо́ всмя́тку	yay-tso fsmyat-koo
Fried eggs	Яи́чницу	ya-eech-nee-tsoo
An omelette	Омле́т	am-lyét
A bun with a curd cheese centre	Ватру́шку	va-troosh-koo
A curd cheese ball	Сыро́к	si-rok
One pastry	Одно́ пиро́жное	ad-no pee-rozh-na-yé
A slice of cake	Кусо́чек то́рта	koo-so-chyék tor-ta
A bar of chocolate	Шокола́дку	sha-ka-lat-koo

A sweet	Конфéту	kan-fyé-too
Two/three/four sweets	Две/три/четы́ре конфéты	dvyé/tree/che-ti-ryé kan-fyé-ti
An ice-cream	Морóженое	ma-ro-zhé-na-yé
How much does it cost?	Скóлько э́то стóит?	skol'-ka é-ta sto-eet

SHOPPING & SERVICES

SHOP SIGNS

The purpose of this alphabetical list is to enable you to look up any sign displayed on a building or kiosk. Since almost all shops and enterprises in the Soviet Union are public and state property, they are usually identified by standardized signs which are descriptive of the goods on sale or services offered. For example, all butcher's shops are identified by the sign МЯСО – Meat, rather than by an owner's name as would be common in the West. Shops, eating places, services, and public buildings usually occupy part of the ground floor of a large block of flats, and can be identified by the signs on the front of the building.

АПТЕКА	Chemist
АТЕЛЬЕ	Dressmaker
БАНК	Bank
БЕРЁЗКА	Beryozka – shop selling goods to foreigners for hard currency
БИБЛИОТЕКА	Library
БЛИННАЯ	Café serving pancakes (see page 78)

БОЛЬНИЦА	Hospital
БУКИНИСТИЧЕСКИЙ МАГАЗИН	Second-hand books
БУЛОЧНАЯ	Baker
БУЛОЧНАЯ – КОНДИТЕРСКАЯ	Bread, cake, and sweet shop
ВИНО	Wine
ГАЗЕТНЫЙ КИОСК	News-stand
ГАЗИРОВАННАЯ ВОДА	Soda water
ГАЛАНТЕРЕЯ	Haberdashery and toilet requisites
ГАСТРОНОМ	General food store
ГРАМПЛАСТИНКИ	Records
ДЕТСКАЯ ОДЕЖДА	Children's clothes
ДИЕТА	Food store specializing in dietetic foods
ДОМ КНИГИ	Bookshop
ЖЕНСКАЯ ОБУВЬ	Women's shoes
ЖЕНСКАЯ ОДЕЖДА	Women's clothes
ЗАКУСОЧНАЯ	Café serving light snacks (see page 78)
ИГРУШКИ	Toys
КАНЦЕЛЯРСКИЕ ТОВАРЫ	Stationery
КАНЦТОВАРЫ	Stationery
КАФЕ	Café
КАФЕ – МОРОЖЕНОЕ	Ice-cream parlour
КИНО	Cinema
КИНОТЕАТР	Cinema
КИНОФОТОТОВАРЫ	Cine-cameras and photographic supplies

КНИГИ	Books
КНИЖНЫЙ МАГАЗИН	Bookshop
КОЛБАСЫ	Sausages
КОМИССИОННЫЙ МАГАЗИН	Second-hand goods shop (clothes or antiques)
КОНДИТЕРСКАЯ	Cake and sweet shop
КОНСЕРВЫ	Tinned foods
КУЛИНАРИЯ	Semi-prepared and cooked foods
КУЛЬТТОВАРЫ	'Culture wares' – stationery, musical instruments, sports goods
МАСТЕРСКАЯ	Repairs
МЕБЕЛЬ	Furniture
МЕЖДУГОРОДНЫЙ ТЕЛЕФОН	Long-distance telephone call office
МЕЛОДИЯ	'Melodiya' – records
МЕТАЛЛОРЕМОНТ	Metal work and repairs (keys cut, locks repaired, umbrellas mended, etc.)
МЕХА	Furs
МОРОЖЕНОЕ	Ice-cream
МУЖСКАЯ ОБУВЬ	Men's shoes
МУЖСКАЯ ОДЕЖДА	Men's clothes
МЯСО	Meat
ОБУВЬ	Shoes
ОВОЩИ – ФРУКТЫ	Vegetables – Fruit
ОДЕЖДА	Clothes
ОПТИКА	Optician
ОТДЕЛЕНИЕ МИЛИЦИИ	Police station
ОТДЕЛЕНИЕ СВЯЗИ	Post office

ПАПИРОСЫ – СИГАРЕТЫ	Cigarettes
ПАРИКМАХЕРСКАЯ	Hairdresser
ПАРФЮМЕРИЯ	Perfumes and toilet requisites
ПЕЛЬМЕННАЯ	Café serving Siberian meat dumplings (see page 78)
ПЕРЕГОВОРНЫЙ ПУНКТ	Long-distance telephone call office
ПИРОЖКОВАЯ	Café serving meat pies (see page 78)
ПИЦЦЕРИЯ	Pizzeria
ПОДАРКИ	Gifts
ПОЛИКЛИНИКА	Out-patients' clinic
ПОЧТА	Post Office
ПОЧТА-ТЕЛЕГРАФ	Post office – Telegraph office
ПОЧТОВОЕ ОТДЕЛЕНИЕ	Local post office
ПРАЧЕЧНАЯ	Laundry
ПРОДМАГ	Food store
ПРОДОВОЛЬСТВЕННЫЙ МАГАЗИН	Food store
ПРОДУКТЫ	Food store
РАДИОТОВАРЫ	Radio and TV goods
РЕМОНТ ОБУВИ	Shoe repairs
РЕМОНТ СУМОК	Repairs to bags
РЕМОНТ ЧАСОВ	Watch repairs
РЕСТОРАН	Restaurant
РЫБА	Fish
РЫНОК	Market
СБЕРЕГАТЕЛЬНАЯ КАССА	Savings bank
СБЕРКАССА	Savings bank
СВЕТ	'Light' – electrical goods
СОКИ	Fruit juices

СОКИ – ВОДЫ	Fruit juices – Mineral waters
СОЮЗПЕЧАТЬ	News-stand
СПОРТТОВАРЫ	Sports goods
СПРАВКИ	Information
СПРАВОЧНОЕ БЮРО	Information bureau
СТОЛОВАЯ	Cafeteria
ТАБАК	Tobacco
ТЕАТР	Theatre
ТЕАТРАЛЬНАЯ КАССА	Theatre booking office
ТЕЛЕГРАФ	Telegraph office
ТЕЛЕФОН	Telephone
ТКАНИ	Fabrics
ТРИКОТАЖ	Knitted fabrics and articles of clothing
УНИВЕРМАГ	Department store
УНИВЕРСАМ	Supermarket
ФОТОАТЕЛЬЕ	Photographer's studio
ФОТОГРАФИЯ	Photographer's studio
ФОТОЛАБОРАТОРИЯ	Photo laboratory
ФОТОМАГАЗИН	Photographic supplies
ФОТОТОВАРЫ	Photographic supplies
ХИМЧИСТКА	Dry cleaning
ХЛЕБ	Bread
ХОЗЯЙСТВЕННЫЙ МАГАЗИН	Household goods (hardware)
ХОЗЯЙСТВЕННЫЕ ТОВАРЫ	Household goods (hardware)
ХУДОЖЕСТВЕННЫЙ САЛОН	Art Salon
ЦВЕТЫ	Flowers

ЧАСЫ	Watches and clocks
ШАШЛЫЧНАЯ	Café serving kebabs (see page 78)
ЭЛЕКТРОТОВАРЫ	Electrical goods
ЮВЕЛИРНЫЙ МАГАЗИН	Jewellery

WHERE TO GO

If you are shopping for a particular item, consult the relevant section below. If you just want to visit a Soviet shop, you will perhaps gain the fullest impression by visiting a department store (УНИВЕРМА́Г – Ooneevyer-mag, i.e. Universal store). In Moscow the two best department stores are ГУМ (GOOM – the initials stand for State Universal Store), on Red Square, and ЦУМ (TsOOM – the initials of Central Universal Store) on the Petrovka behind the Bolshoi theatre. In Leningrad there is the famous ГОСТИ́НЫЙ ДВОР (Gasteeniy Dvor) on Nevsky Prospekt. There are also the foreign-currency Beryozka shops which are reserved for foreigners. You will not get a true impression of a Soviet shop by visiting a Beryozka, but you will find a greater range of luxury goods on sale, and sometimes at cheaper prices in the foreign currency than in roubles in Soviet shops. Beryozkas also accept payment by credit card.

Most shops (apart from food shops, for which see page 119) are closed on Sunday and shut from 2 to 3 p.m. every day. Shops usually open at 9 or 11 a.m., and close at 6, 7, 8, or 9 p.m.

МАГАЗИН РАБОТАЕТ с 11ч. до 20ч.	The shop is open from 11 a.m. to 8 p.m.
ПЕРЕРЫВ с 14ч. до 15ч.	Midday closing from 2 p.m. to 3 p.m.
ВЫХОДНОЙ ДЕНЬ: ВОСКРЕСЕНЬЕ	Closed on: Sunday

Where is there a department store near here?	Где здесь универмáг?	gdyé zdyés' oo-nee-vyér-mak
Where can I buy ...?	Где мóжно купи́ть ...? (+ acc.)	gdyé mozh-na koo-peet' ...
How can I get there?	Как тудá попáсть?	kak too-da pa-past'
When does the shop open?	Когдá открывáется магази́н?	kag-da at-kri-va-yét-sa ma-ga-zeen
When does the shop shut?	Когдá закрывáется магази́н?	kag-da za-kri-va-yét-sa ma-ga-zeen

IN THE SHOP[1]

КАССА	Cash desk
САМООБСЛУЖИВАНИЕ	Self-service

Excuse me, please ...	Извини́те, пожáлуйста ...	eez-vee-nee-tyé, pa-zha-loo-sta ...
Do you have ...?	У вас есть ...?	oo-vas yést' ...
Which section is ... sold in?	В какóм отдéле продаётся ...?	fka-kom at-dyé-lyé pra-da-yot-sa ...
I would like to buy ...	Я хочý купи́ть ... (+ acc.)	ya ha-choo koo-peet' ...
Please show that to me	Покажи́те, пожáлуйста, э́то	pa-ka-zhi-tyé, pa-zha-loo-sta, é-ta

1. Everything for sale is usually on display, so there is little point in asking for something if you cannot see it.

'hat one, please	Вот э́то, пожа́луйста	vot é-ta, pa-zha-loo-sta
t's in the window	Э́то в витри́не	é-ta vvee-tree-nyé
)o you have another one?	У вас есть друго́й?	oo-vas yést' droo-goy
)o you have anything cheaper/like this?	У вас есть что-нибу́дь дешёвле/вро́де э́того?	oo-vas yést' shto nee-boot dyé-shév-lyé/vro-dyé é-ta-va
No, it's not what I want	Нет, мне э́то не ну́жно	nyét, mnyé é-ta nyé noozh-na
'es, I'll take that	Да, я э́то возьму́	da, ya é-ta vaz'-moo
ιnother one, please	Ещё оди́н, пожа́луйста	yé-sho a-deen, pa-zha-loo-sta
Γhat's all	Э́то всё	é-ta fsyo
Vrap it up, please	Заверни́те, пожа́луйста	za-vyér-nee-tyé, pa-zha-loo-sta

RETURNING GOODS

This isn't working	Э́то не рабо́тает	é-ta nyé ra-bo-ta-yét
May I exchange this?	Мо́жно э́то поменя́ть?	mozh-na é-ta pa-myé-nyat'
would like to return this. Here is the receipt	Я хочу́ э́то верну́ть. Вот чек	ya ha-choo é-ta vyér-noot'. vot chyék
'lease call the manager	Позови́те заве́дующего	pa-za-vee-tyé za-vyé-doo-yoo-she-va

PAYING[1]

In Soviet shops there are three stages to making a purchase. You must fir find out what you want to buy, whether it is in stock, and how much costs. The shop-assistant will tell you the price; if you do not understan ask her to write it down for you. In some shops, if you are buying manufac tured goods, the shop-assistant will write out a sales-slip for you to take t the cash desk. In this case, the phrase 'please write me out a sales-slip' the standard phrase for indicating that you wish to buy the item. When yo have established the cost of the item, go to the КАССА (**kassa**) or cas desk, and repeat the price of the item to the cashier. She may ask you i which section you are making your purchase; you can either point or giv the name or number of the relevant section of the shop. The cashier wi then ring up the sum of money on the till, and give you a chyék – a receip – which you must take back to the first shop-assistant, and hand over i return for your purchase. In large department stores, purchases are some times collected from a counter marked ВЫДАЧА ПОКУ́ПОК (**Vidach pakoopak**) or КОНТРО́ЛЬ (**Kantrol'**).

How much does it cost?	Ско́лько э́то сто́ит?	**skol'-ka é-ta sto-eet**
Would you write the price down, please	Напиши́те це́ну, пожа́луйста	**na-pee-shi-tyé tsé-noo, pa-zha-loo-sta**
Please write me out a sales-slip	Вы́пишите, пожа́луйста	**vi-pee-shi-tyé, pa-zha-loo-sta**
Pay at the cash desk	*Плати́те в ка́ссу	**pla-tee-tyé fkas-soo**

1. For a description of Soviet money see p. 17.

Where/which section?	*Куда́/в како́й отде́л?	koo-da/fka-koy at-dyel
Over there	Туда́	too-da
In the milk section	В моло́чный отде́л	fma-loch-niy at-dyél
Your receipt, please	*Ваш чек, пожа́луйста	vash chyék, pa-zha-loo-sta
Who is last in the queue?	Кто после́дний?	kto pa-slyéd-neey

SOUVENIRS

Traditional Russian handicrafts are sold in souvenir shops, or at the souvenir counters of large department stores. In these shops you can buy wooden spoons and bowls from Khokhloma (painted brightly in red, gold, and black, and varnished), Russian wooden dolls which fit inside each other (matryoshkee), ivory bone carvings from the North, Palekh ware (lacquered boxes or brooches made from papier mâché with brightly coloured miniatures painted on them), Russian lace, wooden carvings, shawls and scarves, and amber jewellery from the Baltic republics. In Moscow, there are two particularly good areas for souvenir shopping. One is on Kutuzovsky Prospekt, opposite the Ukraina hotel. Set back from the road is an Art Salon which specializes in pottery, weavings, rugs, and amber jewellery. Near by, at 9 Kutuzovsky Prospekt, is a large souvenir shop, РУ́ССКИЙ СУВЕНИ́Р (**Roosskeey soovyéneer** – Russian Souvenir), next to which there is a Beryozka shop. Across the road is a large toy shop ДОМ ИГРУ́ШКИ (Dom **eegrooshkee** – The House of Toys).

The other good shopping centre is on the Petrovka, a street which starts behind the Bolshoi Theatre. Here is Moscow's Central Department Store (known by its initials as TsOOM), and a shopping arcade ПЕТРО́ВСКИЙ

ПАССА́Ж (Pyétrovskeey passazh) with souvenir shops; a little further up the street there is an Art Salon and a shop called РУ́ССКИЙ УЗО́Р (Roosskeey oozor – Russian Design) which sells jewellery as well as handicrafts.

There are shops which specialize in watches and clocks, and jewellery shops (usually with individual names referring to precious stones). Fur hats can be purchased in hat shops or in large department stores (ГОЛОВНЫ́Е УБО́РЫ – Galavniyé oobori – Hats). However, all these items are often on sale in Beryozka shops at a foreign-currency price which is lower than the rouble price in Soviet shops.

There are also official state shops selling second-hand goods – usually clothes or antiques. These shops are called Kameesseeonniy magazeen because of the commission which the state deducts for selling the property of individuals. Paintings, china, and samovars are on sale (see 'Arrival and Customs', page 19), and, although the prices are high, the shops are interesting to browse in.

Posters and postcards are sold in bookshops (see page 116).

Where is there a	Где	gdyé
souvenir shop?	магази́н сувени́ров?	ma-ga-zeen soo-vyé-nee-raf
watches and clocks shop?	магази́н часо́в?	ma-ga-zeen cha-sof
jewellery shop?	ювели́рный магазин?	yoo-vyé-leer-niy ma-ga-zeen
second-hand goods shop?	комиссио́нный магази́н?	ka-mees-see-on-niy ma-ga-zeen
Do you have any	У вас есть	oo-va yést'
toys?	игру́шки?	ee-groosh-kee

Russian wooden dolls?	матрёшки?	ma-tryosh-kee
wooden dishes?	деревя́нная посу́да?	dyé-ryé-vyan-na-ya pa-soo-da
wooden spoons?	деревя́нные ло́жки?	dyé-ryé-vyan-ni-yé losh-kee
Palekh ware?	изде́лия из Па́леха?	eez-dyé-lee-ya eez pa-lyé-ha
headscarves/shawls?	платки́/ша́ли?	plat-kee/sha-lee
fur hats?	меховы́е ша́пки?	myé-ha-vi-yé shap-kee
things made of amber?	изде́лия из янтаря́?	eez-dyé-lee-ya eez yan-ta-rya
Is this real	Э́то настоя́щее	é-ta nas-ta-ya-shé-yé
silver/gold?	серебро́/зо́лото?	syé-ryé-bro/zo-la-ta

BOOKS AND RECORDS

It is generally very difficult to find good books on sale in ordinary Soviet bookshops since they are in great demand, and sell out very quickly. The biggest bookshop in Moscow is ДОМ КНИ́ГИ (Dom kneegee, meaning 'The House of Books') on Prospekt Kalinina. Interesting books can be found in the second-hand bookshops, but they are usually expensive. The Beryozka shops carry a selection of books; in Moscow, on Kropotkinskaya Ulitsa, there is a Beryozka which specializes in books.

One of the best record shops in Moscow, МЕЛО́ДИЯ (Melodiya), is near 'The House of Books' on Prospekt Kalinina. Records are also sold in large bookshops, department stores, and Beryozka shops. Russian records are extremely good value – a long-playing record usually costs about 2 roubles 50 kopecks.

Where is there a bookshop?	Где кни́жный магази́н?	gdyé kneezh-niy ma-ga-zeen
Where are books	Где кни́ги	gdyé knee-gee
on art?	по иску́сству?	pa-ees-koos-stvoo
by Tolstoy?	Толсто́го (or any author's name in gen. case)?	tal-sto-va
in English?	на англи́йском языке́?	na-an-gleey-skam ya-zi-kyé
for children?	для дете́й?	dlya dyé-tyéy
on the Russian language?	по ру́сскому языку́?	pa-roos-ska-moo ya-zi-koo
Do you have	У вас есть	oo-vas yést'
a guide book?	путеводи́тель?	poo-tyé-va-dee-tyél'
an English-Russian dictionary?	англо-русский слова́рь?	an-gla-rooss-kiy sla-var'
any posters?	плака́ты?	pla-ka-ti
Where is there a record shop?	Где магази́н пласти́нок?	gdyé ma-ga-zeen plas-tee-nak
Do you have any records (of ...)?	У вас есть пласти́нки ... ? (+ gen.)	oo-vas yést' pla-steen-kee ...

Iay I listen to this record?	Мóжно послýшать эту пластúнку?	mozh-na pa-sloo-shat' é-too pla-steen-koo

NEWSPAPERS AND STATIONERY

Iewspapers are displayed for the public to read on special stands in the :reets; they are also sold at news-stands or in automatic vending machines, sually found in metro stations. Western newspapers are not generally available, but may be on sale at the news-stand in the hotel lobby. *Moscow News*, n English-language Soviet publication, carries useful information about 'hat is on in Moscow, and is usually available in hotels.

Maps, paper, postcards, pens, envelopes, and stamps are also sold at ews-stands. A wider range of stationery articles can be found in stationery hops. Postcards of paintings or buildings are sold in bookshops, sometimes ı the poster section.

Vhere is the nearest news-stand?	Где ближáйший газéтный киóск?	gdyé blee-zhay-sheey ga-zyét-niy kee-osk
'ravda, please	*Прáвду*, пожáлуйста	prav-doo, pa-zha-loo-sta
)o you have any English newspapers?	У вас есть англúйские газéты?	oo-vas yést' an-gleey-skee-yé ga-zyé-ti
'lease give me	Дáйте, пожáлуйста	day-tyé, pa-zha-loo-sta
some drawing paper	бумáгу для рисовáния	boo-ma-goo dlya ree-sa-va-nee-ya
an envelope	конвéрт	kan-vyért
an exercise book	тетрáдь	tyé-trat'
a note pad	блокнóт	blak-not

paperclips	скрéпки	skryép-kee
a pen	рýчку	rooch-koo
a pencil	карандáш	ka-ran-dash
a pencil sharpener	точи́лку	ta-cheel-koo
a postcard	откры́тку	at-krit-koo
a rubber	рези́нку	ryé-zeen-koo
some writing paper	почтóвую бумáгу	pach-to-voo-yoo boo-ma-goo
Do you have ... ?	У вас есть ... ?	oo-vas yést' ...
Where can I buy	Где мóжно купи́ть	gdyé mozh-na koo-peet
a map of the town?	план гóрода?	plan go-ra-da
a public transport map of the town?	план городскóго трáнспорта?	plan go-rad-sko-va tran-spar-ta
a plan of the metro?	план метрó?	plan mé-tro
a road map?	кáрту автомоби́льных дорóг?	kar-too af-ta-ma-beel'-nih da-rok
Where is there a stationery shop?	Где магази́н канцеля́рских товáров?	gdyé ma-ga-zeen kan-tsé lyar-skeeh ta-va-raf

TOBACCONIST

Cigarettes and tobacco are sold at news-stands and tobacco kiosks. Popula brands of filter-tips are Столи́чные (Staleechniyé – 'Metropolitan') an

Но́вость (Novast – 'News'). The Russians also smoke papeerosi – long hollow-tipped cigarettes – the most popular brands are Казбе́к (Kazbyék – 'Kazbek') and Беломо́р (Byélamor – 'White Sea'). The best filter-tips are Золото́е руно́ (Zalatoyé roono – 'Golden Fleece') and Я́ва (Yava – 'Java'). Western cigarettes can only be purchased in Beryozka shops.

Smoking is not allowed in public places – in the underground, on buses, in shops, in museums, in theatres and cinemas, etc.

Where is there a tobacco kiosk?	Где́ здесь таба́чный кио́ск?	gdyé zdyés' ta-**bach**-niy kee-**osk**
Could I please have	Да́йте мне, пожа́луйста	**day**-tyé mnyé, pa-**zha**-loo-sta
some filter-tip cigarettes	сигаре́ты с фи́льтром	see-ga-**ryé**-ti **sfeel'**-tram
some cigarettes without filters	сигаре́ты без фи́льтра	see-ga-**ryé**-ti byéz **feel'**-tra
some pipe tobacco	таба́к для тру́бки	ta-**bak** dlya **troop**-kee
a box of cigars	коро́бку сига́р	ka-**rop**-koo see-**gar**
some matches/a cigarette lighter	спи́чки/зажига́лку	**speech**-kee/ za-zhi-**gal**-koo

FOOD AND DRINK

For general food shopping, it is best to go to a Gastranom or general food store. Department stores often have a food section on the ground floor, and there are also supermarkets. Most towns have a market where many items not available in shops are on sale. In Moscow there are two markets which are well worth a visit – the Central market at 15 Tsvetnoy Boulevard, and the Cheryomooshkeenskeey market at 1/42 Lomonosovsky Prospekt (within a short tram or trolleybus ride of the Ooneevyérseetyét or Prafsayooznaya metro stations).

Individual shops which sell particular categories of food are described in the sections which follow. All food shops are open every day of the year, and close from 1 p.m. to 2 p.m. for the midday break. When shopping for food, it is wise to carry a supply of plastic bags, since no paper or bags are provided in the shops.

Where is the nearest	Где здесь	gdyé zdyés'
general food store?	гастроно́м?	gas-tra-nom
food store?	продово́льственный магази́н?	pra-da-vol'-stvyén-niy ma-ga-zeen
department store?	универма́г?	oo-nee-vyér-mak
supermarket/market?	универса́м/рынок?	oo-nee-vyér-sam/ ri-nak

BREAD AND CAKES

In the Soviet Union, there are both bread shops and combined bread and cake shops. White bread is usually baked in long stick-shaped loaves; the price varies according to the quality of the flour. There are many different kinds of 'black' bread: arlofskeey, baradeenskeey, rzhanoy, to name but a few. It is possible to buy a whole, a half, or a quarter of a loaf of black bread.

Bread shops are almost always self-service. You choose your bread from the racks, testing its freshness with the forks provided for this purpose; then you take it to the cashier.

Cakes tend to have standard names such as 'Prague' or, more fancifully, 'Goose's feet', and are sold in bread and cake shops or Kooleenareeya

('Semi-prepared and cooked foods') shops. The best shop in Moscow for cakes and biscuits is at 11 Stoleshnikov Pereulok. Bread and cake shops also sell a great variety of sweets and chocolates. They are usually priced per 100 grams.

Tea and coffee are also sold in bread and cake shops. If you want anything out of the ordinary, such as green tea, there are specialized tea and coffee shops in Moscow (at 19 Ulitsa Kirova) and in Leningrad (at 81 Nevsky Prospekt).

Where is the nearest bread shop?	Где здесь бу́лочная?	gdyé zdyés' boo-lach-na-ya
Where is the nearest bread and cake shop?	Где здесь бу́лочная-конди́терская?	gdyé zdyés' boo-lach-na-ya kan-dee-tyér-ska-ya
Is the bread fresh?	Хлеб све́жий?	hlyep svyé-zhiy
Please give me a/some	Да́йте, пожа́луйста	day-tyé, pa-zha-loo-sta
loaf	буха́нку	boo-han-koo
half-loaf/quarter (of a loaf)	пол-буха́нки/че́тверть	pal-boo-han-kee/chét-vyért'
of white bread/black bread	бе́лого хле́ба/чёрного хле́ба	byé-la-va hlyé-ba/chyor-na-va hlyé-ba
long loaf	бато́н	ba-ton
small loaf	бу́лку	bool-koo
roll	бу́лочку	boo-lach-koo
cake	торт	tort
pastry	пиро́жное	pee-rozh-na-yé

packet of biscuits	па́чку пече́нья	**pach-koo pyé-chyé-nya**
200 grams/half a kilo of sweets	две́сти грамм/ полкило́ конфе́т	**dvyés-tee gramm/ pal-kee-lo kan-fyét**
box of chocolates	коро́бку шокола́дных конфе́т	**ka-rop-koo sha-ka-lat-nih kan-fyét**
bar of chocolate	шокола́дку	**sha-ka-lat-koo**
packet/tin of coffee	па́чку/ба́нку ко́фе	**pach-koo/ban-koo ko-fyé**
packet of (green) tea	па́чку (зелёного) ча́я	**pach-koo (zyé-lyo-na-va) cha-ya**

MILK AND EGGS

Dairy products, mayonnaise, and eggs are sold in milk shops, or in the milk section of general food stores. Cheese and butter are sold in packets in supermarkets, but are cut and weighed individually for each customer in smaller shops. Eggs are sold loose or in boxes of ten.

There are many excellent milk products in the Soviet Union which we do not have in the West. Amongst these are **kéfeer**, a type of yoghurt, **rya-zhénka**, made from boiled fermented milk, and **smyétana**, sour cream, which is thick, and not at all sour in taste. It is much more common than ordinary single cream (**sleefkee**), and is served with soups, salads and main dishes, or on its own. These milk products are sold in large or small unlabelled bottles; they can be identified by the colour of the bottle top, although practice is not always consistent even within the same town. In Moscow, blue is usually used for yoghurt, greeny blue for **kéfeer**, pink for **ryazhénka**, and silver or gold and white stripes for **smyétana**. Milk is sold in cartons, or in bottles with silver tops.

Tvorag, a fresh curd cheese, is usually eaten with sour cream and a sprinkling of sugar. It is sold in packets in shops, but the best place to buy it is at the market, where peasant women preside over huge enamel bowls of their home-made tvorag which they will allow you to taste. They also sell fresh sour cream.

The ice-cream in the Soviet Union is excellent; it is on sale at numerous kiosks, which display the different kinds together with their prices.

Where is the nearest milk shop?	Где здесь моло́чный магази́н?	gdyé zdyés' ma-locn-niy ma-ga-zeen
Where is the milk section?	Где моло́чный отде́л?	gdyé ma-loch-niy at-dyél
Please give me a bottle/carton	Да́йте, пожа́луйста, буты́лку/па́чку ...	day-tyé, pa-zha-loo-sta, boo-til-koo/pach-koo ...
of milk/yoghurt	молока́/простоква́ши	ma-la-ka/pra-sta-kva-shi
of kefir/ryazhenka	кефи́ра/ря́женки	ké-fee-ra/rya-zhén-kee
of sour cream/single cream	смета́ны/сли́вок	smyé-ta-ni/slee-vak
Please give me	Дайте, пожа́луйста	day-tyé, pa-zha-loo-sta
a packet of curd cheese	па́чку тво́рога	pach-koo tvo-ra-ga
a curd cheese ball	сыро́к	si-rok
100/200 grams/a packet	сто/две́сти грамм/па́чку	sto/dvyé-stee gram/pach-koo
of butter/cheese	ма́сла/сы́ра	mas-la/si-ra

10 eggs	деся́ток яиц	dyé-sya-tak ya-eets
a pot of mayonnaise	ба́нку майоне́за	ban-koo ma-yo-né-za
Where can I buy some ice-cream near here?	Где здесь мо́жно купи́ть моро́женое?	gdyé zdyés' mozh-na koo- peet' ma-ro-zhé-na-yé

VEGETABLES AND FRUIT

Vegetables and fruit are sold together, in shops, or at kiosks. There is not a very great variety available. At the market the choice is much wider, but the prices are considerably higher.

Vegetable and fruit shops also sell dried fruits, bottled fruits and vegetables, and jam, as well as the traditional salted cucumbers and cabbage in barrels.

Where is the nearest greengrocer's shop?	Где здесь овощно́й магази́н?	gdyé zdyés' a-vash-noy ma-ga-zeen
Please give me	Да́йте, пожа́луйста	day-tyé, pa-zha-loo-sta
½ kilo/a kilo	полкило́/кило́	pal-kee-lo/kee-lo
1½ kilos/2 kilos	полтора́ кило́/два кило́	pal-ta-ra kee-lo/dva kee-lo
a bunch	пучо́к	poo-chok
of carrots/ cucumbers	морко́ви/огурцо́в	mar-ko-vee/ a-goor-tsof
of dill/lettuce	укро́па/сала́та	oo-kro-pa/sa-la-ta
of onions/potatoes	лу́ка/карто́шки	loo-ka/kar-tosh-kee
of radishes	реди́ски	ryé-dees-kee

of salted cabbage	квашеной капусты	kva-shé-noy ka-poos-ti
of salted cucumbers	солёных огурцов	sa-lyo-nih a-goor-tsof
of spring onions	зелёного лука	zyé-lyo-na-va-loo-ka
of tomatoes	помидоров	pa-mee-do-raf
a cabbage	кочан капусты	ka-chan ka-poos-ti
a jar of peas	банку гороха	ban-koo ga-ro-ha
a jar of jam	банку варенья	ban-koo va-ryén'-ya
a jar of preserved fruit	банку компота	ban-koo kam-po-ta
a melon	дыню	di-nyoo
a bottle of fruit juice	бутылку фруктового сока	boo-til-koo frook-to-va-va so-ka
Please give me ½ kilo/a kilo	Дайте, пожалуйста, полкило/кило	day-tyé, pa-zha-loo-sta, pal-kee-lo/kee-lo
of apples/apricots	яблок/абрикосов	ya-blak/a-bree-ko-saf
of red cherries/white cherries	вишен/черешни	vee-shen/chyé-ryésh-nee
of dates/dried apricots	фиников/урюка	fee-nee-kaf/oo-ryoo-ka
of dried fruit/figs	сушёных фруктов/инжира	soo-sho-nih frook-taf/een-zhi-ra

of grapes/lemons	виногра́да/ лимо́нов	vee-na-gra-da/ lee-mo-naf
of oranges/peaches	апельси́нов/ пе́рсиков	a-pyél'-see-naf/ pyér-see-kaf
of pears/plums	груш/слив	groosh/sleef
of pomegranates/ prunes	грана́тов/ черносли́ва	gra-na-taf/chyér-na-slee-va
of raisins/ strawberries	изю́ма/клубни́ки	eez-yoo-ma/ kloop-nee-kee
of tangerines	мандари́нов	man-da-ree-naf
Are they ripe?	Они́ спе́лые?	a-nee spyé-li-yé?
Can I help myself?	Мо́жно мне самому́/само́й *f* вы́брать?	mozh-na mnyé sa-ma-moo/sa-moy vi-brat'

MEAT

Meat shops only sell large chunks of meat on the bone. To buy meat in any other form you must go to a Kooleenareeya, a shop which sells semi-prepared and cooked foods. These shops or kiosks are more like a butcher's shop than the meat shops are. They sell stewing meat of various qualities, steaks, meat or chicken rissoles, minced beef, liver, and chickens. Cooked meats, fish and chicken, and prepared salads or vegetables may also be on sale. Beef is usually the only meat available, although sometimes it is possible to get mutton. If you want to buy fresh meat which hasn't been frozen, you must go to the market.

Boiled and smoked sausages, frankfurters, and ham are sold in the delicatessen section of a Gastranom, often next to the milk and cheeses.

Where is the nearest	Где здесь	gdyé zdyés'
meat shop?	мясной магазин?	myas-noy ma-ga-zeen
semi-prepared foods shop?	кулинария?	koo-lee-na-ree-ya
Where is the sausage section?	Где здесь колбасный отдел?	gdyé zdyés' kal-bas-niy at-dyél
What kind of meat is this?	Какое это мясо?	ka-ko-yé é-ta mya-sa
Please give me	Дайте, пожалуйста	day-tyé, pa-zha-loo-sta
a chicken	курицу	koo-ree-tsoo
... steaks/meat rissoles[1]	... антрекотов/котлет	... an-tryé-ko-taf/kat-lyét
½ kilo/a kilo	полкило/кило	pal-kee-lo/kee-lo
of this meat	этого мяса	é-ta-va mya-sa
of beef/mutton/pork	говядины/баранины/свинины	ga-vya-dee-ni/ba-ra-nee-ni/svee-nee-ni
of stewing meat	гуляша/азу[2]	goo-lya-sha/a-zoo
of lean chopped beef	бефстроганова	byéf-stro-ga-no-va
of fried fish	жареной рыбы	zha-ryé-noy ri-bi
of fried meat	жареного мяса	zha-ryé-na-va mya-sa

1. Sold individually. For numbers see p. 235.
2. The second is better quality and more expensive than the first.

of liver/of minced beef	печёнки/фа́рша	pyé-chyon-kee/ far-sha
of frankfurters/of ham	соси́сок/ветчины́	sa-see-sak/ vyét-chee-ni
of smoked sausage	копчёной колбасы́	kap-chyo-noy kal-ba-si
of boiled sausage	варёной колбасы́	va-ryo-noy kal-ba-si

FISH

Almost all the fish on sale is frozen. In the summer a few shops have live fish (usually carp or sheat-fish) on sale in tanks. Herring is usually only available smoked, salted or in tins.

Where is the nearest fish shop?	Где здесь ры́бный магази́н?	gdyé zdyés' rib-niy ma-ga-zeen
What kind of fish is this?	Кака́я э́то ры́ба?	ka-ka-ya é-ta ri-ba
Please give me	Да́йте пожа́луйста	day-tyé, pa-zha-loo-sta
a salted herring	селёдку	syé-lyot-koo
a smoked herring	копчёную сельдь	kap-chyo-noo-yoo syél'd'
½ kilo/a kilo	полкило́/кило́	pal-kee-lo/kee-lo
of this fish	э́той ры́бы	é-toy ri-bi
of cod/halibut/ sprats	трески́/па́лтуса/ ки́лек	tryés-kee/pal-too-sa/ kee-lyék

a tin	ба́нку	ban-koo
of sprats/herring/ sardines	шпрот/са́йры/ сарди́й	shprot/say-ri/ sar-deen

GROCERIES

Most food stores have a groceries section which sells dried goods – flour, cereals, noodles and macaroni, sugar, spices, and tea (sugar and tea are also sold in bread shops).

Where is the groceries section/shop?	Где бакале́я?	gdyé ba-ka-lyé-ya
Please give me some	Да́йте, пожа́луйста	day-tyé, pa-zha-loo-sta
granulated sugar/ lump sugar	песо́к/са́хар	pyé-sok/sa-har
salt/macaroni	соль/макаро́ны	sol'/ma-ka-ro-ni
rice/flour/tea	рис/муку́/чай	rees/moo-koo/chay

WINES AND SPIRITS

The best wine shops in Moscow are at 7 Stoleshnikov Pereulok and 4 Gorky Street. Georgian wines, Armenian cognacs, Crimean port, and vodka are amongst the best buys. Western spirits are only available in Beryozka shops. Soft drinks are sold in supermarkets and general food stores; fruit juices are also sold in vegetable and fruit shops.

Where is the nearest wine shop?	Где здесь ви́нный магази́н?	gdyé zdyés' veen-niy ma-ga-zeen
Please give me a bottle	Да́йте, пожа́луйста, буты́лку	day-tyé, pa-zha-loo-sta, boo-til-koo

of beer/champagne	пи́ва/шампа́нского	pee-va/sham-pan-ska-va
of cognac/port	коньяка́/портве́йна	kan'-ya-ka/part-vyéy-na
of vermouth/vodka	ве́рмута/во́дки	vyér-moo-ta/vot-kee
of red/white wine	кра́сного/бе́лого вина́	kras-na-va/byé-la-va vee-na
of sweet/dry wine	сла́дкого/сухо́го вина́	slat-ka-va/soo-ho-va vee-na
of Georgian wine	грузи́нского вина́	groo-zeen-ska-va vee-na

CLOTHES AND SHOES

Clothes and shoes are generally very expensive in the Soviet Union. It is best to travel with a good supply of stockings and tights, since these are extremely costly to replace. Some items of clothing, including fur hats, scarves, and shawls, are available more cheaply in the Beryozka shops.

Most clothes and shoe shops can be identified by the sign ОДЕ́ЖДА (Adyézhda – Clothes) or О́БУВЬ (Oboof – Shoes), sometimes preceded by МУЖСКА́Я (Moozhskaya – Men's), ЖЕ́НСКАЯ (Zhénskaya – Women's) or ДЕ́ТСКАЯ (Dyétskaya – Children's).

All the clothes and shoes which are for sale are on display. You should not therefore need to say very much to the shop-assistant. If you need to ask for anything in particular, the names of items of clothing and footwear are given in the general vocabulary.

The sizing system is confusing because it is similar to the continental system but not identical. Tables of clothing sizes are given below to serve as a rough guide, but it is always best to try something on before buying it, since sizes can vary tremendously.

МУЖСКАЯ ...	Men's ...
ЖЕНСКАЯ ...	Women's ...
ДЕТСКАЯ ...	Children's ...
ОДЕЖДА	Clothes
ОБУВЬ	Shoes

Where is there a shop for	Где здесь магази́н	gdyé zdyés' ma-ga-zeen
men's/women's	мужско́й/ же́нской	moozh-skoy/ zhen-skoy
clothes/shoes?	оде́жды/ о́буви?	a-dyézh-di/o-boo-vee
Is this my size?	Э́то мой разме́р?	é-ta moy raz-myér
Which is my size?	Како́й мой разме́р?	ka-koy moy raz-myér
Can you measure me?	Вы не могли́ бы изме́рить меня́?	vi nyé ma-glee bi eez-myé-reet' me-nya
It's for a three-year-old	Это для трёхлетнего ребёнка	é-ta dlya tryoh-lyét-nyé-va ryé-byon-ka
Have you got it	У вас есть	oo-vas yést'
in size ...?[1]	... разме́р?	... raz-myér
in another colour/style?	друго́го цве́та/ фасо́на?	droo-go-va tsvyé-ta/ fa-so-na
It's too small/too big	Э́то мало́/велико́	é-ta ma-lo/vyé-lee-ko
Do you have a bigger/smaller size?	У вас есть бо́льший/ ме́ньший разме́р?	oo-vas yést' bol'-shiy/ myén'-shiy raz-myér

1. Use the ordinal number (see p. 239).

May I try it on?	Мóжно примéрить?	**mozh-na pree-myé-reet'**
Do you have a mirror?	У вас есть зéркало?	**oo-vas-yést' zyér-ka-la**
Is it washable?	Мóжно э́то стирáть?	**mozh-na é-ta stee-rat'**
Will it shrink?	Э́то сади́тся?	**é-ta sa-deet-sa**
Is it colour-fast?	Э́то линя́ет?	**é-ta lee-nya-yét**
Is it	Э́то	**é-ta**
handmade?	ручнáя рабóта?	**rooch-na-ya ra-bo-ta**
cotton?	хлóпок?	**hlo-pak**
lace?	кружевá?	**kroo-zhe-va**
leather	кóжа	**ko-zha**
linen?	лён?	**lyon**
silk?	шёлк?	**sholk**
suede?	зáмша?	**zam-sha**
synthetic (fibres)?	синтéтика?	**seen-tyé-tee-ka**
wool?	шерсть?	**shérst'**

CLOTHING SIZES

WOMEN'S DRESSES, ETC.

American	8	10	12	14	16	18	20
British	10	12	14	16	18	20	22
Russian	42	44	46	48	50	52	54

MEN'S SUITS

British and American	36	38	40	42	44	46
Russian	46	48	50	52	54	56

MEN'S SHIRTS

British and American	14	14½	15	15½	16	16½	17
Russian	36	37	38	39	41	42	43

WAIST, CHEST/BUST AND HIPS

Inches	28	30	32	34	36	38	40
Centimetres	71	76	81	87	92	97	102
Inches	42	44	46	48	50	52	54
Centimetres	107	112	117	122	127	132	137

SHOES[1]

British	3	4	5	6	7	8	9	10	11	12
American	4½	5½	6½	7½	8½	9½	10½	11½	12½	13⅓
Russian	34	35	36	37	41	42	43	44	45	46

CHEMIST

Chemist's shops do not sell any toilet requisites, apart from a few basic items such as toothbrushes, toothpaste, and soap. Medicines which are bought on prescription must be paid for. There are all-night chemist's shops, and stalls or kiosks (in department stores, at stations, and in the metro) which sell medical goods. Large chemist's shops also often have an optician's section where it is possible to have new spectacles fitted and old ones repaired.

1. Shoe sizes can also be used for buying stockings and socks.

Where is the nearest (all-night) chemist's?	Где ближайшая (дежурная) аптека?	gdyé blee-zhay-sha-ya (dyé-zhoor-na-ya) ap-tyé-ka
I would like to have this prescription made up	Я хочу́ заказа́ть лека́рство по э́тому реце́пту	ya ha-choo za-ka-zat' lyé-kar-stva pa-é-ta-moo ryé-tsép-too
How long will it take?	Ско́лько вре́мени э́то займёт?	skol'-ka vryé-myé-nee é-ta zay-myot
Can you give me something for	У вас е́сть что-нибу́дь от	oo-vas yést' shto-nee-boot-at
a headache?	головно́й бо́ли?	ga-lav-noy bo-lee
a migraine/sore throat?	мигре́ни/го́рла?	mee-gryé-nee/gor-la
a cough/cold?	ка́шля/просту́ды?	kash-lya/pra-stoo-di
food poisoning?	отравле́ния?	at-rav-lyé-nee-ya
indigestion?	несваре́ния желу́дка?	nyé-sva-ryé-nee-ya zhe-loot-ka
diarrhoea?	расстро́йства желу́дка?	ras-stroy-stva zhe-loot-ka
constipation?	запо́ра?	za-po-ra
sickness?	тошноты́?	tash-na-ti
sunburn?	со́лнечного ожо́га?	sol-nyéch-na-va a-zho-ga
Could I have a/some	Да́йте мне, пожа́луйста	day-tyé mnyé, pa-zha-loo-sta

antiseptic cream	антисепти́ческое сре́дство	an-tee-syép-tee-chyés-ka-yé sryéd-stva
aspirins	аспири́н	as-pee-reen
bandages	бинт	beent
contraceptives *male*	презервати́вы	pryé-zyér-va-tee-vi
contraceptives *general term*	противозача́точные сре́дства	pra-tee-va-za-cha-tach- ni-yé sryéd-stva
cotton wool	ва́ту	va-too
disinfectant	дезинфици́рующее сре́дство	dyé-zeen-fee-tsi-roo-yoo-shyé-yé sryéd-stva
hot-water bottle	гре́лку	gryél-koo
iodine	йод	yot
mosquito repellent	сре́дство от комаро́в	sryéd-stva at-ka-ma-rof
mouthwash	полоска́ние для рта	pa-las-ka-nee-yé dlya rta
nose drops	ка́пли для но́са	kap-lee dlya no-sa
sanitary towels	гигиени́ческие салфе́тки	gee-gyé-nee-chyés-kee-yé sal-fyét-kee
sticking plaster	пла́стырь	plas-tir'
thermometer	гра́дусник	gra-doos-neek
Where can I get some?	Где я могу́ э́то найти́?	gdyé ya ma-goo é-ta nay-tee

I have broken my glasses	Я сломáл очкѝ	ya sla-mal ach-kee
Can you mend them?	Вы мóжете их починѝть?	vi mo-zhé-tyé eeh pa-chee-neet'
I need to buy some glasses	Мне нýжно купѝть очкѝ	mnyé noozh-na koo-peet' ach-kee

TOILET ARTICLES

Toilet articles are sold in a variety of different shops. For creams, shampoos, soaps, perfumes, and cosmetics, go to a perfumery (ПАРФЮМÉРИЯ – parfyoomyéreeya). Cosmetics shops (КОСМÉТИКА – kasmyéteeka) specialize in make-up. A third type of shop, the ГАЛАНТЕРÉЯ (galantyéryéya), sells haberdashery and miscellaneous toilet requisites such as combs, razor blades, toothbrushes, toothpaste, soap, and washing powder. In large department stores there is often a haberdashery section next to or combined with a perfumery.

Toilet paper is sometimes sold in 'Culture Wares' shops, in the stationery section, or in 'Household Goods' shops, where you can also find washing powder.

Many toiletry and cosmetic articles, common in the West, are not manufactured in the U.S.S.R., so it is advisable to travel with a basic supply of your own.

Where is there a perfumery?	Где парфюмéрия?	gdyé par-fyoo-myé-ree-ya

a haberdashery shop?	галантерéя?	ga-lan-tyé-ryé-ya
a household goods shop?	хозя́йственный магази́н?	ha-zyay-stvyén-niy ma-ga-zeen
Please give me some/a	Дáйте мне, пожáлуйста	day-tyé mnyé, pa-zha-loo-sta
comb	расчёску	ras-chyos-koo
hand cream	крем для рук	kryém dlya rook
lipstick	губнýю помáду	goob-noo-yoo pa-ma-doo
lotion	лосьóн	la-tsi-on
razor blades	лéзвия для бритья́	lyéz-vee-ya dlya bree-tya
shampoo	шампýнь	sham-poon'
shaving cream	крем для бритья́	kryém dlya breet-ya
soap	мы́ло	mi-la
sun-tan cream	крем для загáра	kryém dlya za-ga-ra
toilet paper	туалéтную бумáгу	too-a-lyét-noo-yoo boo-ma-goo
toothbrush	зубнýю щётку	zoob-noo-yoo shyot-koo
toothpaste	зубнýю пáсту	zoob-noo-yoo pas-too
washing powder	стирáльный порошóк	stee-ral'-niy pa-ra-shok

PHOTOGRAPHY

In Moscow, the best shops for cameras and photographic supplies are ЮПИ́ТЕР (yoopeeter – Jupiter) at 27 Prospekt Kalinina and КИНОФОТОТОВА́РЫ (keenofotatavari – cine-cameras and photographic supplies) at 25 Gorky Street, 15 Petrovka Street, and 44 Komsomolsky Prospekt. Camera shops often have a developing and printing service for which you pay separately, but you will probably find it quicker and simpler to have this done when you return home.

Cameras and films are also sold in the Beryozka shops. The sensitivity of Soviet films is measured in GOST units (GOST is the abbreviation for State All-Union Standards), or in ASA or DIN units.

Where is there a camera shop?	Где фотомагази́н?	gdyé fo-to-ma-ga-**zeen**
I would like to buy	Я хочу́ купи́ть	ya ha-**choo** koo-**peet'**
a camera	фотоаппара́т	fo-ta-ap-pa-**rat**
a cine-camera	киноаппара́т	kee-no-ap-pa-**rat**
I need	Мне нужна́	mnyé noozh-**na**
a black and white film	чёрно-бе́лая плёнка	**chor**-na **byé**-la-ya **plyon**-ka
a colour film	цветна́я плёнка	tsvyét-**na**-ya **plyon**-ka
for slides	для сла́йдов	dlya **slay**-daf
for this camera	для э́того аппара́та	dlya **é**-ta-va ap-pa-**ra**-ta

Size ...	Размéр ...	raz-myér ...
Sensitivity ... (forty) units	Чувстви́тельность ... (сóрок) едини́ц	choov-stvee-tel'-nast' ... (so-rak) yé-dee-neets
100/400/1000 ASA	сто/четы́реста/ ты́сяча ASA	sto/chyé-ti-ryés-ta/ ti-sya-cha ASA
Could you put it in for me?	Мóжете ли вы егó заряди́ть?	mo-zhé-tyé-lee vi yé-vo za-rya-deet'
Can you develop/print this film?	Мóжно прояви́ть/ отпечáтать э́ту плёнку?	mozh-na pra-ya-veet'/at-pyé-cha-tat' e-too plyon-koo
Can you print enlargements of this negative?	Мóжно сдéлать увели́ченные отпечáтки э́того негати́ва?	mozh-na zdyé-lat' oo-vyé-lee-chyé-ni-yé at-pyé-chat-kee e-ta-va nyé-ga-tee-va
When will it be ready?	Когдá э́то бýдет готóво?	kag-da e-ta boo-dyét ga-to-va
My camera isn't working. Can you mend it?	Мой аппарáт не рабóтает. Мóжете ли вы почини́ть?	moy ap-pa-rat nyé ra-bo-ta-yét. mo-zhé-tyé-lee vi yé-vo pa-chee-neet'
There is something wrong	Чтó-то не так	shto-ta nyé tak
with the flash	со вспы́шкой	sa-fspish-koy
with the light meter	с экспонóметром	sek-spa-no-myé-tram
The film is jammed	Плёнку заéло	plyon-koo za-yé-la

REPAIRS[1]

The key term for any type of repair work is РЕМО́НТ (ryé-mont). The kiosks which deal with shoe repairs are commonly found near the entrance to stations and the metro; it is also possible to have one's shoes cleaned at these kiosks.

Where is the nearest place for shoe repairs?	Где ближа́йший ремо́нт о́буви?	gdyé blee-zhay-sheey ryé-mont o-boo-vee
This isn't working	Э́то не рабо́тает	é-ta nyé ra-bo-ta-yét
This is broken	Э́то слома́лось	é-ta sla-ma-las'
Can you mend this?	Вы мо́жете э́то почини́ть?	vi mo-zhé-tyé é-ta pa-chee-neet'
While I wait?	При мне?	pree-mnyé
When will it be ready?	Когда́ э́то бу́дет гото́во?	kag-da é-ta boo-dyét ga-to-va
I would like to have my shoes cleaned	Я хочу́ почи́стить о́бувь	ya ha-choo pa-chees-teet' o-boof'

ELECTRICAL GOODS

Where is there an electrical goods shop?	Где магази́н электротова́ров?	gdyé ma-ga-zeen e-lyék-tra-ta-va-raf

1. For repairs to glasses, see 'Chemist', p. 133.

I need an electric plug	Мне нужна́ ште́псельная ви́лка	mnyé noozh-na shtep-syél'-na-ya veel-ka
Do you have batteries for this?	У вас есть батаре́и для э́того?	oo-vas yést' ba-ta-ryé-ee dlya é-ta-va

HAIRDRESSER AND BARBER

Where is the nearest hairdresser?	Где ближа́йшая парикма́херская?	gdyé blee-zhay-sha-ya pa-reek-ma-hyér-ska-ya
Can I make an appointment	Мо́жно записа́ться	mozh-na za-pee-sat'-sa
for today/for tomorrow?	на сего́дня/на за́втра?	na-sye-vod-nya/na-zav-tra
for the morning/for the afternoon?	на у́тро/на день?	na-oo-tra/na-dyén
At what time?	*На како́е вре́мя?	na-ka-ko-yé vryé-mya
Can you do my hair now?	Мо́жно ли сейча́с сде́лать причёску?	mozh-na-lee seey-chas zdyé-lat' pree-chyos-koo
How long will I have to wait?	Ско́лько вре́мени ну́жно ждать?	skol'-ka vryé-myé-nee noozh-na zhdat'
I'm in a hurry	Я спешу́	ya spyé-shoo

Please cut my hair	Постригúте меня́, пожáлуйста	pa-stree-gee-tyé me-nya, pa-zha-loo-sta
short/not very short	кóротко/не óчень кóротко	ko-rat-ka/nyé o-chyén' ko-rat-ka
Please trim my hair	Подравня́йте мне вóлосы, пожáлуйста	pad-rav-nyay-tyé mnyé vo-la-si, pa-zha-loo-sta
A little shorter here please	Покорóче здесь, пожáлуйста	pa-ka-ro-chyé zdyés', pa-zha-loo-sta
That's enough off	Так достáточно	tak da-sta-tach-na
It isn't straight here	Здесь нерóвно	zdyés' nyé-rov-na
Do my parting here	Сдéлайте мне пробóр здесь	zdyé-lay-tyé mnyé pra-bor zdyés'
A razor-cut, please	Брúтвой, пожáлуйста	breet-voy, pa-zha-loo-sta
Please wash my hair	Вы́мойте мне гóлову, пожáлуйста	vi-moy-tyé mnyé go-la-voo, pa-zha-loo-sta
I have greasy/dry hair	У меня́ жúрные/сухúе вóлосы	oo-me-nya zhir-ni-yé/soo-hee-yé vo-la-si
The water is too hot/cold	Водá слúшком горя́чая/холóдная	va-da sleesh-kam ga-rya-cha-ya/ ha-lod-na-ya
Please blow-dry my hair	Уложúте мне вóлосы фéном, пожáлуйста	oo-la-zhi-tyé mnyé vo-la-si fyé-nam, pa-zha-loo-sta

Please set my hair	Уложи́те мне во́лосы, пожа́луйста	oo-la-zhi-tyé mnyé vo-la-si, pa-zha-loo-sta
Please tint my hair	Покра́сьте мне во́лосы	pa-kras'-tyé mnyé vo-la-si
auburn	в кашта́новый цвет	fkash-ta-na-viy tsvyét
blond	под блонди́нку	pad-blan-deen-koo
brown	под брюне́тку	pad-bryoo-nyét-koo
Please don't put any beer on my hair	Пожа́луйста, не сма́зывайте во́лосы пи́вом	pa-zha-loo-sta, nyé sma-zi-vay-tyé vo-la-si pee-vam
I don't want any hairspray	Ла́ка не ну́жно	la-ka nyé noozh-na
The dryer is too hot	Суши́лка сли́шком горя́чая	soo-shil-ka sleesh-kam ga-rya-cha-ya
I want a manicure	Сде́лайте мне, пожа́луйста, маникю́р	zdyé-lay-tyé mnyé, pa-zha-loo-sta, ma-nee-kyoor
I want a shave	Побре́йте меня́, пожа́луйста	pa-bréy-tyé me-nya, pa-zha-loo-sta
Please trim my beard/moustache	Пожа́луйста, подстриги́те бо́роду/усы́	pa-zha-loo-sta, pad-stree-gee-tyé bo-ra-doo/oo-si
Please don't put any dressing on my hair	Пожа́луйста, ниче́м не сма́зывайте	pa-zha-loo-sta, nee-chyém nyé sma-zi-vay-tyé

That's fine	Это хорошó	**é-ta ha-ra-sho**
Thank you, I like it very much	Спасúбо, так óчень хорошó	**spa-see-ba, tak o-chyén' ha-ra-sho**

POST OFFICE

Most Intourist hotels have a post office on the premises. Large post offices are usually organized according to a system of numbered windows which offer different services – the signs identifying these services are given in the individual sections which follow.

In Moscow, the main post office is at 26 Ulitsa Kirova (near the Keerav-skaya metro station).

Where's the main post office ?	Где Главпочта́мт?	gdyé glaf-pach-tamt
Where's the nearest post office?	Где ближа́йшая по́чта?	gdyé blee-zhay-sha-ya poch-ta
When does	В кото́ром часу́	fka-to-ram cha-soo
the post office open?	открыва́ется по́чта?	at-kri-va-yét-sa poch-ta
the post office close?	закрыва́ется по́чта?	za-kri-va-yét-sa poch-ta

LETTERS

Postcards, envelopes, stamps, and writing paper are sold at news-stands on the streets, in hotels, and in post offices. Postcards and envelopes often already have a stamp printed on them. The rates for internal or foreign mail differ; an envelope for surface or airmail within the Soviet Union costs 6 kopecks, whereas the rate for an envelope to a foreign country is 50 kopecks.

The order in which Russian addresses are written is the reverse of ours. Correspondence to people in the Soviet Union should be addressed in the way described in the section on Russian addresses (see page 54). The post code of the addressee should be written in the box on the lower left-hand side of the envelope; the lower half of the envelope is reserved for the sender's address.

In Moscow, red letter-boxes are reserved for correspondence within the city, and blue letter-boxes should be used for all other mail.

SIGNS IN THE POST OFFICE

ПРОДАЖА МАРОК, КОНВЕРТОВ, ОТКРЫТОК	Sale of stamps, envelopes, postcards
ПРИЁМ МЕЖДУНАРОДНОЙ КОРРЕСПОНДЕНЦИИ	Letters for abroad

Where is the nearest news-stand?	Где ближа́йший газе́тный кио́ск?	gdyé blee-zhay-sheey ga-zyét-niy kee-osk
Where are letters for abroad handed in?	Где приём междунаро́дной корреспонде́нции?	gdyé pree-yom myézh-doo-na-rot-nay kar-ryés-pan-dyén-tsi-ee

How much does it cost to send	Ско́лько сто́ит	**skol'-ka sto-eet**
an airmail letter to ...?	а́виа-письмо́ в ...? (+ acc.)	**a-vee-a pees'-mo v ...**
an airmail postcard to ...?	а́виа-откры́тка в ...? (+ acc.)	**a-vee-a at-krit-ka v ...**
Please give me	Да́йте, пожа́луйста	**day-tyé, pa-zha-loo-sta**
a postcard	откры́тку	**at-krit-koo**
two/three airmail envelopes	два/три а́виа-конве́рта	**dva/tree a-vee-a-kan-vyér-ta**
with stamps for England	с ма́рками для А́нглии	**smar-ka-mee dlya an-glee-ee**
stamps	ма́рки	**mar-kee**
for an air-letter to England	для а́виа-письма́ в А́нглию	**dlya a-vee-a pees'-ma van-glee-yoo**
for an airmail postcard to America	для а́виа-откры́тки в Аме́рику	**dlya a-vee-a at-krit-kee va-myé-ree-koo**
some writing paper	почто́вую бума́гу	**pach-to-voo-yoo boo-ma-goo**
I want to send this letter	Я хочу́ посла́ть э́то письмо́	**ya ha-choo pa-slat' é-ta pees'-mo**
express	экспре́ссом	**ék-sprés-sam**
by registered post	заказны́м	**za-kaz-nim**
Where is the post box?	Где почто́вый я́щик?	**gdyé pach-to-viy ya-shcheek**

TELEGRAMS

The Moscow Central Telegraph Office is at 7 Gorky Street, near the Intourist Hotel. Telegrams can also be sent from post offices which have a telegraph department. The forms are usually kept by the window where telegrams are handed in.

Where is the nearest telegraph office?	Где ближáйший телегрáф?	gdyé blee-zhay-sheey tyé-lyé-**graf**
Where are telegrams handed in?	Где приём телегрáмм?	gdyé pree-**yom** tyé-lyé-**gramm**
I want to send	Я хочý послáть	ya ha-**choo** pa-**slat'**
a telegram	телегрáмму	tyé-lyé-**gram**-moo
an international telegram	междунарóдную телегрáмму	myézh-doo-na-**rod**-noo-yoo tyé-lyé-**gram**-moo
an express telegram	срóчную телегрáмму	**sroch**-noo-yoo tyé-lyé-**gram**-moo
May I have a form please?	Дáйте мне бланк, пожáлуйста	**day**-tyé mnyé blank, pa-**zha**-loo-sta
How should I fill in this form?	Как мне запóлнить э́тот бланк?	kak mnyé za-**pol**-neet' **é**-tat blank
What is the charge per word?	Скóлько стóит кáждое слóво?	**skol'**-ka **sto**-eet **kazh**-da-yé **slo**-va
How long will a telegram take to get to London?	Скóлько врéмени идёт телегрáмма в Лóндон?	**skol'**-ka **vryé**-myé-nee ee-**dyot** tyé-lyé-**gram**-ma **flon**-don

Can I send a telex?	Могу́ ли я посла́ть те́лекс?	ma-goo lee ya pa-slat' tyé-lyéks

PARCELS

There is a basic distinction between a small packet (бандеро́ль – band-yérol') and a parcel (посы́лка – pasilka). Books and records are usually sent by small packet post (бандеро́лью – bandyérol'yoo) or by registered small packet post (заказно́й бандеро́лью – zakaznoy band-yérol'yoo). They should be taken to the 'small packets' window of the post office, and handed in to the clerk who will wrap them up for you. You must then write the address to which the packet is to be sent and your return address on the packet, and hand it back to the clerk who will weigh it and glue on the correct stamps. You are then charged for the stamps, and receive a receipt if the packet has been registered.

Miscellaneous small objects are usually sent as a small packet of valuables (це́нной бандеро́лью – tsennoy bandyérol'yoo). You should pack them in a box, and address the packet. At the post office you must fill in a form listing the contents of the packet.

Larger items are sent by parcel post, and are usually dealt with in a separate part of the post office. They must be wrapped in advance, and the addresses of sender and addressee must be filled in on a post office form.

ПРИЁМ И ВЫДАЧА БАНДЕРОЛЕЙ	Small packets
ПРИЁМ И ВЫДАЧА ПОСЫЛОК	Parcels

Where can I hand in	Где приём	gdyé pree-yom
a small packet/a parcel?	бандеро́лей/посы́лок?	ban-dyé-ro-lyéy/pa-si-lak

Please wrap this up	Заверни́те, пожа́луйста	za-vyér-nee-tyé, pa-zha-loo-sta
I would like to send	Я хочу́ посла́ть что-то	ya ha-choo pa-slat' shto-ta
a small packet	бандеро́лью	ban-dyé-rol'-yoo
a small registered packet	заказно́й бандеро́лью	za-kaz-noy ban-dyé-rol'yoo
a small packet of valuables	це́нной бандеро́лью	tsén-noy ban-dyé-rol'-yoo
I would like to send a parcel	Я хочу́ посла́ть посы́лку	ya ha-choo pa-slat' pa-sil-koo
Should I fill in a customs declaration form?	Ну́жно ли мне заполня́ть тамо́женную деклара́цию?	noozh-na-lee mnyé za-pal-nyat' ta-mo-zhén-noo-yoo dyé-kla-ra-tsi-yoo
Could I please have a receipt?	Да́йте мне квита́нцию, пожа́луйста	day-tyé mnyé kvee-tan-tsi-yoo, pa-zha-loo-sta

POSTE RESTANTE

Poste restante facilities are available for tourists who are not sure at which hotel they will be staying. For Moscow, letters should be addressed c/o Intourist, Moscow K.600. This is the address of the post office in the Intourist hotel at the foot of Gorky Street. For Leningrad, the address is C.400, 6 Nevsky Prospekt, Leningrad. Messages for tourists staying in other cities should be addressed c/o Intourist, followed by the city's name.

Where is the poste restante section?	Где вы́дача пи́сем до востре́бования?	gdyé vi-da-cha pee-syém da-vas-tryé-ba-va-nee-ya
Are there any letters for me? My name is ...	Есть ли для меня́ пи́сьма? Моя́ фами́лия ...	yést'-lee dlya me-nya pees'-ma. ma-ya fa-mee-lee-ya ...
May I see your identification?	*Ваш докуме́нт, пожа́луйста	vash da-koo-myént, pa-zha-loo-sta
Here is my passport	Вот па́спорт	vot pas-part

TELEPHONING

MAKING A TELEPHONE CALL

Local telephone calls can be made free of charge from the hotel. There are also many public telephone booths on the streets, in the metro, in cinemas etc. To use a public telephone:

1. Insert a 2-kopeck coin, or two 1-kopeck coins, into the slot at the top of the telephone.
2. Lift the receiver from the hook, and wait until you hear the dialling tone (a continuous purring); start dialling.
3. Long signals indicate the normal ringing tone; if somebody answers, the money in the slot will automatically drop down, and you will be connected.
4. If nobody answers, or if the number is engaged (in which case you will hear short rapid signals), replace the receiver and take your money back.

The Soviet Union is currently in the process of changing over to a time-based system of charges for local calls. New telephone booths have been installed which do not allow one to speak for more than three minutes. From many public telephone booths it is still possible to speak for as long as one likes for the price of 2 kopecks. However, there is a generally accepted rule that people should limit themselves to four minutes if there is a queue of other people waiting to use the telephone. If this is not observed, the people in the queue are likely to express their impatience by banging on the door of the telephone booth.

Telephone directories listing the telephone numbers of private individuals are not generally available in the Soviet Union. If you know the full name and address of a person, it is possible to find out their telephone number by dialling directory inquiries (in Moscow the number for this service is 09).

Where is the nearest phone box?	Где ближáйший телефóнавтомáт?	gdyé blee-zhay-sheey tyé-lyé-fon af-ta-mat
Could you give me change in two-kopeck coins please?	Разменя́йте по две копéйки, пожáлуйста	raz-myé-nyay-tyé pa-dvyé ka-pyéy-kee, pa-zha-loo-sta
May I make a phone call from here?	Мóжно ли от вас позвони́ть?	mozh-na-lee at-vas pa-zva-neet'
Do you have a telephone directory?	У вас есть телефóнный спрáвочник?	oo-vas yést' tyé-lyé-fon-niy spra-vach-neek
I would like to find out the telephone number of an address ...	Я хочý узнáть телефóн по áдресу ...	ya ha-choo oo-znat' tyé-lyé-fon pa-a-dryé-soo ...
the surname is ...	фами́лия ...	fa-mee-lee-ya ...
the address is ...	áдрес ...	a-dryés ...
What is the code for ... ?	Какóй код для ... ? (+gen.)	ka-koy kod dlya ...
You're wanted on the telephone	*Вас прóсят к телефóну	vas pro-syat ktyé-lyé-fo-noo
Hallo!	Аллó!	al-lo

Please give me extension number ...	Да́йте, пожа́луйста, доба́вочный ...	day-tyé, pa-zha-loo-sta, da-ba-vach-niy ...
Who's speaking?	*Кто э́то?/Кто говори́т?	kto é-ta/kto ga-va-reet
May I speak to ...?	Попроси́те, пожалуйста, ...	pa-pra-see-tyé, pa-zha-loo-sta ...
He/she isn't here	*Его́/её нет	yé-vo/yé-yo nyét
When will he (she) be back?	Когда́ он (она́) бу́дет?	kag-da on (a-na) boo-dyét
You have the wrong number	*Вы не туда́ попа́ли/ Вы оши́блись	vi nyé too-da pa-pa-lee/vi a-shi-blees'
Can I take a message?	*Что переда́ть?	shto pyé-ryé-dat'
Please say	Переда́йте, пожа́луйста	pyé-ryé-day-tyé, pa-zha-loo-sta
that ... telephoned	что звони́л/ звони́ла *f* ...	shto zva-neel/zva-nee-la ...
that I will ring again	что я позвоню́ ещё раз	shto ya pa-zva-nyoo yé-sho raz
in an hour/later/ tomorrow	че́рез час/по́зже/ за́втра	che-ryéz chas/po-zhé/ zav-tra
Please ask him/her to telephone me	Попроси́те его́/её позвони́ть мне, пожа́луйста	pa-pra-see-tyé yé-vo/yé-yo pa-zva-neet' mnyé, pa-zha-loo-sta
What is your telephone number?	*Како́й ваш телефо́н?	ka-koy vash tyé-lyé-fon

My telephone number is ...	Мой телефóн ...	moy tyé-lyé-fon
How can I get in touch with him?	Как я могý с ним связáться?	kak ya ma-goo sneem svya-zat'-sa?
I can't hear you	Я вас не слы́шу	ya vas nyé sli-shoo
Please speak more loudly	Пожáлуйста, говори́те грóмче	pa-zha-loo-sta, ga-va-ree-tyé grom-ché

BOOKING A TELEPHONE CALL

Long-distance and international calls can be booked by telephone from your hotel, or at a telegraph or long-distance call office. In Moscow, the International Telephone Exchange is in the building of the Central Telegraph Office at 7 Gorky Street, near the Intourist Hotel. Some towns in the Soviet Union can be dialled direct from special long-distance public telephones in the telegraph office. Otherwise you must book your call at the counter for a given time, stating in advance the number of minutes you will speak for; then you must wait in the general hall until your call is put through; an announcement over the loudspeaker will tell you the number of the booth (kabeena) which you must go to to hold your conversation.

Where is the nearest telegraph office?	Где ближáйший телегрáф?	gdyé blee-zhay-sheey tyé-lyé-graf?
I would like to book a telephone call	Я хочý заказáть телефóнный разговóр	ya ha-choo za-ka-zat' tyé-lyé-fon-niy raz-ga-vor
to London (to ...)	с Лóндоном (с ... + instr.)	slon-da-nam (s ...)
for ... minutes	на ... минýт	na ... mee-noot

How much will it cost?	Ско́лько э́то бу́дет сто́ить?	skol'-ka é-ta boo-dyét sto-eet'
When do you want to speak?	*Когда́ вы хоти́те говори́ть?	kag-da vi ha-ti-tyé ga-va-reet'
Wait for the call to come through during the next hour	*В тече́ние ча́са – жди́те звонка́	ftyé-chyé-nee-yé cha-sa – zhdee-tyé zvan-ka
How long do you want to talk for?	*Ско́лько мину́т вы бу́дете разгова́ривать?	skol'-ka mee-noot vi boo- dyé-tyé raz-ga-va-ree-vat'
I want to speak for ... minutes	Я бу́ду говори́ть ... мину́т	ya boo-doo ga-va-reet' ... mee-noot
Whom do you want to speak to?	*Кого́ позва́ть?	ka-vo pa-zvat'
It doesn't matter	Всё равно́ кого́	fsyo rav-no ka-vo
Hold the line	*Не ве́шайте тру́бку	nyé vyé-shay-tyé troob-koo
I'm putting you through. Go ahead	*Соединя́ю. Говори́те	sa-yé-dee-nya-yoo. Ga-va-ree-tyé
The line's engaged	*За́нято	za-nya-ta
There's no answer	*Никто́ не отвеча́ет	nee-kto nyé at-vyé-cha-yét
The phone is out of order	*Телефо́н не рабо́тает	tyé-lyé-fon nyé ra-bo-ta-yét
One minute left	*Оста́лась одна́ мину́та	a-sta-las' ad-na mee-noo-ta

Your time is up	*Ва́ше вре́мя истекло́	va-she vryé-mya ees-tyé-klo
Please extend the call for three minutes	Продли́те, пожа́луйста, на три мину́ты	pra-dlee-tyé, pa-zha-loo-sta, na tree mee-noo-ti
Don't disconnect us	Не разъединя́йте	nyé raz-yé-dee-nyay-tyé
We were cut off, can you reconnect us?	Нас разъедини́ли, вы мо́жете опя́ть соедини́ть?	nas raz-yé-dee-nee-lee, vi mo-zhé-tyé a-pyat' sa-yé-dee-neet'
You gave me the wrong number	Вы меня́ непра́вильно соедини́ли	vi me-nya nyé-pra-veel'-na sa-yé-dee-nee-lee

SIGHTSEEING

Intourist organizes a wide variety of sightseeing tours and excursions for foreigners. These can be useful for visiting places which are otherwise difficult to get into or to reach. However, it is often more interesting, and considerably cheaper, to do one's sightseeing independently. Information about museum opening times and directions can be obtained at the service bureau in your hotel, or at an Information kiosk (see page 51).

СПРАВКИ/СПРАВОЧНОЕ БЮРО	Information bureau

THE TOWN

Where is the tourist office?	Где бюро́ тури́зма?	gdyé byoo-ro too-reez-ma
What are the main things to see here?	Каки́е здесь достопримеча́тельности?	ka-kee-yé zdyés' da-sta-pree-myé-cha-tyél'- nas-tee

Is there a map/plan of the places to visit?	Есть ли план с указáнием досто-примечáтель-ностей?	yést' lee plan soo-ka-za-nee-yém da-sta-pree-myé-cha-tyél'-na-styéy
I would like to visit ...	Я хочý посмотрéть ... (+ acc.)	ya ha-choo pa-sma-tryet' ...
How can I get there?[1]	Как мне тудá попáсть?	kak mnyé too-da pa-past'
Is it far to walk?	Далекó ли тудá идтѝ?	da-lyé-ko lee too-da ee-tee
Is it an easy walk?	Легкó ли тудá идтѝ?	lyéh-ko lee too-da ee-tee
Can I get there by car?	Мóжно ли тудá добрáться на машѝне?	mozh-na lee too-da da-brat'-sa na ma-shi-nyé
Is there access for wheelchairs?	Мóжно ли тудá пойтѝ в инвалѝдном крéсле?	mozh-na lee too-da pai-tee veen-va-leed-nam kryés-lyé
Is there a sightseeing tour to ...?	Есть ли экскýрсия в ...? (+ acc.)	yést'-lee ék-skoor-see-ya v ...
How long does the tour take?	Как дóлго длѝтся экскýрсия?	kak dol-ga dleet-sa ék-skoor-see-ya
How much does the tour cost?	Скóлько стóит экскýрсия?	skol'-ka sto-eet ék-skoor-see-ya

1. See 'Asking the Way' (p. 51).

Does it include lunch?	Сюда́ вхо́дит сто́имость обе́да?	syoo-da vho-deet sto-ee-mast' a-byé-da
Are there reductions	Есть ли ски́тки	yést' lee skeet-kee
for children?	для дете́й?	dlya dyé-tyéy
for students?	для студе́нтов?	dlya stoo-dyén-taf
for the elderly?	для пенсионе́ров?	dlya pyén-see-a-nyé-raf
Have you got a ticket?	*У вас есть биле́т?	oo-vas yést bee-lyét
I'd like to walk round the old town	Я хочу́ гуля́ть по ста́рому го́роду	ya ha-choo goo-lyat' pa-sta-ra-moo go-ra-doo
Is there a good street plan?	Есть ли хоро́ший план го́рода?	yést' lee ha-ro-shiy plan go-ra-da
Where is/are the	Где	gdyé
centre/old town?	центр/ста́рый го́род?	tsentr/sta-riy go-rad
Kremlin/castle?	Кремль/за́мок?	kryéml'/za-mak
walls/gate?	сте́ны/воро́та?	styé-ni/va-ro-ta
church/cathedral?	це́рковь/собо́р?	tser-kaf'/sa-bor
monastery/cemetery?	монасты́рь/кла́дбище?	ma-na-stir'/klad-bee-shé
main square/library?	центра́льная пло́щадь/библиоте́ка	tsen-tral'-na-ya plo-shad'/bee-blee-a-tyé-ka

park/botanical gardens?	парк/ботани́ческий сад?	park/ba-ta-nee-chyés-keey sat
lake/fountain?	о́зеро/фонта́н?	o-zyé-ra/fan-tan
market/harbour?	ры́нок/порт?	ri-nak/port
What is that building?	Что э́то за зда́ние?	shto é-ta za-zda-nee-yé
What is that monument?	Что э́то за па́мятник?	shto é-ta za-pa-myat-neek
When was it built?	Когда́ э́то бы́ло постро́ено?	kag-da é-ta bi-la pa-stro-yé-na
Who built it?	Кто э́то постро́ил?	kto e-ta pas-tro-eel
May we go up the tower?	Мо́зжно ли подня́ться на ба́шню?	mazh-na lee pad-nyat'-sa na bash-nyoo

RELIGIOUS SERVICES

Many churches in the Soviet Union have been closed down or converted to other use, for example as museums of art or atheism, or warehouses. Churches which are still open for worship are referred to as 'functioning' churches ('dyéy-stvoo-yoo-sha-ya tsér-kaf''). The seat of the Moscow Patriarchate is in the Novodevichy convent (near Sporteevnaya metro station), and the main theological academy of the Russian Orthodox Church is in the beautiful monastery of St Sergius, just outside Moscow at Zagorsk. At Russian Orthodox services it is customary for men to remove their hats and for women to cover their heads.

What is the name of this church?	Как называ́ется э́та це́рковь?	kak na-zi-va-yét-sa é-ta tsér-kaf
Is the church still used for worship?	Э́та це́рковь де́йствующая?	é-ta tsér-kaf dyéy-stvoo-yoo-sha-ya
Is there a church where services are held near here?	Здесь есть побли́зости де́йствующая це́рковь?	zdyés' yést' pa-blee-za-stee dyéy-stvoo-yoo-sha-ya tsér-kaf'
When is the church open?	Когда́ це́рковь откры́та?	kag-da tsér-kaf at-kri-ta
When are the services?	Когда́ быва́ет слу́жба?	kag-da bi-va-yet sloozh-ba
Where is the Catholic/Protestant church?	Где католи́ческая/протеста́нтская це́рковь?	gdyé ka-ta-lee-chyés-ka-ya/pra-tyés-tant-ska-ya tsér-kaf
Where is the mosque/the synagogue?	Где мече́ть/синаго́га?	gdyé myé-chyét'/see-na-go-ga
May we see inside the building?	Мо́жно осмотре́ть э́то зда́ние внутри́?	mozh-na a-sma-tryét' é-ta zda-nee-yé vnoo-tree

MUSEUMS

МУЗЕЙ РАБОТАЕТ С 10 Ч. ДО 18 Ч.	The museum is open from 10 a.m. to 6 p.m.
ВЫХОДНОЙ ДЕНЬ ПОНЕДЕЛЬНИК	Closed on Monday

ВХОД БЕСПЛАТНЫЙ/ ВХОД СВОБОДНЫЙ	Admission free
ВХОД ПО БИЛЕТАМ	Admission by tickets
КАССА	Ticket office
ФОТОГРАФИРОВАТЬ ВОСПРЕЩАЕТСЯ	Photography forbidden

Where is the museum of ...?	Где музе́й ...? (+ gen.)	gdyé moo-zyéy ...
Where is the art gallery?	Где музе́й жи́вописи?	gdyé moo-zyéy zhi-va-pee-see
Where is the house of ...?[1]	Где дом-музе́й ...? (+ gen.)	gdyé dom-moo-zyéy ...
What exhibitions are on at the moment?	Каки́е вы́ставки сейча́с устра́иваются?	ka-kee-yé vi-staf-kee seey-chas oo-stra-ee-va-yoot-sa
Where is the ... collection/ exhibition?	Где собра́ние/ вы́ставка ...?	gdyé sa-bra-nee-yé/ vi-stav-ka ...
When does the museum open?	Когда́ открыва́ется музе́й?	kag-da at-kri-va-yét-sa moo-zyéy
When does the museum shut?	Когда́ закрыва́ется музе́й?	kag-da za-kri-va-yét-sa moo-zyéy
What day is the museum shut?	Когда́ выходно́й день?	kag-da vi-had-noy dyén’

1. In the Soviet Union there are excellent museums (called dom-moozyéy – house-museum) devoted to the lives and works of famous writers. In Moscow you can visit the houses of Tolstoy, Dostoyevsky, Chekhov, and many others.

Where is the ticket office?	Где ка́сса?	gdyé kas-sa
How much does a ticket cost?	Ско́лько сто́ит биле́т?	skol'-ka sto-eet bee-lyét
One student's ticket, please	Оди́н студе́нческий биле́т, пожа́луйста	a-deen stoo-dyén-chyés-keey bee-lyét, pa-zha-loo-sta
One child's ticket, please	Оди́н де́тский биле́т, пожа́луйста	a-deen dyét-skeey bee-lyét, pa-zha-loo-sta
Are there guided tours of the museum?	Есть ли экску́рсия с экскурсово́дом по музе́ю?	yést' lee ek-skoor-see-ya sek-skoor-sa-vo-dam pa-moo-zyé-yoo
Does the guide speak English?	Экскурсово́д говори́т по-англи́йски?	ek-skoor-sa-vod ga-va-reet pa-an-gleey-skee
We don't need a guide	Нам не ну́жен экскурсово́д	nam nyé noo-zhen ek-skoor-sa-vod
I would prefer to go round alone; is that all right?	Я предпочита́ю всё осмотре́ть сам/сама́ *f*. Так мо́жно?	ya pryéd-pa-chee-ta-yoo vsyo a-sma-tryét' sam/sa-ma. tak mozh-na
May I take photographs?	Мо́жно ли фотографи́ровать?	mozh-na-lee fa-ta-gra-fee-ra-vat'
Where is the cloakroom?	Где гардеро́б?	gdyé gar-dyé-rop
May I leave my bag with you?	Мо́жно у вас оста́вить су́мку?	mozh-na oo-vas as-ta-veet' soom-koo

Where is the toilet?	Где туалéт?	gdyé too-a-lyét
Is there a snack bar here?	Здесь есть буфéт?	zdyés' yést' boo-fyét
Do you have ...?	У вас есть ...?	oo-vas yést' ...
Where can I buy	Где мóжно купи́ть	gdyé mozh-na koo-peet'
a catalogue/postcards?	каталóг/откры́тки?	ka-ta-lok/at-krit-kee
a guide to the museum?	путеводи́тель по музéю?	poo-tyé-va-dee-tyél' pa-moo-zyé-yoo
Will you make photocopies?	Вы смóжете дéлать фотокóпии?	vi smo-zhe-tyé dyé-lat' fa-ta-ko-pee-ee
Could you make me a transparency of this painting?	Вы смóжете дéлать слайд э́той карти́ны?	vi smo-zhe-tyé dyé-lat' slayd e-toy kar-tee-ni
How long will it take?	Скóлько врéмени э́то займёт?	skol'-ka vryé-myé-nee e-ta zay-myot
Where is the way out?	Где вы́ход?	gdyé vi-had
Where is my group?	Где моя́ грýппа?	gdyé ma-ya groop-pa

ENTERTAINMENT

WHAT'S ON

Moscow News appears once a week on Fridays in English and carries information about what is on at the theatres and cinemas. It is usually available at news-stands in hotels. In Moscow there are also large posters giving details of what is on at the theatre, opera, ballet, and concert halls over a period of ten days; these are displayed in the service bureaux of Intourist hotels, on theatre kiosks and in the streets. Fuller details of performances can be found in the booklet *Moscow Theatres* (Театральная Москва – Tyéatral'naya Maskva), usually on sale in theatres.

Information about Moscow cinema programmes is given on posters headed КИНОТЕАТР (Keenotyéatr – Cinema) which are displayed on stands and buildings and replaced every two or three days. The cinemas are listed in alphabetical order, and the films are listed, with details of dates and times, under the name of the cinema where they are showing. The same film is frequently shown in a number of different cinemas, so it is worth combing through the entire list to check that you have found the most convenient location. There is also a weekly newspaper, *Leisure in Moscow* (Досуг в Москве – Dasoog fmaskvyé) which appears on Saturdays and carries information and reviews of films, plays, concerts and other events.

What is on	Что идёт	shto ee-dyot
at the ... theatre?	в ... теáтре?	f ... tyé-a-tryé
at the ... cinema?	в кинотеáтре ...?	fkee-na-tyé-a-tryé ...
at the puppet theatre?	в кýкольном теáтре?	fkoo-kal'-nam tyé-a-tryé
at the opera?	в óпере?	vo-pyé-ryé
at the Bolshoi?	в Большóм?	fbal'-shom
today/tomorrow?	сегóдня/зáвтра?	syé-vod-nya/zav-tra
What concerts are on?	Что идёт в концéртных зáлах?	shto ee-dyot fkan-tsert-nih za-lah
What ballet is on today?	Какóй сегóдня балéт?	ka-koy syé-vod-nya ba-lyét
Could you recommend a good film?	Не моглú бы вы посовéтовать хорóший фильм?	nyé ma-glee-bi vi pa-sa-vyé-ta-vat' ha-ro-shiy feel'm
Is that a ballet or an opera?	Э́то балéт úли óпера?	é-ta ba-lyét ee-lee o-pyé-ra
What orchestra is playing?	Какóй оркéстр игрáет?	ka-koy ar-kyéstr ee-gra-yét
Who is	Кто	kto
directing?	режиссёр?	ryé-zhi-syor
conducting?	дирижёр?	di-ri-zhor
singing?	поёт?	pa-yot

BUYING TICKETS

In Moscow particularly, it is generally very difficult to get tickets for the best theatres and performances. Foreign tourists, however, are privileged; a certain quota of tickets is reserved for them, and they are able to order tickets through the service bureau of their hotel. If the service bureau cannot produce the tickets, it is sometimes worth asking at the Intourist bureau in Gorky Street (next to the Intourist hotel) on the day of the performance in case they have any spare unsold tickets.

Otherwise, tickets are sold at the theatre box office, in theatre ticket kiosks (ТЕАТРАЛЬНАЯ КАССА – Tyé**atral**'naya **kassa**) on the street or in metro stations. These kiosks are glass-enclosed stands, displaying posters with details of what is on and handwritten lists of theatres for which tickets are still available on a given date; odd tickets which are for sale are also sometimes taped up.[1] It is always worth asking the woman who sits inside the stand if she has tickets for a particular performance, even if it is not listed; but it is generally unusual to find good tickets on sale at these kiosks.

As a last resort you can adopt a widespread Moscow practice, and attempt to buy a ticket at the theatre itself just before the performance, approaching any likely looking individual, and using the phrase given on page 172. People often sell at the last minute in front of the theatre tickets which they are unable to use. Cinema tickets are easily obtainable and very cheap. They are sold at the cinema box office on the day of the performance, or a day in advance. In all cases, it is worth persevering and being insistent. If you have any difficulties at a theatre or cinema box office, approach the manager who can usually be summoned forth from behind a window labelled АДМИНИСТРАТОР (Admeeneest**ra**tar – Manager).

1. See 'Finding Your Seat', p. 172.

ТЕАТР	Theatre
КИНО/КИНОТЕАТР	Cinema
КАССА	Box office
ТЕАТРАЛЬНАЯ КАССА	Theatre ticket kiosk/box office
ПРОДАЖА БИЛЕТОВ НА СЕГОДНЯ	Sale of tickets for today
ПРЕДВАРИТЕЛЬНАЯ ПРОДАЖА БИЛЕТОВ	Advance booking
АДМИНИСТРАТОР	Manager
ВСЕ БИЛЕТЫ ПРОДАНЫ	All tickets sold

Where is	Где	gdyé
the ... cinema/ theatre?	кинотеáтр/ теáтр ... ?	kee-na-tyé-atr/ tyé-atr ...
a theatre ticket office?	театрáльная кáсса?	tyé-a-tral'-na-ya kas-sa
When does the box office open?	Когдá открывáется кáсса?	kag-da at-kri-va-yét-sa kas-sa
Do you have any tickets ... ?	У вас есть билéты ... ?	oo-vas yést' bee-lyé-ti ...
I would like to book ...	Я хочý заказáть ...	ya ha-choo za-ka-zat' ...
Please give me one ticket	Дáйте мне, пожáлуйста, оди́н билéт	day-tyé mnyé, pa-zha-loo-sta, a-deen bee-lyét
for today/for tomorrow	на сегóдня/на зáвтра	na syé-vod-nya/na zav-tra
for the next showing	на слéдующий сеáнс	na slyé-doo-sheey syé-ans

How much is a ticket ... ?	Ско́лько сто́ит биле́т ...?	skol'-ka sto-eet bee-lyét ...
I would like seats	Я хочу́ места́	ya ha-choo myé-sta
in the stalls	в парте́ре	fpar-té-ryé
in the dress circle	в бельэта́же	fbyél-é-ta-zhé
at the front/back	впереди́/сза́ди	fpyé-ryé-dee/sza-dee
in the middle	в середи́не	fsyé-ryé-dee-nyé
Where are these seats?	Где э́ти места́?	gdyé e-tee myé-sta
The cheapest seats please	Са́мые дешёвые биле́ты, пожа́луйста	sa-mi-yé dyé-sho-vi-yé bee-lyé-ti, pa-zha-loo-sta
Do you have any better (cheaper) seats?	У вас есть лу́чшие (бо́лее дешёвые) места́?	oo-vas yést' looch-shi-yé (bo-lyé-yé dyé-sho-vi-yé) myé-sta
There aren't any tickets	*Биле́тов нет	bee-lyé-taf nyét
Will you have any more tickets later?	У вас бу́дут ещё биле́ты по́зже?	oo-vas boo-doot yé-sho bee-lyé-ti po-zhé
Is there a performance another day?	Идёт ли э́тот спекта́кль в друго́й день?	ee-dyot-lee é-tat spyék-takl' fdroo-goy dyén'
When does the performance begin?	Когда́ начина́ется спекта́кль?	kag-da na-chee-na-yét-sa spyék-takl'
When does the performance end?	Когда́ конча́ется спекта́кль?	kag-da kan-cha-yét-sa spyék-takl'

AT THE THEATRE OR CINEMA

'erformances usually begin at 7 p.m. in theatres, and at 7.30 p.m. in concert ıalls. Matinées are generally held on Sundays at noon. The time is always vritten on the posters and on the back of the tickets. The public is not dmitted to the auditorium after the third bell has announced the beginning f the performance.

Cinemas are open from 9 a.m. till late at night. The public is only admit-ed at the start of the programme, or during the brief interval which eparates the newsreel or short film from the main feature film. The seats re numbered and reserved, and tickets are valid for one showing only.

In theatres, although not in cinemas, it is compulsory to leave one's coat nd hat and any bags in the cloakroom. There is no charge for this service. t is possible to hire opera glasses from the cloakroom attendant at a cost of o kopecks.

For many Russians, an integral part of an outing to the theatre is the visit o the boofyét or refreshment room during the interval. At the end of the irst act, there is often quite a stampede to the refreshment room, where ueues form for drinks, sandwiches, cakes, and ice-cream. Phrases for use in he refreshment room are given on page 101.

Smoking is not allowed in cinemas and theatres except in special smoking ooms.

ФОЙЕ	Foyer
БУФЕТ	Refreshment room
КУРИТЕЛЬНАЯ КОМНАТА	Smoking room
ВХОД В ЗРИТЕЛЬНЫЙ ЗАЛ	Entrance to the auditorium
ВЫХОД	Exit

Do you have a spare ticket?[1]	У вас нет ли́шнего биле́та?	oo-vas nyét leesh-nyé-va bee-lyé-ta
Your ticket, please	*Ваш биле́т, пожа́луйста	vash bee-lyét, pa-zha-loo-sta
We are together	Мы вме́сте	mi vmyé-styé
A programme, please	Програ́мму, пожа́луйста	pra-gram-moo, pa-zha-loo-sta
A pair of opera glasses, please	Бино́кль, пожа́луйста	bee-nokl', pa-zha-loo-sta
Where is my seat?	Где моё ме́сто?	gdyé ma-yo myés-ta
How many intervals are there?	Ско́лько бу́дет антра́ктов?	skol'-ka boo-dyét an-trak-taf
Where is the cloakroom/ refreshment room?[2]	Где гардеро́б/ буфе́т?	gdyé gar-dyé-rop/ boo-fyét

FINDING YOUR SEAT

ПАРТЕ́Р	Stalls	par-tér
ЛЕ́ВАЯ СТОРОНА́	Left side	lyé-va-ya sta-ra-na
ПРА́ВАЯ СТОРОНА́	Right side	pra-va-ya sta-ra-na
СЕРЕДИ́НА	Centre	syé-ryé-dee-na
АМФИТЕА́ТР	Rear stalls	am-fee-tyé-atr

1. See p. 168.
2. See p. 101.

ƂЕЛЬЭТА́Ж	Dress circle	byél'-é-tazh
ƂАЛКО́Н	Circle or balcony	bal-kon
ЯРУС/ЛО́ЖА	Tier/box	ya-roos/lo-zha
РЯД/МЕ́СТО	Row/seat	ryat/myés-ta

SPORTS

ATTENDING SPORTS EVENTS

Information about sports events in Moscow is published once a week in the English-language edition of *Moscow News*, which is usually available in Intourist hotels.

The main sports centre of Moscow is the Lenin Central Stadium, otherwise known as the 'Luzhniki' sports centre ('Luzhniki' refers to the marshy land near the river on which the stadium was built). The centre comprises an open-air stadium, a covered Palace of Sports, skating rinks, tennis courts, and facilities for all the sports in the Olympic calendar.

You can also visit two other large sports centres in Moscow, the Dynamo Stadium and the Central Army Sports Club, situated very near each other in the north of Moscow.

Tickets are on sale at the stadium, or at special desks and kiosks in the metro.

I would like to go to a football (ice-hockey) match	Я хочу́ посмотре́ть футбо́льный (хокке́йный) матч	**ya ha-choo pa-sma-tryét' foot-bol'-niy (hak-kyéy-niy) match**

Where is the stadium/ the race course?	Где стадио́н/ ипподро́м?	gdyé sta-dee-on/eep-pa-drom
would like two/three tickets	Я хочу́ два/три биле́та	ya ha-choo dva/tree bee-lyé-ta
Do you have any better/cheaper tickets?	У вас есть биле́ты полу́чше/ подеше́вле?	oo-vas yést' bee-lyé-ti pa-looch-shé/pa-dyé-shév-lyé
When does it start?	Когда́ начина́ется игра́?	kag-da na-chee-na-yét-sa ee-gra
When does it end?	Когда́ конча́ется игра́?	kag-da kan-cha-yét-sa ee-gra
Who is playing?	Кто игра́ет?	kto ee-gra-yét
What team is it?	Кака́я э́то кома́нда?	ka-ka-ya é-ta ka-man-da
Who is winning?	Кто выи́грывает?	kto vi-ee-gri-va-yét
What is the score/result?	Како́й счёт/ результа́т?	ka-koy-shyot/ ryé-zool'-tat
What sport do you go in for?	Каки́м ви́дом спо́рта вы занима́етесь?	ka-keem vee-dam spor-ta vi za-nee-ma-yé-tyés

TAKING PART IN SPORTS

In Moscow you can go swimming in one of the largest swimming pools in the world – the heated open-air Moscow swimming pool which is open all the year round, whatever the temperature. The pool is situated at the exit from the Krapotkeenskaya metro station, near the Pushkin Museum of Fine Arts.

It is also possible to go skiing or skating in the parks of Moscow during the winter. Inquire about this at the service bureau of your hotel. The equipment can be hired, or bought at a sports shop.

СПОРТТОВАРЫ	Sports goods	
Where can I/we	Где здесь мóжно	gdyé zdyés' mozh-na
play tennis?	игрáть в тéннис?	ee-grat' ftyén-nees
go skiing?	катáться на лы́жах?	ka-tat'-sa na-li-zhah
go skating?	катáться на конькáх?	ka-tat'-sa na-kan'-kah
Where is there a swimming pool?	Где здесь бассéйн?	gdyé zdyés' bas-syéyn
Open air/indoor	Откры́тый/закры́тый	at-kri-tiy/za-kri-tiy
Is it heated?	Он подогревáется?	on pa-da-gryé-va-yét-sa
Where can I hire ... ?	Где мóжно взять напрокáт ... ?	gdyé mozh-na vzyat' na-pra-kat ...
I would like to hire	Я хочý взять напрокáт	ya ha-choo vzyat' na-pra-kat
tennis rackets	тéннисные ракéтки	tyén-nees-ni-yé ra-kyét-kee
skis	лы́жи	li-zhi
skates	конькú	kan'-kee
a boat	лóдку	lot-koo
a bicycle	велосипéд	vyé-la-si-pyéd

What is the charge per hour?	Ско́лько э́то сто́ит в час?	skol'-ka é-ta sto-eet fchas
Where is there a good sports shop?	Где хороший магази́н спорттова́ров?	gdyé ha-ro-shiy ma-ga-zeen sport-ta-va-raf
Is there a good fishing spot near here?	Где здесь мо́жно лови́ть ры́бу?	gdyé zdyés' mozh-na la-veet' ri-boo

ON THE BEACH

КУПАТЬСЯ ВОСПРЕЩАЕТСЯ Bathing forbidden

Where can we go swimming?	Где здесь мо́жно купа́ться?	gdyé zdyés mozh-na koo-pat'-sa
Is it safe to bathe here?	Здесь безопа́сно купа́ться?	zdyés' byé-za-pas-na koo-pat'-sa
Is there a lifeguard?	Есть ли здесь спаса́тельная слу́жба?	yést' lee zdyés' spa-sa-týel'-na-ya sloozh-ba
Where can I change?	Где мо́жно переоде́ться?	gdyé mozh-na pyé-ryé-a-dyét'-sa
Can we water ski here?	Здесь мо́жно ката́ться на во́дных лы́жах?	zdyés' mozh-na ka-tat'-sa na-vod-nih li-zhah
Where can I hire	Где мо́жно взять напрока́т	gdyé mozh-na vzyat' na-pra-kat
a beach chair?	шезло́нг?	shéz-long

a sun canopy/a sun umbrella?	тент/зóнтик?	tyént/zon-teek
a beach bed/a chess set?	топчáн/шáхматы?	tap-chan/shah-ma-ti
a boat/water skis?	лóдку/вóдные лы́жи?	lot-koo/vod-ni-yé li-zhi
a paddle boat?	вóдный велосипéд?	vod-niy vyé-la-see-pyéd
What is the charge per hour?	Скóлько э́то стóит в час?	skol'-ka é-ta sto-eet fchas
Where can I buy a bucket and spade?	Где мóжно купи́ть ведёрку и лопáтку?	gdyé mozh-na koo-peet' vyé-dyor-koo ee la-pat-koo

TRAVELLING WITH CHILDREN

Can you put a cot in our room?	Вы мóжете постáвить дéтскую кровáтку в нáшу кóмнату?	vi **mo**-zhe-tyé pa-**sta**-veet' **dyét**-skoo-yoo kra-**vat**-koo **fna**-shoo **kom**-na-too
Can you give us adjoining rooms?	Вы мóжете нам дать сосéдние кóмнаты?	vi **mo**-zhe-tyé nam dat' sa-**syéd**-nee-ye **kom**-nati
We shall be out for a couple of hours	Мы ухóдим на пáру часóв	mi oo-**ho**-deem na **pa**-roo cha-**sof**
We shall be back at ...	Мы вернёмся в ...	mi vyér-**nyom**-sa v ...
Do you have half-portions for children?	У вас есть пол-пóрции для детéй?	oo-vas yést' pal-**por**-tsi-ee dlya dyé-**tyéy**
Could anyone in the hotel baby-sit for our children?	Мог ли бы ктó-нибýдь в гостúнице посидéть с ребёнком?	mog lee bi kto-nee-**boot'** fgas-**tee**-nee-tsé pa-see-**dyét'** sryé-**byon**-kam

Is there a	Есть ли	yést' lee
children's swimming pool?	дéтский бассéйн?	dyét-skeey bas-syéyn
playground?	дéтская площáдка?	dyét-ska-ya pla-shad-ka
games room?	кóмната игр?	kom-na-ta eegr
Is there near by	Есть ли поблúзости	yést' lee pa-blee-zas-tee
an amusement park?	аттракциóнный парк?	at-trak-tsi-on-niy park
a zoo?	зоопáрк?	zoo-park
a toyshop?	магазúн игрýшек?	ma-ga-zeen ee-groo-shek
I'd like	Я хóчу	ya ha-choo
a ball	мяч	myach
a bucket and spade	ведёрку и лопáтку	vyé-dyor-koo ee la-pat-koo
a doll	кýклу	koo-kloo
some flippers	лáсты	las-ti
some goggles	мáску для плáвания	mas-koo dlya pla-va-nee-ya
some playing cards	игрáльные кáрты	ee-gral'-ni-ye kar-ti
some roller skates	рóликовые конькú	ro-lee-ka-vi-yé kan'-kee
a snorkel	трýбку для плáвания	troop-koo dlya pla-va-nee-ya

Where can I feed/change my baby?	Где я могу́ покорми́ть/переоде́ть ребёнка?	gdyé ya ma-goo pa-kar-meet'/pyé-ryé-a-dyét' ryé-byon-ka
Can you heat this bottle for me?	Вы мо́жете подогре́ть э́ту буты́лку для меня́?	vi mo-zhe-tyé pa-da-gryét' e-too boo-til-koo dlya me-nya?
I want	Я хочу́	ya ha-choo
a feeding bottle	буты́лку для кормле́ния ребёнка	boo-til-koo dlya kar-mlyé-nee-ya ryé-byon-ka
some baby food	еду́ для ребёнка	yé-doo dlya ryé-byon-ka
nappies[1]	пелёнки	pyé-lyon-kee
My daughter suffers from travel sickness	Мою́ дочь ука́чивает	ma-yoo doch' oo-ka-chee-va-yet
She hurt herself	Она уши́блась	a-na oo-shi-blas'
My son is ill	Мой сын заболе́л	moy sin za-ba-lyél
He has lost his toy	Он потеря́л игру́шку	on pa-tyé-ryal ee-groosh-koo
I'm sorry if they have bothered you	Я извиня́юсь, если они́ вас побеспоко́или	ya eez-vee-nya-yoos', yés-lee a-nee vas pa-byés-pa-ko-ee-lee

1. Disposable nappies are not available in the U.S.S.R.

BUSINESS MATTERS

I would like to make an appointment with ...	Я хочу́ прийти́ на приём к ... (+ dat.)	ya ha-choo pree-tee na pree-yom k ...
I have an appointment with ...	У меня́ назна́чена встре́ча с ... (+ instr.)	oo me-nya na-zna-chyé-na vstryé-cha s ...
My name is ...	Меня́ зову́т ...	me-nya za-voot ...
Here is my card	Вот моя́ визи́тная ка́рточка	vot ma-ya vee-zeet-na-ya kar-tach-ka
This is our catalogue	Вот наш катало́г	vot nash ka-ta-lok
I would like to see your products	Я хочу́ ви́деть то, что вы произво́дите	ya ha-choo vee-dyét' to, shto vi pra-eez-vo-dee-tyé
Could you send me some samples?	Мо́жете ли вы присла́ть мне не́которые образцы́?	mo-zhe-tyé lee vi pree-slat' mnyé nyé-ka-ta-ri-yé a-braz-tsi

Can you provide an interpreter/a secretary?	Мóжете ли вы предостáвить перевóдчика/ секретáршу?	**mo**-zhe-**tyé** lee vi pryé-da-**sta**-veet' pyé-ryé-**vot**-cheeka/ syé-kryé-**tar**-shoo
Where can I make some photocopies?	Где мóжно снять фотокóпии?	gdye **mózh**-na snyat' fa-ta-**ko**-pee-ee

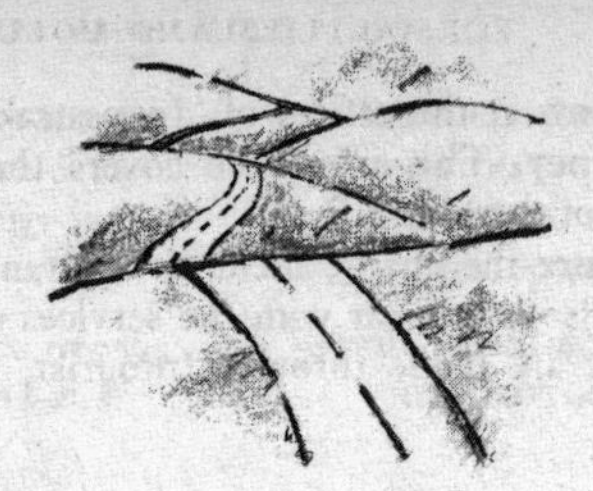

DRIVING

FORMALITIES AND DOCUMENTS

Travelling in the Soviet Union in your own car is possible, but needs careful advance organization, including giving details of your route to Intourist. You are only allowed to drive along approved Intourist itineraries, and cannot cover more than 500 km a day. You must state in advance where you will spend each night; this must be at an Intourist hotel, motel, or official camping site. A visa for a motoring holiday is only granted if you buy vouchers in advance from Intourist to cover every day of your holiday.

You must have a passport, a visa, an international driving licence or a national driving licence with an insert in Russian (this can be obtained at the first Intourist service point at a cost of 50 kopecks), and the car registration papers. Your car must display a nationality sticker and must be registered on entry with customs. You must also fill in a form undertaking to remove the car from the U.S.S.R. on departure. There is a road tax of 10 roubles per car and 5 roubles for a trailer.

You will be given a map of Intourist itineraries, and a document with full details of your itinerary and overnight stops.

Insurance: Insurance is not compulsory, but may be arranged in advance through the Black Sea and Baltic General Insurance Company, or at the border on arrival, or in Moscow at the offices of 'Ingosstrakh', the Soviet State Foreign Insurance Agency. This insurance covers third-party risks and accidents on the territory of the U.S.S.R.

Car hire: For self-drive car hire the charge includes insurance and servicing, but not petrol. You can also hire a car with the services of a chauffeur. All arrangements for car hire are made through Intourist, usually in the service burcau of your hotel.

Here is/are	Вот	vot
my driving licence	мои́ права́	ma-ee pra-va
the car documents	докуме́нты на маши́ну	da-koo-myén-ti na ma-shi-noo
my passport	мой па́спорт	moy pas-part
my visa	моя́ ви́за	ma-ya vee-za
I have an international driving licence	У меня́ междунаро́дные права́	oo-me-nya myézh-doo-na-rod-ni-yé pra-va
Is the car insured?	*Маши́на застрахо́вана?	ma-shi-na za-stra-ho-va-na
My car is insured	Моя́ маши́на застрахо́вана	ma-ya ma-shi-na za-stra-ho-va-na
I would like to insure my car	Я хочу́ застрахова́ть маши́ну	ya ha-choo za-stra-ha-vat' ma-shi-noo
I would like to hire a car	Я хочу́ взять напрока́т маши́ну	ya ha-choo vzyat' na-pra-kat ma-shi-noo

No, the document is not out of date. Here is the renewal stamp	Нет, докуме́нт не просро́чен. Вот штамп о продле́нии	nyét, da-koo-myént nyé pra-sro-chyén. vot shtamp a-pra-dlyé-nee-ee
My route has been approved by Intourist	Мой маршру́т был одо́брен Интури́стом	moy marsh-root bil a-do-bryén een-too-rees-tam
All the arrangements were made by Intourist	Всё бы́ло организо́вано Интури́стом	fsyo bi-lo ar-ga-nee-zo-va-na een-too-rees-tam
I need an interpreter	Мне ну́жен перево́дчик	mnyé noo-zhén pyé-ryé-vot-cheek
Thank you. May I go now?	Спаси́бо. Мо́жно е́хать?	spa-see-ba. mozh-na yé-hat'

TRAFFIC REGULATIONS

The traffic police in the Soviet Union are called ГАИ; these are the initials of the State Motor Inspection, and are pronounced ga-ee. The traffic police patrol the roads and are also stationed at permanent posts, marked ГАИ. There is relatively little traffic on Soviet roads, and international road signs are used. It is obviously essential to have mastered the Russian alphabet for reading directions and street signs.

– Traffic drives on the right side of the road.

– In populated areas there is a speed limit of 60 km per hour (37 m.p.h.) and using the horn is not allowed except in an emergency.

– It is compulsory for both front-seat passengers to wear seat-belts.

– In the centre of large towns, drivers use their sidelights when driving after dark, and not their headlights (even dipped).

– There are virtually no restrictions on parking. Except in a few areas in the centre of Moscow, you can park your car wherever you like, and leave it for an unlimited time. If you see a sign with a large P on it outside an official building, this means that parking is restricted to members of that institution.

СТОП	Stop	
ОБЪЕЗД	Diversion	
I'm sorry. Is something wrong?	Извини́те. Что́-то не в поря́дке?	eez-vee-nee-tyé. shto-ta nyé fpa-ryat-kyé
This is a one-way street	*Здесь односторо́ннее движе́ние	zdyés' ad-na-sta-ron-nyé-yé dvee-zhé-nee-yé
You're driving too fast	*Вы е́дете сли́шком бы́стро	vi yé-dyé-tyé sleesh-kam bis-tra
You crossed a red light	*Вы е́хали на кра́сный свет	vi yé-ha-lee na kras-niy svyét
You made a turn where it is forbidden	*Вы поверну́ли в запрещённом ме́сте	vi pa-vyér-noo-lee fza-pryé-shon-nam myés-tyé
I'm sorry. I didn't realize	Изини́те. Я не знал/зна́ла *f*	eez-vee-nee-tyé. ya nyé znal/zna-la
I didn't see the sign	Я не ви́дел/ви́дела *f* зна́ка	ya nyé vee-dyél/vee-dyé-la zna-ka
I will observe the speed limit in future	Я не бу́ду превыша́ть ско́рость	ya nyé boo-doo pryé-vi-shat' sko-rast'
I have only just arrived	Я то́лько что прие́хал/прие́хала *f*	ya tol'-ka-shto pree-yé-hal/pree-yé-ha-la

What is the speed limit?	Какáя предéльная скóрость?	ka-ka-ya pryé-dyél'-na-ya sko-rast'
Where can I park my car?	Где мóжно постáвить машѝну?	gdyé mozh-na pa-sta-veet' ma-shi-noo
May I park my car here?	Мóжно тут постáвить машѝну?	mozh-na toot pa-sta-veet' ma-shi-noo
Parking is forbidden here	*Стоя́нка здесь запрещенá	sta-yan-ka zdyés' za-pryé-shé-na

FINDING YOUR WAY

A list of towns open to foreign tourists is given on page 47. This may help you either to recognize the name of a town on a direction sign, or to pronounce it correctly if asking for directions.

Please help me	Помогѝте мне, пожáлуйста	pa-ma-gee-tyé mnyé, pa-zha-loo-sta
I'm lost	Я заблудѝлся/заблудѝлась *f*	ya za-bloo-deel-sa/za-bloo-dee-las'
Please show me on the map	Покажѝте мне на кáрте, пожáлуйста	pa-ka-zhi-tyé mnyé na kar-tyé, pa-zha-loo-sta
where I am/ where … is	где я нахожýсь/ где …	gdyé ya na-ha-zhoos'/gdyé …
Could you please tell me …	Скажѝте, пожáлуйста …	ska-zhi-tyé, pa-zha-loo-sta …

How far is it to . . . ?	Как далекó до . . . ? (+ gen.)	**kak da-lyé-ko da . . .**
How many kilometres to . . . ?[1]	Скóлько километров до . . . ? (+ gen.)	**skol'-ka kee-la-myé-traf da . . .**
How long will it take to drive from here to . . . ?	Скóлько врéмени éхать отсю́да до . . . ? (+ gen.)	**skol'-ka vryé-myé-nee yé-hat' at-syoo-da da . . .**
How can I get to	Как доéхать до (+ gen.)	**kak da-yé-hat' da**
the centre/ . . . hotel?	цéнтра/ гости́ницы . . . ?	**tsén-tra/gas-tee-nee-tsi . . .**
the next restaurant?	слéдующего ресторáна?	**slyé-doo-shé-va ryés-ta-ra-na**
the next village?	слéдующей дерéвни?	**slyé-doo-shéy dyé-ryév-nee**
How can I get	Как проéхать	**kak pra-yé-hat'**
to the motorway/to the main road?	к магистрáли/к шоссé?	**kma-gee-stra-lee/ kshas-syé**
Am I going the right way for . . . ?	Я прáвильно éду к . . . ? (+ dat.)	**ya pra-veel'-na yé-doo k . . .**
Go straight ahead/back	*Поезжáйте пря́мо/назáд	**pa-yéz-zhay-tyé prya-ma/na-zat**

1. See p. 240 for distance conversion table.

Go as far as	*Доезжáйте	da-yéz-zhay-tyé
the traffic lights	до светофóра	da-svyé-ta-fo-ra
the first intersection	до пéрвого перекрёстка	da pyér-va-va pyé-ryé-kryost-ka
Turn right/left	*Повернúте напрáво/налéво	pa-vyér-nee-tyé na-pra-va/na-lyé-va
by the traffic lights	у светофóра	oo-svyé-ta-fo-ra
at the crossroads	на перекрёстке	na-pyé-ryé-kryost-kyé
Where does this road go?	Кудá идёт э́та дорóга?	koo-da ee-dyot é-ta da-ro-ga
Which is the road for ...?	Какáя дорóга на ...? (+ acc.)	ka-ka-ya da-ro-ga na ...
What is this place called?	Как называ́ется э́то мéсто?	kak na-zi va-yét-sa é-ta myés-ta
Is there black ice on the road?	Есть ли на дорóге гололёд?	yést'-lee na da-ro-gyé ga-la-lyot
Can I get through on this road?	Мóжно ли проéхать по э́той дорóге?	mozh-na-lee pra-yé-hat' pa-é-toy da-ro-gyé

AT THE PETROL STATION

There are petrol stations and service stations on Intourist motoring routes and at all official stopping-points. They are marked on the map of motoring routes which Intourist issues at the border. Petrol stations can be recognized by a sign with a picture of a pump, or with the letters АЗС (the initials of 'car filling station' in Russian).

• Various grades of petrol are available; the most common are 76 octane and 93 octane. At some petrol stations you pay with coupons, at others you pay with money (some will accept both). Coupons for petrol will be issued to you at the border; they can also be purchased at tobacco shops, sports shops and hardware stores.

All petrol stations are self-service; you hand your money or coupons to the person on duty, and then fill up your tank with the amount you have paid for. Since petrol stations are not very numerous, it is a good idea to carry a spare can of petrol in your car. Petrol cans are sold in hardware stores; the top is sometimes sold separately at the counter.

Occasionally you can buy oil at a petrol station, but, again, you must have your own container, or be prepared to put the oil in yourself. In general, however, for all routine maintenance as well as for repairs you must go to a service station; the phrases which you will need for general maintenance are therefore given in the next section.

How do I get to the petrol station?	Как доéхать до бензоколóнки?	**kak da-yé-hat' da-byén-za-ka-lon-kee**
Where is there a petrol station near here?	Где здесь бензоколóнка?	**gdyé zdyes' byén-za-ka-lon-ka**
How far is the petrol station?	Как далекó до бензоколóнки?	**kak da-lyé-ko da-byén-za-ka-lon-kee**
What kind of petrol do you have?	Какóй у вас бензи́н?	**ka-koy oo-vas byén-zeen**
Could I have	Дáйте, пожáлуйста	**day-tyé, pa-zha-loo-sta**
93 octane petrol?	девянóсто трéтий?	**dyé-vya-nos-ta tryé-teey**
76 octane petrol?	сéмьдесят шестóй?	**syém'-dyé-syat shés-toy**

ten/twenty litres?[1]	де́сять/два́дцать ли́тров?	dyé-syat'/dvat-tsat' lee-traf
thirty-five litres?	три́дцать пять ли́тров?	treet-tsat pyat' lee-traf
Please fill the petrol tank	По́лный бак, пожа́луйста	pol-niy bak, pa-zha-loo-sta
Do you take coupons or money?	Вы принима́ете тало́ны и́ли де́ньги?	vi pree-nee-ma-yé-tyé ta-lo-ni ee-lee dyén'-gee
How many coupons do I owe you?	Ско́лько тало́нов я вам до́лжен/должна́ *f*?	skol'-ka ta-lo-naf ya vam dol-zhén/dalzh-na
Do you have any oil?	У вас есть ма́сло?	oo-vas yést' mas-la
I need some water	Мне нужна́ вода́	mnyé noozh-na va-da
for the radiator	для радиа́тора	dlya ra-dee-a-ta-ra
for the windscreen washers	для стекло-промыва́телей	dlya styé-kla-pra-mi-va-tyé-lyéy
to wash the windscreen	что́бы помы́ть пере́днее стекло́	shto-bi pa-mit' pyé-ryéd-nyé-yé styék-lo
Can you give me a rag?	Мо́жете ли вы мне дать тря́пку?	mo-zhe-tyé-lee vi mnyé dat' tryap-koo
Do you have . . . ?	У вас есть ...	oo-vas yést' ...

1. See p. 242 for liquid measures conversion table.

Please give me	Дайте, пожалуйста	**day-tyé, pa-zha-loo-sta**
petrol coupons	талоны на бензин	**ta-lo-ni na-byén-zeen**
for ... litres	на ... литров	**na ... lee-traf**

AT THE SERVICE STATION

A service station (АВТОСТАНЦИЯ – aftastantsiya – in Russian) can be recognized by a sign with a picture of a spanner or by the words СТАНЦИЯ ТЕХОБСЛУЖИВАНИЯ (service station). There are service stations at all main stopping-points on Intourist motoring routes, usually near motels or camping sites. In Moscow, the service stations are all outside the centre, usually near the outer ring road.

MAINTENANCE

All general maintenance work is carried out at service stations. You can buy oil, but you must have your own container. Distilled water can sometimes be obtained at service stations, but if you have difficulty try a chemist. You can check the pressure of your tyres at a service station; many drivers also carry their own tyre pressure gauge, and you can ask to borrow this if necessary. It is also possible to have your car washed or to clean it yourself at a car washing-point; the sign for this service is АВТОМОЙКА.

It is a good idea to take with you a supply of whatever engine oil you use, distilled water for the battery, and any special items such as brake fluid, oil for the automatic transmission, windscreen washer additive, etc.

How do I get to the service station?	Как доéхать до автостáнции?	**kak da-yé-hat' da-af-ta-stan-tsi-ee**

Where is there a service station near here?	Где здесь автоста́нция?	gdyé zdyés' af-ta-**stan**-tsi-ya
How far is the service station?	Как далеко́ до автоста́нции?	kak da-lyé-**ko** da-af-ta-**stan**-tsi-ee
I need to check the oil and the water	Ну́жно прове́рить ма́сло и во́ду	**noozh**-na pra-**vyé**-reet' **mas**-la ee **vo**-doo
The oil needs changing	Ну́жно смени́ть ма́сло	**noozh**-na smyé-**neet'** **mas**-la
What kind of oil do you have?	Како́е ма́сло у вас?	ka-**ko**-yé **mas**-la oo-vas
I would like to buy some spare petrol/some oil	Я хочу́ купи́ть запасно́й бензи́н/ма́сло	ya ha-**choo** koo-**peet'** za-pas-**noy** byén-**zeen**/**mas**-la
I have a can	У меня́ есть кани́стра	oo-me-**nya** yest' ka-**nee**-stra
Do you have a can?	У вас есть кани́стра?	oo-vas yest' ka-**nee**-stra
Could I please have	Да́йте, пожа́луйста	**day**-tyé, pa-**zha**-loo-sta
... litres of oil[1]	... ли́тра ма́сла	... **lee**-tra **mas**-la
Do you have distilled water (for the battery)?	У вас есть дистилли́ро́ванная вода́ (для аккумуля́тора)?	oo-vas yést' dees-teel-lee-**ro**-van-na-ya va-**da** (dlya ak-koo-moo-**lya**-ta-ra)

1. See p. 242 for liquid measures conversion table.

Please check	Пожáлуйста, провéрьте	pa-zha-loo-sta, pra-vyér'-tyé
the battery	аккумуля́тор	ak-koo-moo-lya-tar
the brakes	тормозá	tar-ma-za
the oil	мáсло	mas-la
the tyre pressure	давлéние в ши́нах	dav-lyé-nee-yé fshi-nah
The tyre pressure should be ...	Давлéние должнó быть ...	dav-lyé-nee-yé dalzh-no bit' ...
... at the front/ ... at the back	... впереди́/ ... сзáди	... fpyé-ryé-dee/ ... sza-dee
The spare tyre also needs to be checked	Нýжно тóже провéрить запаснóе колесó	noozh-na to-zhé pra-vyé-reet' za-pas-no-yé ka-lyé-so
I need to put some air in the tyres	Нýжно накачáть ши́ны	noozh-na na-ka-chat' shi-ni
Do you have a tyre pressure gauge?	У вас есть манóметр?	oo-vas yést' ma-no-myétr?
Where can I wash my car?	Где мóжно помы́ть маши́ну?	gdyé mozh-na pa-mit' ma-shi-noo
Can you wash my car?	Мóжете ли вы помы́ть маши́ну?	mo-zhé-tyé-lee vi pa-mit' ma-shi-noo
Is there a toilet here?	Здесь есть туалéт?	zdyés' yést' too-a-lyét

REPAIRS

Since the Soviet Union produces its own cars and imports virtually none, it is unlikely that you will be able to find any spare parts there for your vehicle. It is a common-sense precaution to take a tool kit and a simple set of spares, such as the makers of your car, or the R.A.C. or A.A., would recommend. A spare fanbelt, radiator hose, light bulbs and wiper blades would figure on your list. While in the Soviet Union, it is, incidentally, a good plan to adopt the local custom of removing windscreen wipers (arms as well as blades) and any other removable parts when leaving the car unattended. Unless all your spark plugs are new, take spares. Make sure your spare wheel with tyre and tube are in good shape and take a spare inner tube as well. You may also wish to take an emergency replacement windscreen. If you are likely to encounter wintry conditions, take a snow shovel, chains, and a spray for clearing ice from the windows.

Is there a mechanic here?	Здесь есть меха́ник?	**zdyés' yést' myé-ha-neek**
I don't understand what is wrong	Я не зна́ю, в чём де́ло	**ya nyé zna-yoo fchyom dyé-la**
I think that something is wrong with the ...[1]	Я ду́маю, что ... не в поря́дке	**ya doo-ma-yoo shto ... nyé fpa-ryat-kyé**
... isn't working[1]	... не рабо́тает	**... nyé ra-bo-ta-yét**
... has broken[1]	... слома́лся	**... sla-mal-sa**
I have a flat tyre	У меня́ ло́пнула ши́на	**oo me-nya lop-noo-la shi-na**

1. Use these phrases in conjunction with 'Driver's Vocabulary' (p. 202).

The tyre needs to be changed	Ну́жно смени́ть ши́ну	noozh-na smyé-neet' shi-noo
I have a spare wheel in the boot	У меня́ в бага́жнике запасно́е колесо́	oo me-nya fba-gazh-nee-kyé za-pas-no-yé ka-lyé-so
The tyre is tubeless	Ши́на беска́мерная	shi-na byés-ka-myér-na-ya
My car won't start	Маши́на не заво́дится	ma-shi-na nyé za-vo-deet-sa
The battery needs charging	Ну́жно подзаряди́ть аккумуля́тор	noozh-na pad-za-rya-deet' ak-koo-moo-lya-tar
The engine is overheating	Мото́р перегрева́ется	ma-tor pyé-ryé-gryé-va-yét-sa
The engine is firing badly	Мото́р рабо́тает с перебо́ями	ma-tor ra-bo-ta-yet spyé-ryé-bo-ya-mee
The clutch engages too quickly	Сцепле́ние сли́шком ре́зкое	stsé-plyé-nee-yé sleesh-kam ryéz-ko-yé
The radiator is leaking	Радиа́тор течёт	ra-dee-a-tar tyé-chyot
There is	В маши́не	fma-shi-nyé
a petrol leak	уте́чка бензи́на	oo-tyéch-ka byén-zee-na
an oil leak	уте́чка ма́сла	oo-tyéch-ka mas-la
There's a smell of petrol/rubber	Па́хнет бензи́ном/рези́ной	pah-nyét byén-zee-nam/ryé-zee-noy
There is a noise	Что́-то шуми́т	shto-ta shoo-meet

The car is locked, and the keys are inside it	Маши́на за́перта, а ключи́ внутри́	ma-shi-na za-pyér-ta, a klyoo-chee vnoo-tree
I have lost the car key	Я потеря́л/потеря́ла *f* ключ от маши́ны	ya pa-tyé-ryal/pa-tyé-rya-la klyooch at-ma-shi-ni
It is necessary to adjust	Ну́жно отрегули́ровать	noozh-na at-ryé-goo-lee-ra-vat'
the idling speed	холосто́й ход	ha-las-toy hot
the brakes/the pedal	тормоза́/педа́ль	tar-ma-za/pyé-dal'
It is necessary to replace ...	Ну́жно замени́ть ...	noozh-na za-myé-neet'
a faulty plug	неиспра́вную свечу́	nyé-ees-praf-noo-yoo svyé-choo
the fanbelt	вентиляцио́нный реме́нь	vyén-tee-lya-tsi-on-niy ryé-myén'
I have a spare ...	У меня́ есть запасно́й ...	oo-me-nya yést' za-pas-noy ...
Do you have the spare parts?	У вас есть запча́сти?	oo-vas yést' zap-chas-tee
Where can I get the spare parts?	Где мо́жно доста́ть запча́сти?	gdyé mozh-na da-stat' zap-chas-tee
When will the spare parts arrive?	Когда́ бу́дут запча́сти?	kag-da boo-doot zap-chas-tee
Have you found the trouble?	Вы нашли́ поло́мку?	vi nash-lee pa-lom-koo

What has happened?	Что случи́лось?	shto sloo-chee-las'
Can you mend it?	Вы мо́жете испра́вить?	vi mo-zhé-tyé ees-pra-veet'
How long will it take to repair it?	Ско́лько вре́мени займёт ремо́нт?	skol'-ka vryé-myé-nee zay-myot ryé-mont
Can you do a temporary repair?	Мо́жете ли вы сде́лать вре́менный ремо́нт?	mo-zhe-tyé-lee vi zdyé-lat' vryé-myén-niy ryé-mont
I must reach ... by tonight	Я до́лжен/должна́ *f* дое́хать до ... (+ gen.) сего́дня ве́чером	ya dol-zhén/dalzh-na da-yé-hat' da ... syé-vod-nya vyé-chyé-ram
When should I come back?	Когда́ мне прийти́?	kag-da mnyé preey-tee
How much will it cost?	Ско́лько э́то бу́дет сто́ить?	skol'-ka é-ta boo-dyét sto-eet'
I would like to speak to the manager	Я хочу́ поговори́ть с нача́льником	ya ha-choo pa-ga-va-reet' sna-chal'-nee-kam
Thank you. You have been very helpful	Спаси́бо. Вы мне о́чень помогли́	spa-see-ba. vi mnyé o-chyén' pa-ma-glee

ACCIDENT AND BREAKDOWN

If you have an accident or a breakdown on the road, you should contact the nearest traffic police station (ГАИ – Ga-ee) or Intourist service point.

There's been an accident	Произошёл несча́стный слу́чай	pra-ee-sa-shol nyé-shas-niy sloo-chay
There are injured people	Есть ра́неные	yést' ra-nyé-ni-yé
My car has broken down	У меня́ останови́лась маши́на	oo-me-nya a-sta-na-vee-las' ma-shi-na
Where is the nearest telephone?	Где ближа́йший телефо́н?	gdyé blee-zhay-sheey tyé-lyé-fon
May I use your telephone?	Мо́жно от вас позвони́ть?	mozh-na at-vas pa-zva-neet'
Please call	Вы́зовите, пожа́луйста	vi-za-vee-tyé, pa-zha-loo-sta
the police	мили́цию	mee-lee-tsi-yoo
an ambulance	ско́рую по́мощь	sko-roo-yoo po-mash
Could you inform the next traffic police station?	Вы мо́жете сообщи́ть в ближа́йшую ГАИ́?	vi mo-zhe-tyé sa-ab-sheet' fblee-zhay-shoo-yoo ga-ee

Could you send a mechanic?	Пришли́те, пожалуйста, меха́ника	pree-shlee-tyé, pa-zha-loo-sta, myé-ha-nee-ka
Could you send a breakdown truck to tow away my car?	Мо́жно присла́ть грузови́к и взять на букси́р мо́ю маши́ну?	mozh-na pree-slat' groo-za-veek ee vzyat' na book-seer ma-yoo ma-shi-noo
I am	Я	ya
on the ... road	на доро́ге ...	na da-ro-gyé ...
at ... kilometres from ...	в ... киломе́трах от ... (+ gen.)	v ... kee-la-myé-trah at ...
not far from ...	недалеко́ от ... (+ gen.)	nyé-da-lyé-ko ot ...
How long will I have to wait?	Ско́лько ну́жно ждать?	skol'-ka noozh-na zhdat'
I have run out of petrol	У меня́ ко́нчился бензи́н	oo-me-nya kon-cheel-sa byén-zeen
Could you sell me some petrol?	Вы мо́жете мне прода́ть бензи́н?	vi mo-zhe-tyé mnyé pra-dat' byén-zeen
My car is stuck	Моя́ маши́на застря́ла	ma-ya ma-shi-na za-strya-la
in the snow/in the mud	в снегу́/в грязи́	fsnyé-goo/fgrya-zee
Could you possibly tow me to the next town?	Вы не могли́ бы меня́ взять на букси́р до сле́дующего го́рода?	vi-nyé ma-glee-bi me-nya vzyat' na-book-seer da-slyé-doo-shé-va go-ra-da

I have a tow-rope	У меня́ есть трос	oo-me-nya yést' tros
I don't have a tow-rope	У меня́ нет тро́са	oo-me-nya nyét tro-sa

DRIVER'S VOCABULARY

The words in this section can be used with the phrases on page 196.

accelerator	акселера́тор	ak-syé-lyé-ra-tar
air filter	возду́шный фильтр	vaz-doosh-niy feel'tr
air pump	возду́шный насо́с	vaz-doosh-niy na-sos
alternator	альтерна́тор	al'-tyér-na-tar
anti-freeze	антифри́з	an-tee-freez
axle	ось	os'
battery	аккумуля́тор	ak-koo-moo-lya-tar
bearings	подши́пники	pad-ship-nee-kee
bonnet/hood	капо́т	ka-pot
boot/trunk	бага́жник	ba-gazh-neek
brake	то́рмоз	tor-maz
brake lining	тормозна́я подкла́дка	tar-maz-na-ya pad-klat-ka
brushes	щётки	shyot-kee
bulb	ла́мпа	lam-pa
bumper	ба́мпер	bam-pyér
cable	трос	tros
camshaft	кулачко́вый вал	koo-lach-ko-viy val
carburettor	карбюра́тор	kar-byoo-ra-tar

choke	возду́шная засло́нка	vaz-doosh-na-ya za-slon-ka
clutch	сцепле́ние	stsé-plyé-nee-yé
clutch pedal	педаль сцепле́ния	pyé-dal' stsé-plyé-nee-ya
contact	конта́кт	kan-takt
cooling system	систе́ма охлажде́ния	sees-tyé-ma a-hlazh-dyé-nee-ya
crankcase	ка́ртер коле́нчатого ва́ла	kar-tyér ka-lyén-cha-ta-va va-la
crankshaft	коле́нчатый вал	ka-lyén-cha-tiy val
cylinder	цили́ндр	tsi-leendr
cylinder head	голо́вка цили́ндра	ga-lof-ka tsi-leen-dra
de-mister	приспособле́ние про́тив запотева́ния	pree-spa-sab-lyé-nee-yé pro-teef za-pa-tyé-va-nee-ya
differential gear	дифференциа́л	deef-fyé-ryén-tsi-al
dip-stick	сте́ржень для измере́ния у́ровня жи́дкости	styér-zhén' dlya eez-myé-ryé-nee-ya oo-rav-nya zhid-kas-tee
distilled water	дистиллиро́ванная вода́	dee-steel-lee-ro-va-na-ya va-da
distributor	распредели́тель	ras-pryé-dyé-lee-tyél'
door	дверь	dvyér'
doorhandle	дверна́я ру́чка	dvyér-na-ya rooch-ka
dynamo	дина́мо	dee-na-ma
electrical system	электрообору́дование	é-lyék-tra-a-ba-roo-da-va-nee-yé
engine	мото́р	ma-tor
exhaust	выхлопна́я тру́ба	vi-hlap-na-ya troo-ba

fan	вентиля́тор	vyén-tee-lya-tar
fanbelt	вентиляцио́нный реме́нь	vyén-tee-lya-tsi-on-niy ryé-myén’
footbrake	ножно́й то́рмоз	nazh-noy tor-maz
fusebox	закры́тый пла́вкий предохрани́тель	za-kri-tiy plaf-keey pryé-da-hra-nee-tyél’
gasket	прокла́дка	pra-klat-ka
gear box	коро́бка ско́ростей	ka-rop-ka sko-ras-tyéy
gear lever	рыча́г	ri-chak
gears	переда́чи/ско́рости	pyé-ryé-da-chee/ sko-ras-tee
handbrake	ручно́й то́рмоз	rooch-noy tor-maz
heater	отопи́тель ку́зова	a-ta-pee-tyél’ koo-za-va
horn	гудо́к	goo-dok
hose	шланг	shlang
ignition	зажига́ние	za-zhi-ga-nee-yé
ignition key	ключ зажига́ния	kylooch za-zhi-ga-nee-ya
indicator	указа́тель поворо́та	oo-ka-za-tyél’ pa-va-ro-ta
jack	домкра́т	dam-krat
lights		
headlights	фа́ры	fa-ri
main beams	да́льние	dal’-nee-yé
dipped beams	бли́жние	bleezh-nee-yé
front sidelights	подфа́рники	pad-far-nee-kee
rear (tail) lights	за́дние фонари́	zad-nee-yé fa-na-ree
brake (stop) lights	стоп-сигна́л	stop-seeg-nal
emergency flashing lights	авари́йные фонари́	a-va-reey-ni-yé fa-na-ree
lock	замо́к	za-mok

lubrication system	систе́ма сма́зки	sees-tyé-ma smaz-kee
mirror	зе́ркало	zyér-ka-la
number plate	номерно́й знак	na-myér-noy znak
nut	га́йка	gay-ka
oil	ма́сло	mas-la
oil filter	маслофи́льтр	mas-la-feel'tr
oil gauge	масломе́р	mas-la-myér
oil pump	ма́сляный насо́с	mas-lya-niy na-sos
pedal	педа́ль	pyé-dal'
petrol	бензи́н	byén-zeen
petrol can	бидо́н	bee-don
petrol filter	бензофи́льтр	byén-za-feel'tr
petrol gauge	бензиноме́р	byén-zee-na-myér
petrol pump	бензи́новый насо́с	byén-zee-na-viy na-sos
piston	по́ршень	por-shén'
piston ring	поршнево́е кольцо́	par-shnyé-vo-yé kal'-tso
pump	насо́с	na-sos
puncture	проко́л	pra-kol
radiator	радиа́тор	ra-dee-a-tar
rear axle	за́дняя ось	zad-nya-ya os'
reflectors	отража́тели	at-ra-zha-tyé-lee
reverse	за́дний ход	zad-neey hot
(sliding) roof	сдвига́ющаяся кры́ша	sdvee-ga-yoo-sha-ya-sa kri-sha
screwdriver	отвёртка	at-vyort-ka
seat	ме́сто	myés-ta
shaft	вал	val
shock absorber	амортиза́тор	a-mar-tee-za-tar
silencer	глуши́тель	gloo-shi-tyél'

spanner	гáечный ключ	ga-yéch-niy klyooch
spare parts	запчáсти	zap-chas-tee
spare wheel	запаснóе колесó	za-pas-no-yé ka-lyé-so
sparking plugs	свéчи	svyé-chee
sparking plug leads	кáбель свéчи	ka-byél' svyé-chee
speed	скóрость	sko-rast'
speedometer	спидóметр	spee-do-myétr
spring	рессóра	ryés-so-ra
starter	стáртер	star-tyér
steering	рулевóе управлéние	roo-lyé-vo-yé oo-prav-lyé-nee-yé
steering box	кáртер рулевóго управлéния	kar-tyér roo-lyé-vo-va oo-prav-lyé-nee-ya
steering column	колóнка руля́	ka-lon-ka roo-lya
steering wheel	руль	rool'
suspension	подвéска	pad-vyés-ka
tank	бак	bak
tappets	толкáтели клáпана	tal-ka-tyé-lee kla-pa-na
thermostat	термостáт	tyér-ma-stat
transmission	передáча	pyé-ryé-da-cha
(inner) tube	кáмера	ka-myé-ra
tubeless tyre	бескáмерная ши́на	byés-ka-myér-na-ya shi-na
tyre	ши́на	shi-na
tyre pressure	давлéние в ши́нах	da-vlyé-nee-yé fshi-nah
tyre pressure gauge	манóметр	ma-no-myétr
valve	клáпан	kla-pan

wheel – back	колесó – зáднее	ka-lyé-so – zad-na-yé
front	перéднее	pyé-ryéd-nyé-yé
spare	запаснóе	za-pas-no-yé
window	боковóе стеклó	ba-ka-vo-yé styé-klo
windscreen	перéднее стеклó	pyé-ryéd-nyé-yé styé-klo
windscreen washers	стеклопромывáтели	styé-kla-pra-mi-va-tyé-lee
windscreen wipers	двóрники	dvor-nee-kee

CAMPING

If you go on a motoring holiday to the Soviet Union, you have the choice of staying overnight at a hotel, motel, or camping site. Foreign tourists are allowed to camp only at official sites, and must arrange their itinerary and overnight stops in advance with Intourist.

The camping sites are open from June until October. You can either rent a space for your own tent or caravan, or you can sleep in a two- to four-berth tent or hut. You will almost certainly find someone who speaks English in the administration quarters of the camping site. Here you can also hire tents, folding beds, sports equipment, bedding, and kitchen utensils. Facilities include a kitchen, a cafeteria or restaurant, a laundry, a food shop, showers and washrooms, lavatories, a post office, and sometimes a cinema and sports area. You will be provided with a parking space for your car, either in a communal car park or by your tent or hut. There are also facilities for washing cars, and car inspection pits. There is normally a petrol station near by.

Payment is made by vouchers, issued in advance by Intourist.

ПИТЬЕВАЯ ВОДА	Drinking water
НЕ ПИТЬЕВАЯ ВОДА	Not for drinking

How can I get to the camping site?	Как доéхать до кéмпинга?	kak da-yé-hat' da-kém-peen-ga
How far is the camping site?	Как далекó до кéмпинга?	kak da-lyé-ko da-kém-peen-ga
Where is the administration?	Где админи-стрáция?	gdyé ad-mee-nee-stra-tsi-ya
Is there an interpreter here?	Есть ли здесь перевóдчик?	yést'-lee zdyés' pyé-ryé-vot-cheek
Where can I park my car?	Где мóжно постáвить маши́ну?	gdyé mozh-na pa-sta-veet' ma-shi-noo
Can I park the car here?	Мóжно постáвить маши́ну здесь?	mozh-na pa-sta-veet' ma-shi-noo zdyés'
next to the tent?	óколо палáтки?	o-ka-la pa-lat-kee
What is your car registration number?	*Какóй нóмер вáшей маши́ны?	ka-koy no-myér va-shéy ma-shi-ni
Where should we put our tent/caravan?	Где мóжно постáвить палáтку/дом-автофургóн?	gdyé mozh-na pa-sta-veet' pa-lat-koo/ dom-af-ta-foor-gon
I would like a place	Я хочý мéсто	ya ha-choo myés-ta
in a hut/in a tent	в дóмике/в палáтке	fdo-mee-kyé/ fpa-lat-kyé
Where is my hut/my tent?	Где мой дóмик/моя́ палáтка?	gdyé moy do-meek/ma-ya pa-lat-ka

I'm afraid the camp site is full	*К сожалéнию в кéмпинге все местá зáняты	ksa-zha-lyé-nee-yoo fkyém-peen-gyé vsyé myés-ta za-nya-ti
Can I hire	Мóжно взять напрокáт	mozh-na vzyat' na-pra-kat
a saucepan/a frying pan?	кастрю́лю/ сковороду́?	kas-tryoo-lyoo/ ska-va-ra-doo
some crockery?	посу́ду?	pa-soo-doo
a tent?	палáтку?	pa-lat-koo
some bed-linen?	постéльное бельё?	pa-styél'-na-ye byé-lyo
Is there a . . . ?	Здесь есть . . . ?	zdyés yést . . .
Where is the . . .	Где . . .	gdyé . . .
kitchen/cafeteria?	ку́хня/столóвая?	kooh-nya/sta-lov-va-ya
restaurant/laundry?	ресторáн/ прáчечная?	ryés-ta-ran/ pra-chyésh-na-ya
food shop/post office?	магази́н/ отделéние свя́зи?	ma-ga-zeen/ at-dyé-lyé- nee-ye svya-zee
shower/wash-room?	душевáя/ умывáльники?	doo-shé-va-ya/oo-mi-val'-nee-kee
lavatory?	туалéт?	too-a-lyét
power point?	розéтка?	ra-zyét-ka
cinema?	кинозал?	kee-na-zal

Is there somewhere to dry clothes/ equipment?	Где мóжно суши́ть бельё/ обору́дование?	gdye mozh-na soo-shit' bye-lyo/a-ba-roo-do-va-nee-yé
The toilet is blocked	Туалéт засори́лся	too-a-lyét za-sa-reel-sa
The shower doesn't work	Душ не рабóтает	doosh nyé ra-bo-ta-yét
Where can I buy paraffin/butane gas?	Где мóжно купи́ть керoси́н/ бутáновый газ?	gdyé mozh-na koo-peet' kyé-ra-seen/ boo-ta-na-viy gaz
My camping gas has run out	У меня́ кóнчился газ	oo-me-nya kon-cheel-sa gaz
When is the shop open?	Когдá рабóтает магази́н?	kag-da ra-bo-ta-yét ma-ga-zeen
When is the cafeteria open?	Когдá рабóтает столóвая?	kag-da ra-bo-ta-yét sta-lo-va-ya
Is this drinking water?	Э́то питьевáя водá?	e-ta pee-tyé-va-ya va-da
May I light a fire?	Мóжно разжéчь костёр?	mozh-na raz-zhéch ka-styor
Where can I dispose of rubbish?	Кудá мóжно вы́бросить му́сор?	koo-da mozh-na vi-bra-seet' moo-sar
Where is the petrol station?	Где бензоколóнка?	gdyé byén-za-ka-lon-ka
Where can I wash my car?	Где мóжно помы́ть маши́ну?	gdyé mozh-na pa-mit ma-shi-noo

Where is the car inspection pit?	Где я́ма для осмо́тра автомоби́лей?	gdyé ya-ma dlya a-smo-tra af-ta-ma-bee-lyéy
Please prepare the bill. We are leaving today	Подгото́вьте, пожа́луйста, счёт. Мы сего́дня уезжа́ем	pad-ga-tof-tyé, pa-zha-loo-sta, shot. mi syé-vod-nya oo-yez-zha-yem
How many coupons do I owe you?	Ско́лько тало́нов я вам до́лжен/должна́ *f*?	skol'-ka ta-lo-naf ya vam dol-zhén/dalzh-na
Thank you and goodbye. We're off	Спаси́бо, до свида́ния. Мы пое́хали	spa-see-ba, da-svee-da-nya, mi pa-yé-ha-lee

AT THE DOCTOR'S

If you feel unwell, notify your Intourist guide or interpreter or the hotel service bureau so that a doctor can be called. Health care in the Soviet Union is free for British tourists.

If you are able to call a doctor through the hotel, you are likely to have the services of an interpreter. But should you find yourself with a Soviet doctor who does not speak English, these phrases may come in useful. If necessary, show the doctor this section of the phrase book, and get him or her to point out to you phrases which apply to your ailments, their diagnosis and treatment.

For minor ailments or for buying medicines which have been prescribed, see the chemist's section, page 133.

ПОЛИКЛИНИКА	Out-patients' clinic
БОЛЬНИЦА	Hospital

AILMENTS

I'm ill	Я бóлен/больнá *f*	ya bo-lyén/bal'-na

I'm not feeling well	Я пло́хо себя́ чу́вствую	ya plo-ha sé-bya choov-stvoo-yoo
Call a doctor (urgently)	Вы́зовите врача́ (сро́чно)	vi-za-vee-tyé vra-cha (sroch-na)
Where is the nearest hospital/out-patients' clinic?	Где ближа́йшая больни́ца/поликли́ника?	gdyé blee-zhay-sha-ya bal'-nee-tsa/ pa-lee-klee-nee-ka
When can the doctor come?	Когда́ врач смо́жет прийти́?	kag-da vrach smo-zhét pree-tee
Does the doctor speak English?	Говори́т ли врач по-англи́йски?	ga-va-reet lee vrach pa-an-gleey-skee
Can I make an appointment for as soon as possible?	Могу́ ли я записа́ться на приём как мо́жно ра́ньше?	ma-goo lee ya za-pee-sat'-sa na pri-yom kak mozh-na ran'-shé
What is wrong with you?	*На что вы жа́луетесь?	na-shto vi zha-loo-yé-tyés
Where does it hurt?	*Где у вас боли́т?	gdyé oo-vas ba-leet
I have a pain here	У меня́ боли́т здесь	oo-me-nya ba-leet zdyés'
Does it hurt here?	*Тут бо́льно?	toot bol'-na
It is very painful	О́чень бо́льно	o-chyén' bol'-na
I think it is infected	Я ду́маю, что у меня́ инфе́кция	ya doo-ma-yoo shto oo-me-nya een-fyék-tsi-ya
I have/He has/ She has	У меня́/У него́/ У неё	oo-me-nya/oo-nyé-vo/ oo-nyé-yo

a headache/a migraine	боли́т голова́/мигре́нь	ba-leet ga-la-va/mee-gryén
an earache/a sore throat	боля́т у́ши/боли́т го́рло	ba-lyat oo-shi/ba-leet gor-la
a bad cough/a cold	си́льный ка́шель/просту́да	seel'-niy ka-shel'/pra-stoo-da
a stomach-ache/constipation	боли́т живо́т/запо́р	ba-leet zhi-vot/za-por
diarrhoea	расстро́йство желу́дка	ras-stroy-stva zhe-loot-ka
sunstroke	со́лнечный уда́р	sol-nyéch-niy oo-dar
a temperature	температу́ра	tyém-pyé-ra-too-ra
back pain	боль в спине́	bol' fspee-nyé
an insect bite/sting	уку́с насеко́мого	oo-koos na-syé-ko-ma-va
a swelling	о́пухоль	o-poo-hal'
I have bruised myself here	Я уши́бся/уши́блась *f* здесь	ya oo-ship-sa/oo-ship-las' zdyés'
I have cut myself here	Я поре́зался/поре́залась *f* здесь	ya pa-ryé-zal-sa/pa-ryé-za-las' zdyés'
I have burnt myself	Я обжёгся/обожгла́сь *f*	ya ab-zhok-sa/a-bazh-glas'
My nose keeps bleeding	У меня́ идёт кровь из но́са	oo-me-nya ee-dyot krof eez-no-sa

I fell over and hurt my back	Я упáл/упáла *f* и повреди́л/повреди́ла *f* себé спи́ну	ya oo-pal/oo-pa-la ee pa-vryé-deel/pa-vryé-dee-la sé-byé spee-noo
I think I've sprained my ankle	Я, кáжется, растянýл/растянýла *f* себé нóгу	ya, ka-zhét-sa, ras-tya-nool/ras-tya-noo-la sé-byé no-goo
I think I've caught flu	Я, кáжется, подхвати́л/подхвати́ла *f* грипп	ya, ka-zhét-sa, pad-hva-teel/pad-hva-tee-la greepp
I think I've got food poisoning	Мне кáжется, я отрави́лся/отрави́лась *f*	mnyé ka-zhét-sa, ya at-ra-veel-sa/ at-ra-vee-las'
I feel dizzy	У меня́ кружи́тся головá	oo-me-nya kroo-zhit-sa ga-la-va
I feel shivery	У меня́ ознóб	oo-me-nya a-znop
I feel sick	Меня́ тошни́т	me-nya tash-neet
I keep vomiting	Меня́ всё врéмя рвёт	me-nya fsyo vryé-mya rvyot
I have difficulty in breathing	Мне трýдно дышáть	mnyé trood-na di-shat'
My heart is beating very fast	У меня́ си́льное сердцебиéние	oo-me-nya seel'-na-yé syérd-tsé-bee-yé-nee-yé
I have lost my appetite	У меня́ пропáл аппети́т	oo-me-nya pra-pal ap-pyé-teet

I can't eat/sleep	Я не могу́ есть/спать	ya nyé ma-goo yést'/spat'
I am/He is/ She is	У меня́/У него́/ У неё	oo-me-nya/oo-nyé-vo/ oo-nyé-yo
diabetic	диабе́т	dee-a-byét
epileptic	эпиле́псия	é-pee-lyép-see-ya
anaemic	малокро́вие	ma-la-kro-vee-yé
I have/He has/ She has	У меня́/У него́/ У неё	oo-me-nya/oo-nyé-vo/ oo-nyé-yo
high blood pressure	гипертони́я	gee-pyér-ta-nee-ya
a bad heart	больно́е се́рдце	bal'-no-yé syérd-tsé
a stomach ulcer	я́зва желу́дка	yaz-va zhe-loot-ka
asthma	а́стма	as-ma
I am pregnant	Я бере́менна	ya byé-ryé-myén-na
I am allergic to ...	У меня́ аллерги́я к ... (+ dat.)	oo-me-nya al-lyér-gee-ya k ...

DIAGNOSIS

What is wrong with me?	Что со мной?	shto sa-mnoy
When did it start?	*Когда́ э́то у вас начало́сь?	kag-da é-ta oo-vas na-cha-los'
It started	Э́то начало́сь	é-ta na-cha-los'
today/yesterday	сего́дня/вчера́	syé-vod-nya/fché-ra

the day before yesterday	позавчера́	pa-zaf-ché-ra
I've had this before	Э́то у меня́ уже́ бы́ло	é-ta oo-me-nya oo-zhé bi-la
What have you eaten?	*Что вы съе́ли?	shto vi syé-lee
Breathe deeply	*Дыши́те глу́бже	di-shi-tyé gloop-zhé
Lie down please	*Ложи́тесь, пожа́луйста	la-zhi-tyés, pa-zha-loo-sta
I must take your blood pressure	*Я вам изме́рю давле́ние	ya vam eez-myé-ryoo dav-lyé-nee-yé
I must do an analysis of your	*Мне ну́жно сде́лать вам ана́лиз	mnyé noozh-na zdyé-lat' vam a-na-leez
urine/blood	мочи́/кро́ви	ma-chee/kro-vee

TREATMENT

You must have an X-ray	*Вам ну́жно сде́лать рентге́н	vam noozh-na zdyé-lat' ryén-gyén
You must have an operation	*Вам нужна́ опера́ция	vam noozh-na a-pyé-ra-tsi-ya
You must go into hospital	*Вам на́до лечь в больни́цу	vam na-da lyéch' fbal'-nee-tsoo
I will put you on a diet	*Я назна́чу вам дие́ту	ya na-zna-choo vam dee-é-too
I will give you an injection	*Я сде́лаю вам уко́л	ya zdyé-la-yoo vam oo-kol

I will give you a prescription for	*Я вы́пишу вам	ya vi-pee-shoo vam
some medicine for ...	лека́рство от ... (+ gen.)	lyé-kar-stva ot ...
some penicillin	пеницилли́н	pyé-nee-tsil-leen
an antibiotic	антибио́тики	an-tee-bee-o-tee-kee
a painkiller	болеутоля́ющее	bo-lyé-oo-ta-lya-yoo-shyé-yé
a sedative	успокои́тельное	oo-spa-ka-ee-tyél'-na-yé
I am taking this medicine	Я принима́ю э́то лека́рство	ya preé-nee-ma-yoo é-ta lyé-kar-stva
Could you please prescribe	Вы́пишите мне, пожа́луйста	vi-pee-shi-tyé mnyé, pa-zha-loo-sta
this medicine	э́то лека́рство	é-ta lyé-kar-stva
some medicine for ...	лека́рство от ... (+ gen.)	lyé-kar-stva ot ...
Where can I buy this medicine?	Где мо́жно купи́ть э́то лека́рство?	gdyé mozh-na koo-peet' é-ta lyé-kar-stva
How many times a day should it be taken?	Ско́лько раз в день его́ принима́ть?	skol'-ka raz fdyén' yé-vo pree-nee-mat'
Take	*Принима́ть	pree-nee-mat'
one pill	по одно́й табле́тке	pa-ad-noy ta-blyét-kyé
two teaspoonfuls	по две ча́йные ло́жки	pa-dvyé chay-ni-yé lozh-kee
once a day	раз в день	raz fdyén'

English	Russian	Pronunciation
twice/three times a day	два ра́за/три ра́за в день	dva ra-za/tree ra-za fdyén'
after meals/before meals	по́сле еды́/пе́ред едо́й	po-slyé yé-di/pyé-ryéd yé-doy
Will you come again?	Вы придёте опя́ть?	vi pree-dyo-tyé a-pyat'
I will call again ...	*Я приду́ опя́ть ...	ya pree-doo a-pyat' ...
Come and see me again	*Приди́те ко мне опя́ть	pree-dee-tyé ka-mnyé a-pyat'
tomorrow	за́втра	zav-tra
the day after tomorrow	послеза́втра	po-slyé-zav-tra
in ... days' time	че́рез ... дня	ché-ryéz ... dnya
Should I stay in bed?	Мне ну́жно лежа́ть?	mnyé noozh-na lyé-zhat'
When will I be better?	Когда́ я попра́влюсь?	kag-da ya pa-pra-vlyoos'
When will I be able to continue my journey?	Когда́ я смогу́ продолжа́ть поéздку?	kag-da ya sma-goo pra-dal-zhat' pa-yézd-koo

AT THE DENTIST'S

If you need to see a dentist urgently, contact your Intourist guide or the hotel service bureau.

I have toothache	У меня́ боли́т зуб	oo-me-nya ba-leet zoop
I need to see a dentist urgently	Мне сро́чно ну́жно к зубно́му врачу́	mnyé sroch-na noozh-na kzoob-no-moo vra-choo
Can I make an appointment with the dentist?	Мо́жно записа́ться на приём к зубно́му врачу́?	mozh-na za-pee-sat'-sa na-pree-yom kzoob-no-moo vra-choo
As soon as possible	Как мо́жно скоре́е	kak mozh-na ska-ryé-yé
Can you do it now?	Вы мо́жете э́то сде́лать сейча́с?	vi mo-zhé-tyé é-ta zdyé-lat' seey-chas
Can you fix it temporarily before I leave?	Вы мо́жете сде́лать что-нибу́дь вре́менно до моего́ отъе́зда?	vi mo-zhé-tyé zdyé-lat' shto-nee-boot vryé-myén-na da-ma-yé-vo at-yéz-da

How long will I have to wait?	Ско́лько на́до ждать?	skol'-ka na-da zhdat'
This tooth hurts	Э́тот зуб боли́т	é-tat zoop ba-leet
My gums are sore	У меня боля́т дёсны	oo-me-nya ba-lyat dyos-ni
I've lost a filling	У меня́ вы́пала пло́мба	oo-me-nya vi-pa-la plom-ba
Can you fill it?	Вы мо́жете запломбирова́ть зуб?	vi mo-zhé-tyé za-plam-bee-ra-vat' zoop
I have a broken tooth	У меня́ слома́лся зуб	oo me-nya sla-mal-sa zoop
Will you take the tooth out?	Вы вы́рвете зуб?	vi vir-vyé-tyé zoop
I do not want you to take the tooth out	Я не хочу́, что́бы вы удали́ли зуб	ya nyé ha-choo shto-bi vi oo-da-lee-lee zoop
Please give me a local anaesthetic	Пожа́луйста, сде́лайте мне обезбо́ливание	pa-zha-loo-sta, zdyé-lay-tyé mnyé a-byéz-bo-lee-va-nee-yé
It hurts	Бо́льно	bol'-na
I've broken my plate; can you repair it?	Я слома́л зубно́й проте́з; вы можете его́ почини́ть?	ya sla-mal zoob-noy pra-tyéz; vi mo-zhé-tyé yé-vo pa-chee-neet'
When will it be ready?	Когда́ он бу́дет гото́в?	kag-da on boo-dyét ga-tof

Please rinse your mouth	*Пожáлуйста, прополощúте рот	pa-zha-loo-sta, pra-pa-la-shee-tyé rot
This tooth needs a filling	*Э́тот зуб нáдо запломбировáть	é-tat zoop na-da za-plam-bee-ra-vat'
This tooth must be taken out	*Э́тот зуб нáдо удалúть	é-tat zoop na-da oo-da-leet'
I will X-ray your teeth	*Я вам сдéлаю рентгéн	ya vam zdyé-la-yoo ryén-gyén
You have an abscess	*У вас нары́в	oo-vas na-rif

PROBLEMS & ACCIDENTS

In case of serious difficulty or accident, contact your Intourist guide, the hotel service bureau, or, if you are in Moscow, the consular section of your Embassy.

American Embassy 19–23 Ulitsa Chaikovskovo
(tel. 252 24 51–59 – 9 lines)

Australian Embassy 13 Kropotkinsky Pereulok
(tel. 246 50 11–16)

British Embassy 14 Naberezhnaya Morisa Toreza
(tel. 231 85 11/12)

Canadian Embassy 23 Starokonyushenniy Pereulok
(tel. 241 90 34/241 91 55)

Irish Embassy 5 Groholsky Pereulok
(tel. 288 41 01)

New Zealand Embassy 44 Ulitsa Vorovskovo
(tel. 290 34 85/290 12 77)

Please help me	Помогите мне, пожалуйста	pa-ma-gee-tyé mnyé, pa-zha-loo-sta
I'm lost	Я заблудился/ заблудилась *f*	ya za-bloo-deel-sa/za-bloo-dee-las'
How can I get to	Как мне попасть	kak mnyé pa-past'
the ... hotel?	в гостиницу ... ?	fgas-tee-nee-tsoo ...
the British Embassy?	в Британское посольство?	fbree-tan-ska-yé pa-sol'-stva
the American Embassy?	в американское посольство?	va-myé-ree-kan-ska-yé pa-sol'-stva
I need to ring the Embassy	Мне нужно позвонить в посольство	mnyé noozh-na pa-zva-neet' fpa-sol'-stva
I have missed	Я опоздал/ опоздала *f*	ya a-paz-dal/a-paz-da-la
my train	на поезд	na-po-yézt
my bus/aeroplane	на автобус/на самолёт	na-af-to-boos/na-sa-ma-lyot
I have lost	Я потерял/ потеряла *f*	ya pa-tyé-ryal/pa-tyé-rya-la
my passport	паспорт	pas-part
my traveller's cheques	дорожные чеки	da-rozh-ni-yé chyé-kee
my luggage	свой багаж	svoy ba-gazh
My bag has been stolen	У меня украли сумку	oo-me-nya oo-kra-lee soom-koo

My money has been stolen	У меня́ укра́ли де́ньги	**oo-me-nya oo-kra-lee dyén'-gee**
My car has been broken into	Кто-то влез в мою́ маши́ну	**kto-ta flyez fma-yoo ma-shi-noo**
I've been robbed/mugged	Меня́ обокра́ли/ поби́ли	**me-nya a-ba-kra-lee/pa-bee-lee**
My son/daughter is lost	Мой сын/моя́ до́чка потеря́лся/ потеря́лась *f*	**moy sin/mo-ya doch-ka pa-tyé-ryal-sa/pa-tyé-rya-las'**
Help!/Fire!/A thief!	На по́мощь!/ Пожар!/Вор!	**na-po-mash/ pa-zhar/vor**
It's urgent	Скоре́е!	**ska-ryé-yé**
I didn't understand the sign	Я не по́нял/поняла́ *f* э́тот знак	**ya nyé po-nyal/pa-nya-la e-tat znak**
Call	Вы́зовите	**vi-za-vee-tyé**
the police	мили́цию	**mee-lee-tsi-yoo**
a doctor/an ambulance	врача́/ско́рую по́мощь	**vra-cha/sko-roo-yoo po-mash**
There has been an accident	Произошёл несча́стный слу́чай	**pra-ee-za-shol nyé-shas-niy sloo-chay**
He/she is badly hurt	Он/она́ си́льно пострада́л/ пострада́ла *f*	**on/a-na seel'-na pa-stra-dal/pa-stra-da-la**
He/she has been run over	Он попа́л/она́ попа́ла под маши́ну	**on pa-pal/a-na pa-pa-la pad-ma-shi-noo**

Her arm is broken	У неё рука́ слома́лась	oo nyé-yo roo-ka sla-ma-las
He/she is seriously ill	Он/она́ серьёзно бо́лен/больна́ *f*	on/a-na syé-ryoz-na bo-lyén/bal'-na
He/she is unconscious	Он потеря́л/она́ потеря́ла *f* созна́ние	on pa-tyé-ryal/a-na pa-tyé-rya-la saz-na-nee-yé
He/she is badly burnt	У него́/у неё си́льный ожо́г	oo-nyé-vo/oo-nyé-yo seel'-niy a-zhok
Somebody's drowning!	Кто́-то то́нет!	kto-to to-nyét!
Please bring	Принеси́те, пожа́луйста	pree-nyé-see-tyé, pa-zha-loo-sta
some water	воды́	va-di
a blanket/some bandages	одея́ло/бинты́	a-dyé-ya-lo/been-ti
Please inform	Сообщи́те, пожа́луйста	sa-ab-shee-tyé, pa-zha-loo-sta
my husband/my wife	моему́ му́жу/мое́й жене́	ma-yé-moo moo-zhoo/ma-yéy zhé-nyé
the Embassy	в посо́льство	fpa-sol'-stva

TIMES & DATES[1]

TIME

Telling the time in Russian is complicated. We suggest that if you want to ask somebody what the time is, you should either ask if you could look at their watch or have them write the time down for you. If you need to name a time, write it down, or use the simpler form '... hours ... minutes'. If you want a free lesson in this way of telling the time, or if you need to find out what the time is, dial 100 in Moscow or 08 in Leningrad, and you will hear the speaking clock.

The word for hour is час (chas) – and for minute минýта (meenoota). These words change their form according to the number which they follow. As in English, two different constructions are used when telling the time, one for the first half of the hour ('so many minutes past ...') and another for the second half of the hour ('so many minutes to the hour'). A few examples are given below:

Six o'clock	Шесть часóв	shést' cha-sof (*literally* six hours)

1. This section contains expressions of time rather than individual words – e.g. 'on Monday' is given instead of 'Monday'. Individual words are in the general vocabulary (see p. 254).

Ten past five	Де́сять мину́т шесто́го	dyé-syat' mee-noot shés-to-va (*literally* ten minutes of the sixth hour)
Half past nine	Полови́на деся́того	pa-la-vee-na dyé-sya-ta-va (*literally* half of the tenth hour)
Twenty to eight	Без двадцати́ во́семь	byéz dvat-tsa-tee vo-syém' (*literally* eight hours minus twenty minutes)

To say 'at' a certain time, you use the preposition 'v', except in the case of the last example (expressions for 'so many minutes to the hour') where the form does not change.

What is the time?	Кото́рый час?	ka-to-riy chas
Show me your watch, please	Покажи́те мне, пожа́луйста, ва́ши часы́	pa-ka-zhi-tyé mnyé, pa-zha-loo-sta, va-shi cha-si
At what time?	В кото́ром часу́?	fka-to-ram cha-soo
Please write it down	Напиши́те, пожа́луйста	na-pee-shi-tyé, pa-zha-loo-sta
When does it begin?	Когда́ э́то начина́ется?	kag-da é-ta na-chee-na-yét-sa
When does it end?	Когда́ э́то конча́ется?	kag-da é-ta kan-cha-yét-sa

How long will it take?	Ско́лько вре́мени э́то займёт?	**skol'-ka vryé-myé-nee é-ta zay-myot**
How much time is left?	Ско́лько вре́мени оста́лось?	**skol'-ka vryé-myé-nee a-sta-las'**
When should I come?	Когда́ мне прийти́?	**kag-da mnyé preey-tee**
I'm sorry I'm late	Прости́те за опозда́ние	**pra-stee-tyé za-a-paz-da-nee-yé**
In *e.g. in an hour's time*	Че́рез (+acc.)	**che-ryéz**
a few minutes	не́сколько мину́т	**nyé-skal'-ka mee-noot**
ten minutes	де́сять мину́т	**dyé-syat' mee-noot**
half an hour/an hour	полчаса́/час	**pal-cha-sa/chas**
... ago *e.g. ten minutes ago*	... тому́ наза́д	**... ta-moo na-zat**
A long time ago/recently	Давно́/неда́вно	**dav-no/nyé-dav-na**
Later/earlier	Попо́зже/пора́ньше	**pa-po-zhé/pa-ran'-shé**
Now/soon	Сейча́с	**seey-chas**
Often/seldom	Ча́сто/ре́дко	**chas-ta/ryéd-ka**
Once/twice	Оди́н раз/два́жды	**a-deen raz/dvazh-di**
After ...	По́сле ... (+ gen.)	**pos-lyé ...**
Until/before ...	До ... (+ gen.)	**do ...**

DATES

What is the date today?[1]	Какóе сегóдня числó?	ka-ko-yé syé-vod-nya chees-lo
The first of July	Пéрвое ию́ля	pyer-va-yé ee-yoo-lya
What date will it be on?	Какóго числá э́то бýдет?	ka-ko-va chees-la é-ta boo-dyét
On the first of July	Пéрвого ию́ля	pyér-va-va ee-yoo-lya

DAY

On Monday	В понедéльник	fpa-nyé-del'-neek
On Tuesday	Во втóрник	va-vtor-neek
On Wednesday	В срéду	fsryé-doo
On Thursday	В четвéрг	fchét-vyérg
On Friday	В пя́тницу	fpyat-nee-tsoo
On Saturday	В суббóту	fsoob-bo-too
On Sunday	В воскресéнье	vvas-kryé-syén'-yé
In the morning/during the day	У́тром/днём	oo-tram/dnyom
After lunch/in the afternoon	Пóсле обéда	pos-lyé a-byé-da
In the evening/at night	Вéчером/нóчью	vyé-chyé-ram/noch'-yoo

1. To indicate the date of the month, use the neuter form of the ordinal (p. 239) followed by the month in the genitive. To translate 'on such and such a date', put the ordinal number into the genitive. See 'Numbers' (p. 235).

Today/yesterday	Сего́дня/вчера́	syé-vod-nya/fchyé-ra
The day before yesterday	Позавчера́	pa-zaf-chyé-ra
Tomorrow/the day after tomorrow	За́втра/послеза́втра	zav-tra/po-slyé-zav-tra
In a few days	Че́рез не́сколько дней	che-ryéz nyé-skal'-ka dnyéy
Every day/all day	Ка́ждый день/весь день	kazh-diy dyén'/vyés' dyén'

WEEK

This week	На э́той неде́ле	na-é-toy nyé-dyé-lyé
Last week	На про́шлой неде́ле	na-prosh-lay nyé-dyé-lyé
Next week	На сле́дующей неде́ле	na-slyé-doo-shéy nyé-dyé-lyé
In a week's time	Че́рез неде́лю	ché-ryéz nyé-dyé-lyoo
In a fortnight's time	Че́рез две неде́ли	ché-ryéz dvyé nyé-dyé-lee

MONTH[1]

In January	В январе́	vyan-va-ryé
In February	В феврале́	vfyé-vra-lyé
In March	В ма́рте	fmar-tyé

1. Months are written without capital letters in Russian.

In April	В апре́ле	va-pryé-lyé
In May	В ма́е	fma-yé
In June	В ию́не	vee-yoo-nyé
In July	В ию́ле	vee-yoo-lyé
In August	В а́вгусте	vav-goos-tyé
In September	В сентябре́	fsyén-tya-bryé
In October	В октябре́	vak-tya-bryé
In November	В ноябре́	fna-ya-bryé
In December	В декабре́	fdyé-ka-bryé
This month	В э́том ме́сяце	vé-tam myé-sya-tsé
Last month	В про́шлом ме́сяце	fprosh-lam myé-sya-tsé
Next month	В сле́дующем ме́сяце	fslyé-doo-shém myé-sya-tsé
In a month's time	Че́рез ме́сяц	ché-ryéz myé-syats

SEASON

In the spring	Весно́й	vyés-noy
In the summer	Ле́том	lyé-tam
In the autumn	О́сенью	o-syén'-yoo
In the winter	Зимо́й	zee-moy

YEAR

This year	В э́том году́	vé-tam ga-doo
Last year	В про́шлом году́	fprosh-lam ga-doo

Next year	В слéдующем годý	**fslyé-doo-shém ga-doo**
In a year's time	Чéрез год	**ché-ryéz got**

PUBLIC HOLIDAYS

1 January	New Year's Day
8 March	International Women's Day
1 and 2 May	International Labour Day
9 May	Victory Day
7 October	Constitution Day
7 and 8 November	Anniversary of the Great October Socialist Revolution

Happy holiday!	С прáздником!	**spraz-nee-kam!**
Happy New Year!	С нóвым гóдом!	**sno-vim go-dam!**

NUMBERS

CARDINAL

0	ноль	nol'
1	оди́н *m*, одна́ *f*, одно́ *n*	a-deen, ad-na, ad-no
2	два *m*, *n*, две *f*	dva, dvyé
3	три	tree
4	четы́ре	che-ti-ryé
5	пять	pyat'
6	шесть	shést'
7	семь	syém'
8	во́семь	vo-syém'
9	де́вять	dyé-vyat'
10	де́сять	dyé-syat'

11	оди́ннадцать	a-deen-nat-tsat'
12	двена́дцать	dvyé-nat-tsat'
13	трина́дцать	tree-nat-tsat'
14	четы́рнадцать	ché-tir-nat-tsat'
15	пятна́дцать	pyat-nat-tsat'
16	шестна́дцать	shést-nat-tsat'
17	семна́дцать	syém-nat-tsat'
18	восемна́дцать	va-syém-nat-tsat'
19	девятна́дцать	dyé-vyat-nat-tsat'
20	два́дцать	dvat-tsat'
21	два́дцать оди́н	dvat-tsat' a-deen
22	два́дцать два	dvat-tsat' dva
23	два́дцать три	dvat-tsat' tree
24	два́дцать четы́ре	dvat-tsat' che-ti-ryé
25	два́дцать пять	dvat-tsat' pyat'
26	два́дцать шесть	dvat-tsat' shést'
27	два́дцать семь	dvat-tsat' syém'
28	два́дцать во́семь	dvat-tsat' vo-syém'
29	два́дцать де́вять	dvat-tsat' dyé-vyat'
30	три́дцать	treet-tsat'
31	три́дцать оди́н	treet-tsat' a-deen
40	со́рок	so-rak

50	пятьдеся́т	**pyat'-dyé-syat**
60	шестьдеся́т	**shést'-dyé-syat**
70	се́мьдесят	**syém'-dyé-syat**
80	во́семьдесят	**vo-syém'-dyé-syat**
90	девяно́сто	**dyé-vya-nos-ta**
100	сто	**sto**
101	сто оди́н	**sto a-deen**
200	две́сти	**dvyé-stee**
300	три́ста	**tree-sta**
400	четы́реста	**che-ti-ryé-sta**
500	пятьсо́т	**pyat'-sot**
600	шестьсо́т	**shést'-sot**
700	семьсо́т	**syém'-sot**
800	восемьсо́т	**va-syém'-sot**
900	девятьсо́т	**dyé-vyat'-sot**
1000	ты́сяча	**ti-sya-cha**
2000	две ты́сячи	**dvyé ti-sya-chee**
3000	три ты́сячи	**tree ti-sya-chee**
4000	четы́ре ты́сячи	**che-ti-ryé ti-sya-chee**
5000	пять ты́сяч	**pyat' ti-syach**
1,000,000	миллио́н	**meel-lee-on**

FRACTIONS

half	полови́на	pa-la-vee-na
quarter	че́тверть	chét-vyért'
three quarters	три че́тверти	tree ché-tvyér-tee
one third	треть	tryét'
two thirds	две тре́ти	dvyé tryé-tee
one and a half	полтора́	pal-ta-ra
ten (collective noun)	деся́ток	dyé-sya-tak

NOTES

The number 'one' has a feminine form одна́ (ad-na) and a neuter form одно́ (ad-no), and agrees in gender with the noun following it.
The number 'two' has a feminine form две (dvyé).
Compound numbers are formed as in English, but without the conjunction 'and' or hyphens.

1980 = ты́сяча девятьсо́т во́семьдесят
ti-sya-cha dyé-vyat'-sot vo-syém'-dyé-syat

The unstressed syllables of numbers are very lightly pronounced.
The number 1 or any number ending in 1 is followed by the nominative singular of the noun.
The numbers 2, 3 and 4, and any numbers ending in 2, 3, or 4, are followed by the genitive singular of the noun.
All other numbers are followed by the genitive plural of the noun.
Fractions are followed by the genitive singular of the noun.

ORDINAL

1st	пéрвый	pyér-viy
2nd	вторóй	fta-roy
3rd	трéтий	tryé-teey
4th	четвёртый	chét-vyor-tiy
5th	пятый	pya-tiy
6th	шестóй	shé-stoy
7th	седьмóй	syéd'-moy
8th	восьмóй	vas'-moy
9th	девя́тый	dyé-vya-tiy
10th	деся́тый	dyé-sya-tiy
20th	двадцáтый	dvat-tsa-tiy
21st	двáдцать пéрвый	dvat-tsat' pyér-viy
100th	сóтый	so-tiy

All ordinals are declined like adjectives and agree in case, gender, and number with the noun they qualify.

WEIGHTS & MEASURES

DISTANCE

kilometres – miles

km	*miles or km*	miles	km	*miles or km*	miles
1·6	*1*	0·6	14·5	*9*	5·6
3·2	*2*	1·2	16·1	*10*	6·2
4·8	*3*	1·9	32·2	*20*	12·4
6·4	*4*	2·5	40·2	*25*	15·3
8	*5*	3·1	80·5	*50*	31·1
9·7	*6*	3·7	160·9	*100*	62·1
11·3	*7*	4·4	804·7	*500*	310·7
12·9	*8*	5·0			

A rough way to convert from miles to km: divide by 5 and multiply by 8; from km to miles, divide by 8 and multiply by 5.

LENGTH AND HEIGHT

centimetres – inches

cm	*ins or cm*	ins
2·5	*1*	0·4
5·1	*2*	0·8
7·6	*3*	1·2
10·2	*4*	1·6
12·7	*5*	2·0
15·2	*6*	2·4
17·8	*7*	2·8
20	*8*	3·2
22·9	*9*	3·5
25·4	*10*	3·9
50·8	*20*	7·9
127	*50*	19·7

A rough way to convert from inches to cm: divide by 2 and multiply by 5; from cm to inches, divide by 5 and multiply by 2.

metres – feet

m	*ft or m*	ft
0·3	*1*	3·3
0·6	*2*	6·6
0·9	*3*	9·8
1·2	*4*	13·1
1·5	*5*	16·4
1·8	*6*	19·7
2·1	*7*	23
2·4	*8*	26·3
2·7	*9*	29·5
3	*10*	32·8
6·1	*20*	65·6
15·2	*50*	164
30·5	*100*	328·1

A rough way to convert from ft to m: divide by 10 and multiply by 3; from m to ft, divide by 3 and multiply by 10.

metres – yards

m	*yds or m*	yds	m	*yds or m*	yds
0·9	*1*	1·1	7·3	*8*	8·8
1·8	*2*	2·2	8·2	*9*	9·8
2·7	*3*	3·3	9·1	*10*	10·9
3·7	*4*	4·4	18·3	*20*	21·9
4·6	*5*	5·5	45·7	*50*	54·7
5·5	*6*	6·6	91·4	*100*	109·4
6·4	*7*	7·7	457·2	*500*	546·8

A rough way to convert from yds to m: subtract 10 per cent from the number of yds; from m to yds, add 10 per cent to the number of metres.

LIQUID MEASURES

litres – gallons

litres	*galls or litres*	galls	litres	*galls or litres*	galls
4·6	*1*	0·2	36·4	*8*	1·8
9·1	*2*	0·4	40·9	*9*	2·0
13·6	*3*	0·7	45·5	*10*	2·2
18·2	*4*	0·9	90·9	*20*	4·4
22·7	*5*	1·1	136·4	*30*	6·6
27·3	*6*	1·3	181·8	*40*	8·8
31·8	*7*	1·5	227·3	*50*	11

1 pint = 0·6 litre   1 litre = 1·8 pint

A rough way to convert from galls to litres: divide by 2 and multiply by 9; from litres to galls, divide by 9 and multiply by 2.

WEIGHT

kilograms – pounds

kg	*lb or kg*	lb
0·5	*1*	2·2
0·9	*2*	4·4
1·4	*3*	6·6
1·8	*4*	8·8
2·3	*5*	11·0
2·7	*6*	13·2
3·2	*7*	15·4
3·6	*8*	17·6
4·1	*9*	19·8
4·5	*10*	22·1
9·1	*20*	44·1
22·7	*50*	110·2

A rough way to convert from lb to kg: divide by 11 and multiply by 5; from kg to lb, divide by 5 and multiply by 11.

grams – ounces

grams	oz
100	3·5
250	8·8
500	17·6
1,000 (1 kg)	35

oz	grams
2	56.7
4	114·3
8	228·6
16 (1 lb)	457·2

TEMPERATURE

centigrade (°C) °C	fahrenheit (°F) °F
−10	14
−5	23
0	32
5	41
10	50
15	59
20	68
25	77
30	86
35	95
37	98·4
38	100·5
39	102
40	104
100	212

To convert °F to °C: deduct 32, divide by 9 and multiply by 5; to convert °C to °F: divide by 5, multiply by 9 and add 32.

BASIC GRAMMAR

The phrases in this book can be used by someone who has no knowledge of Russian grammar. However, if you first grasp a few basic principles about how the Russian language works, you will be able to make fuller use of the phrase book, substituting words of your own choice and altering phrases to suit particular needs. The outline of Russian grammar which follows is extremely schematic, and does not include any reference to exceptions or variations from general rules.

NOUNS

GENDER OF NOUNS

There are three genders in Russian: masculine, feminine and neuter. In most cases the gender of a noun can be determined by its ending. Masculine nouns end in a consonant, й, or ь. Feminine nouns end in а, я, or ь. Neuter nouns end in о, е, ё, or мя.

The gender of a noun is always given in the vocabulary.

class	класс *m*	klass
room	ко́мната *f*	**kom**-na-ta
sea	мо́ре *n*	**mo**-rye

There are no articles (the, a) in Russian.

DECLENSIONS

Russian is an inflected language. This means that, as in Latin or Greek, words change their form according to their grammatical function in a sentence. These changes of form follow a pattern called a declension which determines the different endings of a noun according to its case. Each case is used for a certain grammatical function:

the nominative case expresses the subject of a sentence.

the *girl* sings	*дéвушка* поёт	*dyé-voosh-ka* pa-yot

the accusative case expresses the direct object of the verb.

I love a *girl*	я люблю́ *дéвушку*	ya lyoo-blyoo *dyé-voosh-koo*

the genitive case expresses the idea of possession or relation which in English is usually expressed by the preposition 'of'.

the face of a *girl*	лицó *дéвушки*	lee-tso *dyé-voosh-kee*

the dative case is used for the indirect object of an action, and is usually rendered in English by the preposition 'to'.

I'll give it to the *girl*	я э́то дам *дéвушке*	ya e-ta dam *dyé-voosh-kyé*

the instrumental case is used for the agent or means by which an action is accomplished. In English this is usually expressed by the prepositions 'with' or 'by'.

He was killed by the *girl*	он был уби́т *дéвушкой*	on bil oo-beet *dyé-voosh-koy*

the locative case is only used with prepositions, the most common of which are о (about), в (in) and на (on).

I am talking about the *girl*	я говорю́ о *дéвушке*	ya ga-va-ryoo *o dyé-voosh-kyé*

In these examples, the word дéвушка (dyé-voosh-ka – girl) appears in six different forms, each of which corresponds to one of the six cases. These six forms constitute a complete declension of a feminine noun in the singular. There are three basic types of declension, one for masculine, one for feminine, and one for neuter nouns, and these have a singular and a plural form.

The endings which are characteristic of each declension are given below; they are arranged in columns which illustrate the typical declension pattern of a noun ending in the letter which heads the column. Each ending is given twice – first in Cyrillic script, then, immediately below, in transliteration.

Singular	MASCULINE		FEMININE		NEUTER	
nom.	~[1]	~й/~ь	~а	~я/~ь	~о	~е[3]
		~y/~'	~a	~ya/~'	~o	~yé
acc.[2]	~	~й/~ь	~у	~ю/~ь	~о	~е
		~y/~'	~oo	~yoo/~'	~o	~yé
gen.	~а	~я	~ы	~и	~а	~я
	~a	~ya	~i	~ee	~a	~ya
dat.	~у	~ю	~е	~е/~и	~у	~ю
	~oo	~yoo	~yé	~yé/~ee	~oo	~yoo
instr.	~ом	~ем	~ой	~ей/~ью	~ом	~ем
	~om	~yém	~oy	~yéy/~'yoo	~om	~yém
loc.	~е	~е	~е	~е/~и	~е	~е/~и
	~yé	~yé	~yé	~yé/~ee	~yé	~yé/~ee
Plural	MASCULINE		FEMININE		NEUTER	
nom.	~ы	~и	~ы	~и	~а	~я
	~i	~ee	~i	~ee	~a	~ya
acc.[2]	~ы	~и	~ы	~и	~а	~я
	~i	~ee	~i	~ee	~a	~ya
gen.	~ов	~ев/~ей	~	~й/~ей	~	~ей/~ий
	~ov	~yév/~yéy	~	~y/~yéy	~	~yéy/~eey
dat.	~ам	~ям	~ам	~ям	~ам	~ям
	~am	~yam	~am	~yam	~am	~yam
instr.	~ами	~ями	~ами	~ями	~ами	~ями
	~amee	~yamee	~amee	~yamee	~amee	~yamee
loc.	~ах	~ях	~ах	~ях	~ах	~ях
	~ah	~yah	~ah	~yah	~ah	~yah

1. The first column gives the typical declension pattern of a masculine noun ending in a consonant. The endings should be *added* to the noun. In all other cases, the endings should be *substituted* for the letter heading the column.

	m.	*f.*
nom.	класс	ко́мната
	klass	**komnata**
gen.	кла́сса	ко́мнаты
	klassa	**komnati**

2. The accusative of inanimate masculine nouns is the same as the nominative; if, however, the noun refers to an animate being, the accusative is the same as the genitive in both the singular and the plural. This rule also applies to feminine nouns in the plural, but not in the singular.

3. Neuter nouns ending in -ё are declined like neuter nouns ending in -е, but with the endings accented.

ADJECTIVES

Adjectives, like nouns, have three genders, and decline. There is only one form of the plural for all three genders. An adjective must agree with the noun which it accompanies in gender, number and case.

a clever boy	у́мный ма́льчик	**oom-niy mal'-cheek**
an interesting book	интере́сная кни́га	**een-tyé-ryés-na-ya knee-ga**
the blue sky	си́нее не́бо	**see-nyé-yé nyé-ba**

Adverbs are formed from adjectives by removing the last two letters of the adjective in its nominative form, and substituting the letter o.

serious	серьёзный	**syé-ryoz-niy**
seriously	серьёзно	**syé-ryoz-no**

This table shows the typical patterns of endings which adjectives of certain types follow when declined.

	MASCULINE		FEMININE	
nom.	~ый/~ой	~ий	~ая	~яя
	~iy ~oy	~eey	~aya	~yaya
acc.	~ый/~ой	~ий	~ую	~юю
	~iy ~oy	~eey	~ooyoo	~yooyoo
gen.	~ого	~его	~ой	~ей
	~ovo	~yévo	~oy	~yéy
dat.	~ому	~ему	~ой	~ей
	~omoo	~yémoo	~oy	~yéy
instr.	~ым	~им	~ой	~ей
	~im	~eem	~oy	~yéy
loc.	~ом	~ем	~ой	~ей
	~om	~yém	~oy	~yéy

	NEUTER		PLURAL	
nom.	~ое	~ее	~ые	~ие
	~oyé	~yéyé	~iyé	~eeyé
acc.	~ое	~ее	~ые	~ие
	~oyé	~yéyé	~iyé	~eeyé
gen.	~ого	~его	~ых	~их
	~ovo	~yévo	~ih	~eeh
dat.	~ому	~ему	~ым	~им
	~omoo	~yémoo	~im	~eem
instr.	~ым	~им	~ыми	~ими
	~im	~eem	~imee	~eemee
loc.	~ом	~ем	~ых	~их
	~om	~yém	~ih	~eeh

PRONOUNS

The Russian pronouns are:

	nom.	*gen./acc.*
I	я ya	меня́ me-nya
you *familiar*	ты ti	тебя́ te-bya
he	он on	его́ yé-vo
she	она́ a-na	её yé-yo
it	оно a-no	его yé-vo
we	мы mi	нас nas
you *formal*	вы vi	вас vas
they	они́ a-nee	их eeh

As you can see, there are two forms in Russian for the pronoun you: a familiar form ты (ti), and a formal form вы (vi); these correspond to the French forms tu and vous. You should always use the formal form of address, unless you have been invited to use the familiar form.

To express the idea of having or possessing, the Russians use the preposition у (oo) followed by the genitive form of the noun or pronoun referring to the possessor. You can express the idea of possession using the genitive forms of the pronouns given above.

I have	у меня́	oo me-nya
he has	у него́	oo nyé-vo [1]
we have	у нас	oo nas

VERBS

Russian verbs have two forms or aspects, the imperfective and the perfective. The imperfective form is used for an action which is continuous or uncompleted (as in 'the baby is crying at the moment'), or habitual or repeated (as in 'babies cry'). The perfective form is used for an action of limited duration (as in 'the baby cried for an hour'), or for the beginning or end of an action (as in 'the baby began to cry').

In the vocabulary, verbs are given in the two aspects of the infinitive form. Most imperfective verbs have a corresponding perfective form which is usually formed by adding a prefix to or changing the suffix of the imperfective infinitive.

to read	чита́ть *impf.*	chee-tat'
	прочита́ть *pf.*	pra-chee-tat'

If you want to say 'I would like to read lots of books', you must use the *imperfective* infinitive, since the idea of reading is conceived of as general and continuous, not limited in time. If you want to say 'I would like to read this book', you must use the *perfective* infinitive, since the idea of reading is here associated with a specific action which is to be completed.

The imperfective and perfective infinitives are used for the formation of different tenses. The imperfective infinitive is used for the formation of the present (necessarily incomplete), ('I am working'), of the continuous past ('I was working'), and of the continuous future ('I will be working'). The perfective infinitive is used for the formation of the simple past tense ('I

1. If the pronoun starts with a vowel it should be prefixed with the letter н (n) when using this construction.

worked') and future tense ('I will work tomorrow'). The *present tense* and the *simple future tense* are formed in the same way; for the present tense, take the imperfective infinitive, and for the future tense take the perfective infinitive. If the infinitive ends in ать (at') or ять (yat') remove the *two* final letters, and add on the endings which are shown below in italics.

to read	чита́*ть* *impf.*	chee-ta*t'*
I read	я чита́*ю*	ya chee-ta-*yoo*
you read	ты чита́*ешь*	ti chee-ta-*yésh'*
he reads	он чита́*ет*	on chee-ta-*yét*
we read	мы чита́*ем*	mi chee-ta-*yém*
you read	вы чита́*ете*	vi chee-ta-*yé-tyé*
they read	они чита́*ют*	a-nee chee-ta-*yoot*

If the infinitive ends in ить (eet'), remove the *three* final letters, and substitute the endings shown below in italics.

to build	постро́*ить* *pf.*	pa-stro-*eet'*
I will build	я постро́*ю*	ya pa-stro-*yoo*
you will build	ты постро́*ишь*	ti pa-stro-*eesh'*
he will build	он постро́*ит*	on pa-stro-*eet*
we will build	мы постро́*им*	mi pa-stro-*eem*
you will build	вы постро́*ите*	vi pa-stro-*ee-tyé*
they will build	они постро́*ят*	a-nee pa-stro-*yat*

When forming a *past tense*, the imperfective infinitive should be used for the continuous past, and the perfective infinitive for the simple past. There are only four forms of the past tense, the masculine, feminine and neuter singular forms, and one form for all genders in the plural. To form the past tense, take the correct form of the infinitive, remove the two final letters, and substitute the following endings, shown below in italics.

to read	**чита*ть* *impf.***	**chee-tat'**
masculine singular		
I/you/he was reading	**я/ты/он чита́*л***	**ya/ti/on chee-ta*l***
feminine singular		
I/you/she was reading	**я/ты/она́ чита́*ла***	**ya/ti/a-na chee-ta-*la***
neuter singular		
it was reading	**оно́ чита́*ло***	**a-no chee-ta-*lo***
plural for all genders		
we/you/they were reading	**мы/вы/они́ чита́*ли***	**mi/vi/a-nee chee-ta-*lee***

In this phrase book, when a verb occurs in the past tense, it is always given in the masculine form, and followed by the feminine form. A female speaker should always substitute the feminine form for the masculine form.

To form the negative, insert **не** (**nyé**) before the verb.

I am not reading	**я не чита́ю**	**ya nyé chee-ta-yoo**

The verb 'to be' is not used in the present tense, but understood.

I am a student	**я студе́нт**	**ya stoo-dyént**

VOCABULARY

The vocabulary should be used in conjunction with the basic grammar on page 245. Nouns are followed by an indication of their gender. Adjectives are given in the masculine form. Verbs are given in two forms, the imperfective and the perfective, unless the imperfective is the only form commonly used. Some prepositions and verbs are followed by an indication of the case which should be used after them.

More specialized vocabulary can be found in each of the sections of the phrase book.

ABBREVIATIONS

acc	accusative case	*intrans*	intransitive
adj	adjective	*loc*	locative case
adv	adverb	*m*	masculine gender
dat	dative case	*n*	neuter gender
decl as adj	decline as adjective	*opp*	opposite
f	feminine gender	*pf*	perfective form
gen	genitive case	*pl*	plural
impf	imperfective form	*prep*	preposition
indecl	indeclinable	*sing*	singular
instr	instrumental case	*trans*	transitive

A

able (to be)	мочь *impf*, смочь *pf*	**moch', smoch'**
about *approximately*	óколо (+ *gen*)	**o-ka-la**
about *concerning*	о (+ *loc*)	**o**
above	над (+ *instr*)	**nad**
abroad *motion*	за грани́цу	**za gra-nee-tsoo**
abroad *rest*	за грани́цей	**za gra-nee-tsey**
accept (to)	принима́ть *impf*, приня́ть *pf*	**pree-nee-mat', pree-nyat'**
accident	несча́стный слу́чай *m*	**nyé-shas-niy sloo-chay**
ache	боль *f*	**bol'**
acquaintance *female*	знако́мая (*decl as adj*)	**zna-ko-ma-ya**
acquaintance *male*	знако́мый (*decl as adj*)	**zna-ko-miy**
across	че́рез (+ *acc*)	**che-ryéz**
act (to)	де́йствовать *impf*, по~ *pf*	**dyéy-stva-vat', pa~**
add (to)	добавля́ть *impf*, доба́вить *pf*	**da-ba-vlyat', da-ba-veet'**
address	а́дрес *m*	**a-dryés**
admire (to)	любова́ться *impf*, по~ *pf*	**lyoo-ba-vat'-sa, pa~**
admission	вход *m*	**vhot**
aeroplane	самолёт *m*	**sa-ma-lyot**
afraid (to be)	боя́ться (+ *gen*)	**ba-yat'-sa**
after *place*	за (+ *instr*)	**za**
after *time*	по́сле (+ *gen*)	**pos-lyé**
afternoon	день *m*	**dyén'**
again	опя́ть	**a-pyat'**

against	про́тив (+ *gen*)	pro-teef
age	во́зраст *m*	voz-rast
ago	тому́ наза́д	ta-moo na-zat
agree (to)	соглаша́ться *impf*, согласи́ться *pf*	sa-gla-shat'-sa, sa-gla-seet'-sa
ahead *motion*	вперёд	fpyé-ryot
ahead *rest*	впереди́	fpyé-ryé-dee
air	во́здух *m*	voz-dooh
airbed	надувно́й матра́ц *m*	na-doof-noy ma-trats
air-conditioner	кондиционе́р *m*	kan-dee-tsi-a-nyér
airmail	а́виа-по́чта *f*	a-vee-a-poch-ta
airport	аэропо́рт *m*	a-e-ra-port
alarm clock	буди́льник *m*	boo-deel'-neek
alcoholic *drink*	спиртно́й	speert-noy
alike	похо́жий	pa-ho-zhiy
all	весь *m*, вся *f*, всё *n*, все *pl*	vyés', vsya, vsyo, vsyé
allow (to)	позволя́ть *impf*, позво́лить *pf*	paz-va-lyat', paz-vo-leet'
all right	в поря́дке	fpa-ryat-kyé
almost	почти́	pach-tee
alone	оди́н *m*, одна́ *f*	a-deen, ad-na
already	уже́	oo-zhe
also	то́же	to-zhe
alter (to)	изменя́ть *impf*, измени́ть *pf*	eez-myé-nyat', eez-myé-neet'
alternative	альтернати́ва *f*	al'-ter-na-tee-va
although	хотя́	ha-tya
always	всегда́	vsyeg-da
amber	янта́рь *m*	yan-tar'

ambulance	ско́рая по́мощь *f*	**sko-ra-ya po-mash'**
America	Аме́рика *f*	**a-myé-ree-ka**
American *adj*	америка́нский	**a-myé-ree-kan-skeey**
American *man*	америка́нец *m*	**a-myé-ree-ka-nyéts**
American *woman*	америка́нка *f*	**a-myé-ree-kan-ka**
among	среди́ (+ *gen*)	**sryé-dee**
amuse (to)	развлека́ть *impf*, развле́чь *pf*	**raz-vlyé-kat', raz-vlyéch'**
amusing	заба́вный	**za-baf-niy**
ancient	дре́вний	**dryév-neey**
and	и	**ee**
angry	серди́тый	**syér-dee-tiy**
animal	живо́тное *n* (*decl as adj*)	**zhi-vot-na-yé**
ankle	лоды́жка *f*	**la-dish-ka**
anniversary	годовщи́на *f*	**ga-dav-shee-na**
annoyed	раздражённый	**raz-dra-zhon-niy**
another	друго́й	**droo-goy**
answer *noun*	отве́т *m*	**at-vyét**
answer (to)	отвеча́ть *impf*, отве́тить *pf*	**at-vyé-chat', at-vyé-teet'**
antiques	стари́нные ве́щи *f pl*	**sta-reen-ni-yé vyé-shee**
any	како́й-нибу́дь	**ka-koy-nee-boot'**
anyone	кто́-нибу́дь	**kto-nee-boot'**
anything	что́-нибу́дь	**shto-nee-boot'**
anyway	во вся́ком слу́чае	**va vsya-kam sloo-cha-yé**
anywhere	где́-нибу́дь	**gdyé-nee-boot'**
apartment	кварти́ра *f*	**kvar-tee-ra**
apologize (to)	извиня́ться *impf*, извини́ться *pf*	**eez-vee-nyat'-sa, eez-vee-neet'-sa**

appetite	аппети́т *m*	ap-pyé-teet
apple	я́блоко *n*	ya-bla-ka
April	апре́ль *m*	a-pryél'
architect	архите́ктор *m*	ar-hee-tyék-tar
architecture	архитекту́ра *f*	ar-hee-tyék-too-ra
area	райои *m*	ra-yon
arm	рука́ *f*	roo-ka
armchair	кре́сло *n*	kryés-la
army	а́рмия *f*	ar-mee-ya
around	вокру́г (+ *gen*)	va-krook
arrange (to)	устра́ивать *impf*, устро́ить *pf*	oo-stra-ee-vat', oo-stro-eet'
arrival	прибы́тие *n*	pree-bi-tee-yé
arrive (to)	прибыва́ть *impf*, прибы́ть *pf*	pree-bi-vat', pree-bit'
art	иску́сство *n*	ees-koos-stva
art gallery	карти́нная галере́я *f*	kar-teen-na-ya ga-lyé-ryé-ya
artificial	иску́сственный	ees-koost-vyén-niy
artist	худо́жник *m*	hoo-dozh-neek
as	как	kak
ashtray	пе́пельница *f*	pyé-pyél'-nee-tsa
ask (to) *inquire*	спра́шивать *impf*, спроси́ть *pf*	spra-shi-vat', spra-seet'
ask (to) *request*	проси́ть *impf*, по ~ *pf*	pra-seet', pa ~
aspirin	аспири́н *m*	as-pee-reen
as soon as	как то́лько	kak tol'-ka
as well	то́же	to-zhe

at	в (+ *acc or loc*), у (+ *gen*)	v, oo
at last	наконéц	na-ka-nyéts
atmosphere	атмосфéра *f*	at-mos-fyé-ra
at once	срáзу	sra-zoo
attendant *hotel*	дежýрная *f* (*decl as adj*)	dyé-zhoor-na-ya
attendant *train*	проводни́к *m*	pra-vad-neek
attention	внимáние *n*	fnee-ma-nee-yé
attractive	привлекáтельный	pree-vlyé-ka-tyél'-niy
audience	пýблика *f*	poo-blee-ka
August	áвгуст *m*	av-goost
aunt	тётя *f*	tyo-tya
Australia	Австрáлия *f*	af-stra-lee-ya
Australian *man*	австрали́ец *m*	af-stra-lee-yets
Australian *woman*	австрали́йка *f*	af-stra-leey-ka
author	áвтор *m*	af-tar
autumn	óсень *f*	o-syén'
available	достýпный	da-stoop-niy
avenue	проспéкт *m*	pra-spyékt
average	срéдний	sryéd-neey
avoid (to)	избегáть *impf*, избежáть *pf*	eez-byé-gat', eez-byé-zhat'
awful	ужáсный	oo-zhas-niy

B

baby	ребёнок *m*	ryé-byo-nak
baby food	едá *f* для ребёнка	yé-da dlya ryé-byon-ka
baby sitter	приходя́щая ня́ня *f*	pree-ha-dya-sha-ya nya-nya
bachelor	холостя́к *m*	ha-la-styak

back *adv*	наза́д	na-zat
back *noun*	спина́ *f*	spee-na
bad	плохо́й	pla-hoy
bag	су́мка *f*, мешо́к *m*	soom-ka, myé-shok
baggage	бага́ж *m*	ba-gazh
bait	нажи́вка *f*	na-zhiv-ka
balcony	балко́н *m*	bal-kon
ball *sport*	мяч *m*	myach
ballet	бале́т *m*	ba-lyét
balloon	ша́рик *m*	sha-reek
band *music*	орке́стр *m*	ar-kyéstr
bandage	бинт *m*	beent
bank	банк *m*	bank
bar	бар *m*	bar
bare	го́лый	go-liy
basket	корзи́на *f*	kar-zee-na
bath	ва́нна *f*	van-na
bathe (to)	купа́ться *impf*, ис ~ *pf*	koo-pat'-sa, ees ~
bathing cap	купа́льная ша́почка *f*	koo-pal'-na-ya sha-pach-ka
bathing costume	купа́льный костю́м *m*	koo-pal'-niy ka-styoom
bathing trunks	пла́вки *m pl*	plaf-kee
bathroom	ва́нная *f* (*decl as adj*)	van-na-ya
battery	батаре́я *f*	ba-ta-ryé-ya
bay	зали́в *m*	za-leef
be (to)	быть	bit'
beach	пляж *m*	plyash
beard	борода́ *f*	ba-ra-da

beautiful	краси́вый	kra-see-viy
because	потому́ что	pa-ta-moo shto
become (to)	станови́ться *impf*, стать *pf*	sta-na-veet'-sa, stat'
bed	крова́ть *f*	kra-vat'
bedbug	клоп *m*	klop
bedroom	спа́льня *f*	spal'-nya
beer	пи́во *n*	pee-va
before *place*	пе́ред (+ *instr*)	pyé-ryéd
before *time*	до (+ *gen*)	do
begin (to)	начина́ть *impf*, нача́ть *pf*	na-chee-nat', na-chat'
beginning	нача́ло *n*	na-cha-la
behind *prep*	сза́ди (+ *gen*), за (+ *instr*)	sza-dee, za
believe (to)	ве́рить *impf*, по ~ *pf*	vyé-reet', pa ~
bell	звоно́к *m*	zva-nok
belong (to)	принадлежа́ть	pree-nad-lyé-zhat'
below *prep*	под (+ *acc or instr*)	pod
belt	по́яс *m*	po-yas
bench	скаме́йка *f*	ska-myéy-ka
berth	спа́льное ме́сто *n*	spal'-na-yé myés-ta
beside	о́коло (+ *gen*)	o-ka-la
best	лу́чший	looch-sheey
bet	пари́ (*indecl*)	pa-ree
better	лу́чший	looch-sheey
between	ме́жду (+ *instr*)	myézh-doo
bicycle	велосипе́д *m*	vyé-la-see-pyét
big	большо́й	bal'-shoy
bill	счёт *m*	shyot

binoculars	бинóкль *m*	bee-nokl'
bird	птúца *f*	ptee-tsa
birthday	день *m* рождéния	dyén' razh-dyé-nee-ya
bite (to)	кусáть *impf*, укусúть *pf*	koo-sat', oo-koo-seet'
bitter	гóрький	gor'-keey
black	чёрный	chyor-niy
blanket	одеяло *n*	a-dyé-ya-la
bleed (to)	истекáть *impf*, истéчь *pf* крóвью	ees-tyé-kat', ees-tyéch' kro-vyoo
blind	слепóй	slyé-poy
blister	волды́рь *m*	val-dir'
blond	белокýрый	byé-la-koo-riy
blood	кровь *f*	krof'
blouse	блýзка *f*	blooz-ka
blow (to)	дуть *impf*, по ~ *pf*	doot', pa ~
blue	голубóй	ga-loo-boy
(on) board	на бортý	na bar-too
boat	пароxóд *m*	pa-ra-hot
body	тéло *n*	tyé-la
bolt	болт *m*	bolt
bone	кость *f*	kost'
book	кнúга *f*	knee-ga
book (to)	закáзывать *impf*, заказáть *pf*	za-ka-zi-vat', za-ka-zat'
booking office	кáсса *f*	kas-sa
bookshop	кнúжный магазúн *m*	kneezh-niy ma-ga-zeen
boot	сапóг *m*	sa-pok
border *frontier*	гранúца *f*	gra-nee-tsa
boring	скýчный	skoosh-niy

borrow (to)	брать *impf*, взять *pf*, на вре́мя	brat', vzyat', na vryé-mya
both	о́ба *m*, о́бе *f pl*	o-ba, o-byé
bottle	буты́лка *f*	boo-til-ka
bottle-opener	што́пор *m*	shto-par
bottom	дно *n*	dno
bowl	ча́шка *f*	chash-ka
box *container*	коро́бка *f*	ka-rop-ka
box *theatre*	ло́жа *f*	lo-zha
box office	театра́льная ка́сса *f*	tyé-a-tral'-na-ya kas-sa
boy	ма́льчик *m*	mal'-cheek
bracelet	брасле́т *m*	bras-lyét
braces	подтя́жки *m pl*	pad-tyazh-kee
brain	мозг *m*	mozk
branch *tree*	ветвь *f*	vyetv'
brandy	конья́к *m*	kan'-yak
brassière	бюстга́льтер *m*	byoost-gal'-tyér
bread	хлеб *m*	hlyép
break (to)	лома́ть *impf*, с~ *pf*	la-mat', s~
breakfast	за́втрак *m*	zaf-trak
breast	грудь *f*	groot'
breathe (to)	дыша́ть	di-shat'
bridge	мост *m*	most
briefs	тру́сики *m pl*	troo-see-kee
bright	я́ркий	yar-keey
bring (to) *person*	приводи́ть *impf*, привести́ *pf*	pree-va-deet', pree-vyés-tee
bring (to) *thing*	приноси́ть *impf*, принести́ *pf*	pree-na-seet', pree-nyés-tee
Britain	Великобрита́ния	vyé-lee-ka-bree-ta-nee-ya

British	брита́нский	bree-tan-skeey
broken	сло́манный	slo-man-niy
brooch	брошь *f*	brosh'
brother	брат *m* (*pl* бра́тья)	brat (brat'-ya)
brown	кори́чневый	ka-reech-nyé-viy
bruise	синя́к *m*	see-nyak
brush	щётка *f*	shyot-ka
brush (to)	причёсывать *impf*, причеса́ть *pf*	pree-chyo-si-vat', pree-chyé-sat'
bucket	ведро́ *n*	vyé-dro
buckle	пря́жка *f*	pryazh-ka
build (to)	стро́ить *impf*, по ~ *pf*	stro-eet', pa ~
building	зда́ние *n*	zda-nee-yé
bulb	ла́мпочка *f*	lam-pach-ka
bunch *flowers*	буке́т *m*	boo-kyét
bunch *vegetables*	пучо́к *m*	poo-chok
buoy	буй *m*	booy
burn (to) *something*	обжига́ть *impf*, обже́чь *pf*	ab-zhi-gat', ab-zhech'
burn (to) *oneself*	обжига́ться *impf*, обже́чься *pf*	ab-zhi-gat'-sa, ab-zhech'-sa
bus	авто́бус *m*	af-to-boos
bus stop	авто́бусная остано́вка *f*	af-to-boos-na-ya as-ta-nof-ka
business	де́ло *n*	dyé-la
busy	занято́й	za-nya-toy
but	но	no
button	пу́говица *f*	poo-ga-vee-tsa
buy (to)	покупа́ть *impf*, купи́ть *pf*	pa-koo-pat', koo-peet'
by *near*	о́коло (+ *gen*)	o-ka-la

C

cab	такси́ *n* (*indecl*)	tak-see
cabin	каю́та *f*	ka-yoo-ta
cable	телегра́мма *f*	tyé-lyé-gram-ma
café	кафе́ *n* (*indecl*)	ka-fe
cake	пиро́жное *n* (*decl as adj*)	pee-rozh-na-yé
calculator	счётная маши́на *f*	shot-na-ya ma-shi-na
calendar	календа́рь *m*	ka-lyén-dar'
call (to) *summon*	звать *impf*, позва́ть *pf*	zvat', pa ~,
call (to) *telephone*	звони́ть *impf*, по ~ *pf*	zva-neet', pa ~
call (to) *visit*	посеща́ть *impf*, посети́ть *pf*	pa-syé-shat', pa-syé-teet'
call on (to)	заходи́ть *impf*, зайти *pf* (к + *dat*)	za-ha-deet', zay-tee (k)
calm	споко́йный	spa-koy-niy
camera	фотоаппара́т *m*	fo-ta-ap-pa-rat
camp site	ке́мпинг *m*	kem-peeng
can *tin*	консе́рвная ба́нка *f*	kan-syerv-na-ya ban-ka
can (to be able)	мочь *impf*, смочь *pf*	moch', smoch'
Canada	Кана́да *f*	ka-na-da
Canadian	кана́дец *m*, кана́дка *f*	ka-na-dyéts, ka-nad-ka
cancel (to)	аннули́ровать	an-noo-lee-ra-vat'
candle	свеча́ *f*	svyé-cha
canoe	кано́э *n* (*indecl*)	ka-no-e
can opener	консе́рвный нож *m*	kan-syérv-niy nosh
cap	ке́пка	kyep-ka
capable	спосо́бный	spa-sob-niy
capital city	столи́ца *f*	sta-lee-tsa

capitalism	капитали́зм *m*	**ka-pee-ta-leezm**
car	автомоби́ль *m*, маши́на *f*	**af-ta-ma-beel', ma-shi-na**
carafe	графи́н *m*	**gra-feen**
caravan	дом-автофурго́н *m*,	**dom-af-ta-foor-gon**
cards	ка́рты *f pl*	**kar-ti**
care	внима́ние *n*	**vnee-ma-nee-yé**
careful	внима́тельный	**vnee-ma-tyél'-niy**
careless	небре́жный	**nyé-bryézh-niy**
caretaker	дежу́рный *m* (*decl as adj*)	**dyé-zhoor-niy**
car park	автомоби́льная стоя́нка *f*	**af-ta-ma-beel'-na-ya sta-yan-ka**
carpet	ковёр *m*	**ka-vyor**
carry (to)	нести́ *impf*, по~ *pf*	**nyés-tee, pa~**
cash	де́ньги *m pl*	**dyén'-gee**
cash (to)	разменя́ть	**raz-myé-nyat'**
cashier	касси́р *m*	**kas-seer**
cassette	кассе́та *f*	**kas-syé-ta**
cassette recorder	кассе́тный магнитофо́н *m*	**kas-syét-niy mag-ni-ta-fon**
castle	за́мок *m*	**za-mak**
cat	ко́шка *f*	**kosh-ka**
catalogue	катало́г *m*	**ka-ta-lok**
catch (to)	лови́ть *impf*, пойма́ть *pf*	**la-veet', pay-mat'**
cathedral	собо́р *m*	**sa-bor**
catholic	католи́ческий	**ka-to-lee-chyés-keey**
cause	причи́на *f*	**pree-chee-na**
cave	пеще́ра *f*	**pyé-shyé-ra**

cemetery	клáдбище *n*	klad-bee-she
central	центрáльный	tsen-tral'-niy
centre	центр *m*	tsentr
century	век *m*	vyék
ceremony	церемóния *f*	tse-ryé-mo-nee-ya
certain *sure*	увéренный	oo-vyé-ryén-niy
certainly	конéчно	ka-nyésh-na
chair	стул *m*	stool
chambermaid	гóрничная *f* (*decl as adj*)	gor-neech-na-ya
champagne	шампáнское *n* (*decl as adj*)	sham-pan-ska-yé
(by) chance	случáйно	sloo-chay-na
change *coins*	мéлочь *f*	myé-lach'
change (to) *clothes*	переодевáться *impf*, переодéться *pf*	pyé-ryé-a-dyé-vat'-sa, pyé-ryé-a-dyét'-sa
change (to) *money*, *article*, *etc.*	обмéнивать *impf*, обменя́ть *pf*	ab-myé-nee-vat', ab-myé-nyat'
change (to) *trains*	пересáживаться *impf*, пересéсть *pf*	pyé-ryé-sa-zhi-vat'-sa, pyé-ryé-syest'
charge	ценá *f*	tse-na
cheap	дешёвый	dyé-sho-viy
check (to)	проверя́ть *impf*, провéрить *pf*	pra-vyé-ryat', pra-vyé-reet'
cheek	щекá *f*	shyé-ka
cheque	чек *m*	chyék
cherry	ви́шня *f*	veesh-nya
chess	шáхматы *f pl*	shah-ma-ti
child	ребёнок *m* (*pl* дéти)	ryé-byo-nak (dyé-tee)
child's	дéтский	dyét-skeey

chill	просту́да *f*	pra-stoo-da
chin	подборо́док *m*	pad-ba-ro-dak
china	фарфо́р *m*	far-for
chocolate	шокола́д *m*	sha-ka-lat
choice	вы́бор *m*	vi-bar
choose (to)	выбира́ть *impf*, вы́брать *pf*	vi-bee-rat', vi-brat'
Christmas	Рождество́ *n*	razh-dyést-vo
church	це́рковь *f*	tser-kaf'
cigar	сига́ра *f*	see-ga-ra
cigarette	сигаре́та *f*	see-ga-ryé-ta
Russian type	папиро́са *f*	pa-pee-ro-sa
cinema	кино́ *m*	kee-no
(dress) circle	бельэта́ж *m*	byél'-e-tash
(upper) circle	балко́н *m*	bal-kon
circle *theatre*	я́рус *m*	ya-roos
circus	цирк *m*	tsirk
city	го́род *m*	go-rat
class	класс *m*	klass
clean	чи́стый	chees-tiy
clean (to)	чи́стить *impf*, по ~ *pf*	chee-steet', pa ~
clear	я́сный	yas-niy
clerk	слу́жащий *m* (*decl as adj*)	sloo-zha-sheey
cliff	обры́в *m*	ab-rif
climb (to)	поднима́ться *impf*, подня́ться *pf* (на + *acc*)	pad-nee-mat'-sa, pad-nyat'-sa (na)
cloakroom	гардеро́б *m*	gar-dyé-rop

clock	часы́ *m pl*	cha-si
close (to)	закрыва́ть *impf*, закры́ть *pf*	za-kri-vat', za-krit'
closed	закры́тый	za-kri-tiy
cloth	ткань *f*	tkan'
clothes	оде́жда *f*	a-dyézh-da
cloud	о́блако *n*	o-bla-ka
coach	авто́бус *m*	af-to-boos
coast	бе́рег *m*	byé-ryék
coat	пальто́ (*indecl*)	pal'-to
coat hanger	ве́шалка *f*	vyé-shal-ka
cockroach	тарака́н *m*	ta-ra-kan
(dialling) code	код *m*	kod
coffee	ко́фе *m* (*indecl*)	ko-fyé
coin	моне́та *f*	ma-nyé-ta
cold *adj*	холо́дный	ha-lod-niy
cold *medical*	просту́да *f*	pra-stoo-da
collar	воротни́к *m*	va-rat-neek
collar stud	за́понка *f*	za-pan-ka
collect (to)	собира́ть *impf*, собра́ть *pf*	sa-bee-rat', sa-brat'
colour	цвет *m*	tsvyet
comb	расчёска *f*	ras-chyos-ka
come (to)	приходи́ть *impf*, прийти́ *pf*	pree-ha-deet', preey-tee
comedy	коме́дия *f*	ka-myé-dee-ya
come in!	войди́те!	vay-dee-tyé
comfortable	удо́бный	oo-dob-niy
common	о́бщий	ob-sheey
communist *noun*	коммуни́ст *m*	kam-moo-neest

communist *adj*	коммунистúческий	kam-moo-nee-stee-chyés-keey
compartment	купé *n* (*indecl*)	koo-pe
compass	кóмпас *m*	kom-pas
complain (to)	жáловаться *impf*, по ~ *pf*	zha-la-vat'-sa, pa ~
complaint	жáлоба *f*	zha-la-ba
completely	совершéнно	sa-vyér-shen-na
computer	компьютер *m*	kam-pyoo-tyér
concert	концéрт *m*	kan-tsert
concert hall	концéртный зал *m*	kan-tsert-niy zal
condition	услóвие *n*	oo-slo-vee-yé
conductor *bus*	кондýктор *m*	kan-dook-tar
conductor *orchestra*	дирижёр *m*	dee-ree-zhor
congratulations!	поздравля́ю!	pa-zdrav-lya-yoo
connect (to)	свя́зывать *impf*, связáть *pf*	svya-zi-vat', svya-zat'
connection *train*, *etc.*	пересáдка *f*	pyé-ryé-sat-ka
constipation	запóр *m*	za-por
consul	кóнсул *m*	kon-sool
consulate	кóнсульство *n*	kon-sool'-stva
contact lenses	контáктные лúнзы *f pl*	kan-takt-ni-yé leen-zi
contain (to)	содержáть	sa-dyér-zhat'
contraceptives	противозачáточные срéдства *n pl*	pra-tee-va-za-cha-tach-ni-yé sryéd-stva
contrast	контрáст *m*	kan-trast
convenient	удóбный	oo-dob-niy
conversation	разговóр *m*	raz-ga-vor
cook *chef*	пóвар *m*	po-var

cook (to)	гото́вить *impf*, при ~ *pf*	ga-to-veet', pree ~
cool	прохла́дный	pra-hlat-niy
copy *book*	экземпля́р *m*	ek-zyém-plyar
copy *duplicate*	ко́пия *f*	ko-pee-ya
copy (to)	спи́сывать *impf*, списа́ть *pf*	spee-si-vat', spee-sat'
corkscrew	што́пор *m*	shto-par
corner	у́гол *m*	oo-gal
correct	пра́вильный	pra-veel'-niy
correspond (to)	перепи́сываться	pyé-ryé-pee-si-vat'-sa
corridor	коридо́р *m*	ka-ree-dor
cosmetics	косме́тика *f*	kas-myé-tee-ka
cost	цена́ *f*	tse-na
cost (to)	сто́ить	sto-eet'
cot	де́тская крова́тка *f*	dyét-ska-ya kra-vat-ka
cotton *thread*	ни́тка *f*	neet-ka
cotton wool	ва́та *f*	va-ta
couchette	жёсткое спа́льное ме́сто *n*	zhost-ka-yé spal'-na-yé myés-ta
cough	ка́шель *m*	ka-shel'
count (to)	счита́ть *impf*, по ~ *pf*	shee-tat', pa ~
country *nation*	страна́ *f*	stra-na
country *not town*	дере́вня *f*	dyé-ryév-nya
country house	да́ча *f*	da-cha
couple	па́ра *f*	pa-ra
coupon	тало́н *m*	ta-lon
course *dish*	блю́до *n*	blyoo-da
courtyard	двор *m*	dvor

cousin *female*	двою́родная сестра́ *f*	dva-yoo-rad-na-ya syés-tra
cousin *male*	двою́родный брат *m*	dva-yoo-rad-niy brat
cover	кры́шка *f*	krish-ka
cover (to)	покрыва́ть *impf*, покры́ть *pf*	pa-kri-vat', pa-krit'
cow	коро́ва *f*	ka-ro-va
cramp	су́дорога *f*	soo-da-ra-ga
crash *collision*	ава́рия	a-va-ree-ya
cream *milk*	сли́вки *f pl*	sleef-kee
cream *cosmetics*	крем *m*	kryém
credit card	креди́тная ка́рточка *f*	kryé-deet-na-ya kar-tach-ka
crew	экипа́ж *m*	e-kee-pazh
cross	крест *m*	kryést
cross (to)	переходи́ть *impf*, перейти́ *pf*	pyé-ryé-ha-deet', pyé-ryéy-tee
crossing	перехо́д *m*	pyé-ryé-hot
crossroads	перекрёсток *m*	pyé-ryé-kryos-tak
crowd	толпа́ *f*	tal-pa
crowded	перепо́лненный	pyé-ryé-pol-nyén-niy
cry (to) *shout*	крича́ть *impf*, кри́кнуть *pf*	kree-chat', kreek-noot'
cry (to) *weep*	пла́кать *impf*, за ~ *pf*	pla-kat', za ~
crystal	хруста́ль *m*	hroo-stal'
cup	ча́шка *f*	chash-ka
cupboard	шкаф *m*	shkaf
cure (to)	лечи́ть *impf*, вы́лечить *pf*	lyé-cheet', vi-lyé-cheet'
curious	любопы́тный	lyoo-ba-pit-niy

curl	завито́к *m*	za-vee-tok
(hard) currency	валю́та *f*	va-lyoo-ta
current *electric*	электри́ческий ток *m*	e-lyék-tree-chyés-keey tok
curtain	занаве́ска *f*	za-na-vyés-ka
curve	изги́б *m*	eez-geep
cushion	поду́шка *f*	pa-doosh-ka
custom	привы́чка *f*	pree-vich-ka
customs	тамо́жня *f*	ta-mozh-nya
customs officer	тамо́женник *m*	ta-mo-zhen-neek
cut	поре́з *m*	pa-ryez
cut (to) *trans*	ре́зать *impf*, на~ *pf*	ryé-zat', na~
cut (to) *oneself*	поре́заться	pa-ryé-zat'-sa
cutlet	котле́та *f*	kat-lyé-ta
cycling	езда́ *f* на велосипе́де	yez-da na vyé-la-see-pyé-dyé
cyclist	велосипеди́ст *m*	vyé-la-see-pyé-deest

D

daily	ежедне́вный	ye-zhe-dnyév-niy
damaged	неспра́вный	nyé-ees-prav-niy
damp	сыро́й	si-roy
dance	та́нец *m*	ta-nyéts
dance (to)	танцева́ть *impf*	tan-tse-vat'
danger!	опа́сно!	a-pas-na
dangerous	опа́сный	a-pas-niy
dark	тёмный	tyom-niy
date *appointment*	свида́ние *n*	svee-da-nee-yé
date *time*	число́ *n*	chees-lo
daughter	дочь *f* (*pl* до́чери)	doch' (do-chyé-ree)

day	день *m*	dyen'
dead	мёртвый	myort-viy
deaf	глухóй	gloo-hoy
dear	дорогóй	da-ra-goy
December	декáбрь *m*	dye-kabr'
decide (to)	решáть *impf*, решúть *pf*	ryé-shat', ryé-shit'
deck	пáлуба *f*	pa-loo-ba
deckchair	складнóе крéсло *n*	sklad-no-yé kryés-la
declare (to)	объявля́ть *impf*, объяви́ть *pf*	ab-yav-lyat', ab-ya-veet'
deep	глубóкий	gloo-bo-keey
delay	задéржка *f*	za-dyérzh-ka
delicious	вкýсный	fkoos-niy
deliver (to)	доставля́ть *impf*, достáвить *pf*	da-sta-vlyat', da-sta-veet'
delivery	достáвка *f*	da-staf-ka
dentist	зубнóй врач *m*	zoob-noy vrach
dentures	зубнóй протéз *m*	zoob-noy pra-tyéz
depart (to)	уезжáть *impf*, уéхать *pf*	oo-yéz-zhat', oo-yé-hat'
department	отдéл *m*	at-dyél
department store	универмáг *m*	oo-nee-vyér-mak
departure *aircraft*	отлёт *m*	at-lyot
departure *boat*	отплы́тие *n*	at-pli-tee-yé
departure *general*	отъéзд *m*	at-yézd
departure *train*	отхóд *m*	at-hot
dessert	десéрт *m*	dyé-syért
detour	объéзд *m*	ab-yézd
diabetic	диабéтик *m*	dee-a-byé-teek

dial (to)	набира́ть *impf*, набра́ть *pf* но́мер	**na-bee-rat'**, **na-brat' no-myér**
diamond	алма́з *m*	**al-maz**
diarrhoea	расстро́йство *n* желу́дка	**ras-stroy-stva zhe-loot-ka**
dice	игра́льная кость *f*	**ee-gral'-na-ya kost'**
dictionary	слова́рь *m*	**sla-var'**
diet	дие́та *f*	**dee-yé-ta**
diet (to)	соблюда́ть *impf*, соблюсти́ *pf* дие́ту	**sa-blyoo-dat'**, **sa-blyoos-tee dee-yé-too**
different	разный	**raz-niy**
difficult	тру́дный	**trood-niy**
dine (to)	обе́дать *impf*, по ~ *pf*	**a-byé-dat'**, **pa ~**
dining room	столо́вая *f* (*decl as adj*)	**sta-lo-va-ya**
dinner	обе́д *m*	**a-byéd**
direct	прямо́й	**prya-moy**
direction	направле́ние *n*	**na-prav-lyé-nee-yé**
director	нача́льник *m*	**na-chal'-neek**
dirty	гря́зный	**gryaz-niy**
disappointed	разочаро́ванный	**ra-za-cha-ro-van-niy**
dish	блю́до *n*	**blyoo-da**
disinfectant	дезинфици́рующее сре́дство *n*	**dyé-zin-fee-tsi-roo-yoo-she sryéd-stva**
distance	расстоя́ние *n*	**ras-sta-ya-nee-yé**
disturb (to)	беспоко́ить *impf*, по ~ *pf*	**byés-pa-ko-eet'**, **pa ~**
dive (to)	ныря́ть *impf*, нырну́ть *pf*	**ni-ryat'**, **nir-noot'**
diving board	трампли́н *m*	**tram-pleen**

divorce	развóд *m*	raz-vot
divorced	разведённый	raz-vyé-dyon-niy
do (to)	дéлать *impf*, с~ *pf*	dyé-lat', z~
doctor	врач *m*	vrach
dog	собáка *f*	sa-ba-ka
doll	кýкла *f*	koo-kla
dollar	дóллар *m*	dol-lar
dominoes	доминó (*indecl*)	da-mee-no
door	дверь *f*	dvyér'
double	двойнóй	dvoy-noy
down *motion*	вниз	fneez
downstairs *rest*	внизý	fnee-zoo
dozen	дю́жина *f*	dyoo-zhi-na
draughts	шáшки *f pl*	shash-kee
draw (to)	рисовáть *impf*, на~ *pf*	ree-sa-vat', na~
drawer	я́щик *m*	ya-sheek
drawing	рисýнок *m*	ree-soo-nak
dream	сон *m*	son
dress	плáтье *n*	pla-tyé
dressing gown	халáт *m*	ha-lat
dressmaker	портни́ха *f*	part-nee-ha
drink	напи́ток *m*	na-pee-tak
drink (to)	пить *impf*, вы́пить *pf*	peet', vi-peet'
drinking water	питьевáя водá *f*	pee-tyé-va-ya va-da
drive (to) *intrans*	éздить *impf*, съéздить *pf*	yéz-deet', s-yéz-deet'
drive (to) *car*	води́ть маши́ну	va-deet' ma-shi-noo
driver	води́тель *m*	va-dee-tyél'

driving licence	водительские права́ *n pl*	va-dee-tyél'-skee-yé pra-va
drop (to)	роня́ть *impf*, урони́ть *pf*	ra-nyat', oo-ra-neet'
drunk *adj/noun*	пья́ный	pya-niy
dry	сухо́й	soo-hoy
dry cleaner's	химчи́стка *f*	heem-cheest-ka
during	во вре́мя (+ *gen*)	vo vryé-mya
duvet	пододея́льник *m*	pad-a-dyé-yal'-neek
dye	кра́ска *f*	kras-ka

E

each	ка́ждый	kazh-diy
ear	у́хо *n* (*pl* у́ши)	oo-ha (oo-shi)
earache	боль в уша́х	bol' voo-shah
early	ра́но	ra-na
earrings	се́рьги *f pl*	syer'-gee
east	восто́к *m*	vas-tok
Easter	Па́сха *f*	pas-ha
easy	лёгкий	lyoh-keey
eat (to)	есть *impf*, съесть *pf*	yest', s-yést'
edge	край *m*	kray
egg	яйцо́ *n*	yay-tso
elastic	рези́нка *f*	ryé-zin-ka
elbow	ло́коть *m*	lo-kat'
electricity	электри́чество *n*	e-lyék-tree-chyést-va
electric point	розе́тка *f*	ra-zyét-ka
elevator	лифт *m*	leeft
embarrassed	смущённый	smoo-shyon-niy
embassy	посо́льство *n*	pa-sol'-stva

emergency exit	запа́сный вы́ход *m*	za-pas-niy vi-hat
emigrate (to)	эмигри́ровать	e-mee-gree-ra-vat’
empty	пусто́й	poo-stoy
end	коне́ц *m*	ka-nyéts
engaged	за́нятый	za-nya-tiy
engine	мото́р *m*	ma-tor
England	А́нглия *f*	an-glee-ya
English	англи́йский	an-gleey-skeey
Englishman	англича́нин	an-glee-cha-neen
Englishwoman	англича́нка	an-glee-chan-ka
enjoy (to)	наслажда́ться *impf*, наслади́ться *pf*	na-slazh-dat’-sa, na-sla-deet’-sa
enjoy oneself (to)	получа́ть *impf*, получи́ть *pf* удово́льствие	pa-loo-chat’, pa-loo-cheet’ oo-da-vol’-stvee-yé
enough	доста́точно	da-sta-tach-na
enter (to)	входи́ть *impf*, войти́ *pf* (в + *acc*)	vha-deet’, vay-tee (v)
entrance	вход *m*	vhot
entrance fee	входна́я пла́та *f*	fhad-na-ya pla-ta
envelope	конве́рт *m*	kan-vyért
equipment	обору́дование *n*	a-ba-roo-da-va-nee-yé
escalator	эскала́тор *m*	es-ka-la-tar
escape (to)	убега́ть *impf*, убежа́ть *pf* (из + *gen*)	oo-byé-gat’, oo-byé-zhat’ (eez)
Europe	Евро́па *f*	yé-vro-pa
even *opp. odd*	ро́вный	rov-niy
evening	ве́чер *m*	vyé-chyér
event	собы́тие *n*	sa-bi-tee-yé

every	ка́ждый	kazh-diy
everybody	все *pl*	vsyé
everything	всё *n sing*	vsyo
everywhere	везде́	vyéz-dyé
example	приме́р *m*	pree-myér
(for) example	наприме́р	na-pree-myér
excellent	отли́чный	at-leech-niy
except	кро́ме (+ *gen*)	kro-myé
excess	избы́ток *m*	eez-bi-tak
exchange bureau	обме́н *m* валю́ты	ab-myén va-lyoo-ti
exchange rate	валю́тный курс *m*	va-lyoot-niy koors
exciting	замеча́тельный	za-myé-cha-tyél-niy
excursion	экску́рсия *f*	ek-skoor-see-ya
excuse	извине́ние *n*	eez-vee-nyé-nee-yé
exhausted	переутомлённый	pyé-ryé-oo-tam-lyon-niy
exhibition	вы́ставка *f*	vi-staf-ka
exit	вы́ход *m*	vi-hat
expect (to)	ожида́ть	a-zhi-dat'
expensive	дорого́й	da-ra-goy
explain (to)	объясня́ть *impf*, объясни́ть *pf*	ab-yas-nyat', ab-yas-neet'
explanation	объясне́ние *n*	ab-yas-nyé-nee-yé
express letter	экспре́сс	ek-spryéss
extra	дополни́тельный	da-pal-nee-tyél'-niy
eye	глаз *m* (*pl* глаза́)	glass (gla-za)

F

fabric	ткань *f*	tkan'
fabric shop	магази́н *m* тка́ней	ma-ga-zeen tka-nyéy
face	лицо́ *n*	lee-tso

fact	факт *m*	fakt
factory		
heavy industry	заво́д *m*	za-vot
light industry	фа́брика *f*	fa-bree-ka
fade (to)	увяда́ть	oo-vya-dat'
faint (to)	теря́ть *impf*, по ~ *pf* сozна́ние	tyé-ryat', pa ~ saz-na-nee-yé
fair	белоку́рый	byé-la-koo-riy
fair *fête*	я́рмарка *f*	yar-mar-ka
fall (to)	па́дать *impf*, упа́сть *pf*	pa-dat', oo-past'
family	семья́ *f*	syé-mya
far	далеко́	da-lyé-ko
fare	сто́имость *f* прое́зда	sto-ee-mast' pra-yéz-da
farm *collective*	колхо́з *m*	kal-hoz
farther *adv*	да́льше	dal'-she
fashion	мо́да *f*	mo-da
fast *adv*	бы́стро	bis-tra
fast *train*	ско́рый	sko-riy
fat	то́лстый	tol-stiy
father	оте́ц *m*	a-tyéts
fault	вина́ *f*	vee-na
fear	страх *m*	strah
fear (to)	боя́ться	ba-yat'-sa
February	февра́ль *m*	fyé-vral'
feed (to)	корми́ть *impf*, на ~ *pf*	kar-meet', na ~
feeding bottle	буты́лка *f* для кормле́ния	boo-til-ka dlya karm-lyé-nee-ya
feel (to)	чу́вствовать	choof-stva-vat'

female *adj*	же́нский	zhen-skeey
fetch (to)	приноси́ть *impf*, принести́ *pf*	pree-na-seet', pree-nyés-tee
fever	лихора́дка *f*	le-ha-rat-ka
few	не́сколько (+*gen*)	nyé-skal'-ka
fiancé	жени́х *m*	zhe-neeh
fiancée	неве́ста *f*	nyé-vyés-ta
field	по́ле *n*	po-lyé
fight (to)	дра́ться *impf*, по~ *pf*	drat'-sa, pa~
fill (to)	наполня́ть *impf*, напо́лнить *pf*	na-pal-nyat', na-pol-neet'
fill in (to)	заполня́ть *impf*, запо́лнить *pf*	za-pal-nyat', za-pol-neet'
filling *tooth*	пло́мба *f*	plom-ba
film *cinema*	фильм *m*	feel'm
film *photo*	плёнка *f*	plyon-ka
find (to)	находи́ть *impf*, найти́ *pf*	na-ha-deet', nay-tee
fine	штраф *m*	shtraf
finger	па́лец *m*	pa-lyéts
finish (to)	конча́ть *impf*, ко́нчить *pf*	kan-chat', kon-cheet'
finished	зако́нченный	za-kon-chyén-niy
fire	пожа́р *m*	pa-zhar
fire escape	запа́сный вы́ход *m*	za-pas-niy vi-hat
fire extinguisher	огнетуши́тель *m*	ag-nyé-too-shi-tyél'
fireworks	фейерве́рк *m*	fyé-yér-vyérk
first	пе́рвый	pyér-viy
first aid	ско́рая по́мощь *f*	sko-ra-ya po-mash
first class	пе́рвый класс *m*	pyér-viy klass

fish	ры́ба *f*	ri-ba
fisherman	рыба́к *m*	ri-bak
fit *healthy*	здоро́вый	zda-ro-viy
fit (to)	хорошо́ сиде́ть	ha-ra-sho see-dyét'
flag	флаг *m*	flak
flat *adj*	пло́ский	plos-keey
flat *noun*	кварти́ра *f*	kvar-tee-ra
flavour	вкус *m*	fkoos
flight	рейс *m*, полёт *m*	reys, pa-lyot
float (to)	пла́вать *impf*, плыть *pf*	pla-vat', plit'
flood	наводне́ние *n*	na-vad-nyé-nee-yé
floor	пол *m*	pol
floor *storey*	эта́ж *m*	e-tash
flower	цвето́к *m*	tsvyé-tok
fly	му́ха *f*	moo-ha
fly (to)	лете́ть *impf*, по ~ *pf*	lyé-tyét', pa ~
fog	тума́н *m*	too-man
fold (to)	скла́дывать *impf*, сложи́ть *pf*	skla-di-vat', sla-zhit'
follow (to)	сле́довать (за + *instr*)	slyé-da-vat' (za)
food	еда́ *f*	yé-da
food poisoning	пищево́е отравле́ние *n*	pee-shyé-vo-yé at-rav-lyé-nee-yé
food store	магази́н *m* проду́ктов	ma-ga-zeen pra-dook-taf
foot	нога́ *f*	na-ga
footpath	тропи́нка *f*	tra-peen-ka
for	для (+ *gen*)	dlya

forbid (to)	запрещáть *impf*, запретить *pf*	za-pryé-shat', za-pryé-teet'
forehead	лоб *m*	lop
foreign	инострáнный	ee-na-stran-niy
forest	лес *m*	lyés
forget (to)	забывáть *impf*, забыть *pf*	za-bi-vat', za-bit'
fork	вилка *f*	veel-ka
forward *adv*	вперёд	fpyé-ryot
forward (to)	посылáть *impf*, послáть *pf*	pa-si-lat', pa-slat'
fountain	фонтáн *m*	fan-tan
fragile	хрýпкий	hroop-keey
France	Фрáнция *f*	fran-tsi-ya
free	свобóдный	sva-bod-niy
French	францýзский	fran-tsooz-skeey
fresh	свéжий	svyé-zhiy
fresh water	прéсная водá *f*	pryés-na-ya va-da
Friday	пятница *f*	pyat-nee-tsa
friend	друг *m*, подрýга *f*	drook, pa-droo-ga
friendly	дрýжеский	droo-zhes-keey
from *away from*	от (+ *gen*)	ot
from *out of*	из (+ *gen*)	eez
front	перéдняя сторонá *f*	pyé-ryéd-nya-ya sta-ra-na
in front of	пéред (+ *instr*)	pyé-ryét
frontier	граница *f*	gra-nee-tsa
frost	морóз *m*	ma-roz
frozen *food*	заморóженный	za-ma-ro-zhen-niy
frozen *person*	замёрзший	za-myorz-shiy

fruit	фрукт *m*	frookt
fruit juice	фрукто́вый сок *m*	frook-to-viy sok
frying-pan	сковорода́ *f*	ska-va-ra-da
full	по́лный	pol-niy
fun	весе́лье *n*	vyé-syé-lyé
funny	смешно́й	smyésh-noy
fur	мех *m*	myéh
furniture	ме́бель *f*	myé-byél'
further	да́льше	dal'-she
future *adj*	бу́дущий	boo-doo-sheey

G

game	игра́ *f*	ee-gra
garage	гара́ж *m*	ga-rash
garbage	му́сор *m*	moo-sar
garden	сад *m*	sat
gas	газ *m*	gas
gate	воро́та *pl*	va-ro-ta
gentlemen *toilet*	мужско́й туале́т *m*	moozh-skoy too-a-lyét
genuine	настоя́щий	na-sta-ya-sheey
get (to) *obtain*	достава́ть *impf*, доста́ть *pf*	da-sta-vat', da-stat'
get (to) *somewhere*	попада́ть *impf*, попа́сть *pf*	pa-pa-dat', pa-past'
get off (to)	сходи́ть *impf*, сойти́ *pf*	s-ha-deet', say-tee
get on (to)	сади́ться *impf*, сесть *pf* (на + *acc*)	sa-deet'-sa, syést' (na)
gift	пода́рок *m*	pa-da-rak
girdle	корсе́т *m*	kar-syét

girl *little*	де́вочка *f*	dyé-vach-ka
girl *young*	де́вушка *f*	dyé-voosh-ka
give (to)	дава́ть *impf*, дать *pf*	da-vat', dat'
glad	рад	rat
glass	стака́н *m*	sta-kan
glasses	очки́ *pl*	ach-kee
gloomy	мра́чный	mrach-niy
glorious	чуде́сный	choo-dyés-niy
glove	перча́тка *f*	pyér-chat-ka
go (to) *not on foot*	е́хать *impf*, по ~ *pf*	yé-hat', pa ~
go (to) *on foot*	идти́ *impf*, пойти́ *pf*	eet-tee, pay-tee
goal *football*	гол *m*	gol
God	Бог *m*	bog
gold	зо́лото *n*	zo-la-ta
gold plate	позоло́та *f*	pa-za-lo-ta
good	хоро́ший	ha-ro-shiy
government	прави́тельство *n*	pra-vee-tyél'-stva
granddaughter	вну́чка *f*	fnooch-ka
grandfather	де́душка *m* (*decl as f*)	dyé-doosh-ka
grandmother	ба́бушка *f*	ba-boosh-ka
grandson	внук *m*	fnook
grapes	виногра́д *m*	vee-na-grat
grass	трава́ *f*	tra-va
grateful	благода́рный	bla-ga-dar-niy
great	вели́кий	vyé-lee-keey
Great Britain	Великобрита́ния *f*	vyé-lee-ka-bree-ta-nee-ya
green	зелёный	zyé-lyo-niy
grey	се́рый	syé-riy
ground	земля́ *f*	zyém-lya
group	гру́ппа *f*	groop-pa

grow (to)	расти́ *impf*, вы́расти *pf*	ras-tee, vi-rastee
guarantee *noun*	гара́нтия *f*	ga-ran-tee-ya
guard *noun*	часово́й *m* (*decl as adj*)	cha-sa-voy
guest	гость *m*	gost'
guide	гид *m*	geet
guide book	путеводи́тель *m*	poo-tyé-va-dee-tyél'
guided tour	экску́рсия *f*	ek-skoor-see-ya

H

hail	град *m*	grat
it is hailing	идёт град	ee-dyot grat
hair	во́лосы *m pl*	vo-la-si
hair brush	щётка *f* для воло́с	shyot-ka dlya vo-las
hairgrip	зако́лка *f*	za-kol-ka
hairpin	шпи́лька *f*	shpeel'-ka
half	полови́на *f*	pa-la-vee-na
hammer	мо́лот *m*	mo-lat
hand	рука́ *f*	roo-ka
handbag	да́мская су́мка *f*	dam-ska-ya soom-ka
handkerchief	носово́й плато́к *m*	na-sa-voy pla-tok
handmade	ручно́й рабо́ты	rooch-noy ra-bo-ti
hang (to)	ве́шать *impf*, пове́сить *pf*	vyé-shat', pa-vyé-seet
hanger	ве́шалка *f*	vyé-shal-ka
happen (to)	случа́ться *impf*, случи́ться *pf*	sloo-chat'-sa, sloo-cheet'-sa
happy	счастли́вый	shas-lee-viy
happy birthday!	с днём рожде́ния!	sdnyom razh-dyé-nee-ya
harbour	га́вань *f*	ga-van'

hard	твёрдый	tvyor-diy
hard-currency shop	валю́тный магази́н *m*	va-lyoot-niy ma-ga-zeen
hardly	почти́	pach-tee
harmful	вре́дный	vryéd-niy
harmless	безопа́сный	byéz-a-pas-niy
hat	шля́па *f*	shlya-pa
have (to) *possess*	име́ть	ee-myét'
hay-fever	се́нная лихора́дка *f*	syén-na-ya lee-ha-rat-ka
he	он	on
head	голова́ *f*	ga-la-va
headache	головна́я боль *f*	ga-lav-na-ya bol'
headphones	нау́шники *m pl*	na-oosh-nee-kee
health	здоро́вье *n*	zda-ro-vyé
hear (to)	слы́шать *impf*, у ~ *pf*	sli-shat', oo ~
heart	се́рдце *n*	syérd-tse
heat	жара́ *f*	zha-ra
heating	отопле́ние *n*	a-ta-plyé-nee-yé
heavy	тяжёлый	tya-zho-liy
heel *foot*	пя́тка *f*	pyat-ka
heel *shoe*	каблу́к *m*	ka-blook
height	высота́ *f*	vi-sa-ta
helicopter	вертолёт *m*	vyér-ta-lyot
hello	здра́вствуйте	zdrast-vooy-tyé
help (to)	помога́ть *impf*, помо́чь *pf*	pa-ma-gat', pa-moch'
her	её	yé-yo
here	здесь	zdyés'
herring	сельдь *f*	syél'd'
high	высо́кий	vi-so-keey

hill	холм *m*	holm
hire (to)	брать *impf*, взять *pf* напрока́т	brat', vzyat' na-pra-kat
his	его́	yé-vo
history	исто́рия *f*	ees-to-ree-ya
hold (to)	держа́ть	dyér-zhat'
hole	дыра́ *f*	di-ra
holiday *celebration day*	пра́здник *m*	praz-neek
holiday *from work*	о́тпуск *m*	ot-poosk
holidays *school*	кани́кулы *m pl*	ka-nee-koo-li
hollow	пусто́й	poo-stoy
home	дом *m*	dom
(at) home	до́ма	do-ma
honeymoon	медо́вый ме́сяц *m*	myé-do-viy myé-syats
hope	наде́жда *f*	na-dyézh-da
hope (to)	наде́яться	na-dyé-yat-sa
horse	ло́шадь *f*	lo-shat'
horse race	ска́чки *m pl*	skach-kee
horse riding	верхова́я езда́ *f*	vyer-ha-va-ya yéz-da
hospital	больни́ца *f*	bal'-nee-tsa
host	хозя́ин *m*	ha-zya-een
hostel	общежи́тие *n*	ab-shé-zhi-tee-yé
hostess	хозя́йка *f*	ha-zyay-ka
hot	горя́чий	ga-rya-cheey
hotel	гости́ница *f*	ga-stee-nee-tsa
hotel manager	администра́тор *m*	ad-mee-nee-stra-tar
hot-water bottle	гре́лка *f*	gryél-ka
hour	час *m*	chas
house	дом *m*	dom
housewife	хозя́йка *f*	ha-zyay-ka

hovercraft	су́дно *n* на возду́шной поду́шке	sood-na na vaz-doosh-noy pa-doosh-kyé
how?	как?	kak?
how far?	как далеко́?	kak da-lyé-ko?
how much/many?	ско́лько?	skol'-ka?
hungry	голо́дный	ga-lot-niy
hurry (to)	спеши́ть	spyé-shit'
hurt (to) *intrans*	боле́ть	ba-lyét'
husband	муж *m*	moosh
hydrofoil	су́дно *n* на подво́дных кры́льях	sood-na na pad-vod-nih kri-lyah

I

I	я	ya
ice	лёд *m*	lyot
ice cream	моро́женое *n* (*decl as adj*)	ma-ro-zhe-na-yé
icon	ико́на *f*	ee-ko-na
identify (to)	опознава́ть *impf*, опозна́ть *pf*	a-paz-na-vat', a-paz-nat'
if	е́сли	yé-slee
ill	больно́й (*decl as adj*)	bal'-noy
illness	боле́знь *f*	ba-lyézn'
imagine (to)	представля́ть *impf*, предста́вить *pf* себе́	pryéd-sta-vlyat', pryéd-sta-veet' syé-byé
immediately	неме́дленно	nyé-myéd-lyén-na
important	ва́жный	vazh-niy
in, into	в (+ *loc*), в (+ *acc*)	v, v

include (to)	включа́ть *impf*, включи́ть *pf*	**fklyoo-chat', fklyoo-cheet'**
including	включа́я	**fklyoo-cha-ya**
incorrect	непра́вильный	**nyé-pra-veel'-niy**
independent	незави́симый	**nyé-za-vee-see-miy**
indigestion	несваре́ние *n* желу́дка	**nyé-sva-ryé-nee-yé zhe-loot-ka**
indoors	в до́ме	**fdo-myé**
industry	промы́шленность *f*	**pra-mi-shlyé-nast'**
inexpensive	недорого́й	**nyé-da-ra-goy**
infection	инфе́кция *f*	**een-fyék-tsi-ya**
inflammable	горю́чий	**ga-ryoo-cheey**
inflation	инфля́ция *f*	**een-flya-tsi-ya**
influenza	грипп *m*	**greepp**
information	информа́ция *f*, спра́вки *f pl*	**een-far-ma-tsi-ya, spraf-kee**
information bureau	спра́вочное бюро́ *n* (*indecl*)	**spra-vach-na-yé byoo-ro**
injection	инъе́кция *f*	**een-yek-tsi-ya**
ink	черни́ла *n pl*	**chyér-nee-la**
inquiries	спра́вки *f pl*	**spraf-kee**
insect	насеко́мое *n* (*decl as adj*)	**na-syé-ko-ma-yé**
inside	внутри́	**vnoo-tree**
instead of	вме́сто (+ *gen*)	**vmyés-ta**
instructor	инстру́ктор *m*	**een-strook-tar**
insurance	страхова́ние *n*	**stra-ha-va-nee-yé**
insure (to)	страхова́ть *impf*, за~ *pf*	**stra-ha-vat', za~**
interest	интере́с *m*	**een-tyé-ryés**

interested	заинтересо́ванный	za-een-tyé-ryé-so-van-niy
interesting	интере́сный	een-tyé-ryés-niy
international	междунаро́дный	myézh-doo-na-rot-niy
interpreter	перево́дчик *m*	pyé-ryé-vot-cheek
into	в (+ *acc*)	v
introduce (to)	знако́мить *impf*, по ~ *pf* (с + *instr*)	zna-ko-meet', pa ~ (s)
invitation	приглаше́ние *n*	pree-gla-she-nee-yé
invite (to)	приглаша́ть *impf*, пригласи́ть *pf*	pree-gla-shat', pree-gla-seet'
Ireland	Ирла́ндия *f*	eer-lan-dee-ya
Irish	ирла́ндский	eer-land-skeey
iron (to)	гла́дить *impf*, по ~ *pf*	gla-deet', pa ~
island	о́стров *m*	o-straf
Israel	Изра́иль *m*	eez-ra-eel'
it	э́то	é-ta

J

jacket *man's*	пиджа́к *m*	peed-zhak
jacket *outdoor*	ку́ртка *f*	koort-ka
January	янва́рь *m*	yan-var'
jar	ба́нка *f*	ban-ka
jelly fish	меду́за *f*	myé-doo-za
Jew	евре́й *m*	yé-vrey
jewellery	ювели́рные изде́лия *n pl*	yoo-vyé-leer-ni-yé eez-dyé-lee-ya
Jewess	евре́йка *f*	yé-vrey-ka
Jewish	евре́йский	yé-vrey-skeey
job	рабо́та *f*	ra-bo-ta
journey	пое́здка *f*	pa-yézd-ka

July	ию́ль *m*	ee-yool'
jump (to)	пры́гать *impf*, пры́гнуть *pf*	pri-gat', prig-noot'
jumper	дже́мпер *m*	dzhem-per
June	ию́нь *m*	ee-yoon'

K

keep (to)	держа́ть	dyer-zhat'
key	ключ *m*	klyooch
kind	до́брый	do-briy
king	коро́ль *m*	ka-rol'
kiss	поцелу́й *m*	pa-tse-looy
kiss (to)	целова́ть *impf*, по~ *pf*	tse-la-vat', pa~
kitchen	ку́хня *f*	kooh-nya
knee	коле́но *n*	ka-lyé-na
knickers, pants	трусы́ *pl*	troo-si
knife	нож *m*	nosh
knock (to)	стуча́ть *impf*, по~ *pf*	stoo-chat', pa~
know (to)	знать	znat'
Kremlin	кремль *m*	kryéml'

L

label	этике́тка *f*	e-tee-kyét-ka
lace	кру́жево *n*	kroo-zhe-va
ladies *toilet*	же́нский туале́т *m*	zhen-skeey too-a-lyét
lady	да́ма *f*	da-ma
lake	о́зеро *n*	o-zyé-ra
lamp	ла́мпа *f*	lam-pa
land	земля́ *f*	zyem-lya

landing	ле́стничная площа́дка *f*	lyest-neech-na-ya pla-shat-ka
landscape	пейза́ж ***m***	pyéy-zazh
lane	переу́лок ***m***	pyé-ryé-oo-lak
language	язы́к ***m***	ya-zik
large	большо́й	bal'-shoy
last	после́дний	pa-slyéd-neey
late	по́здно *adv*	poz-na
laugh (to)	смея́ться	smyé-yat'-sa
laundry *place*	пра́чечная *f* (*decl as adj*)	pra-chyésh-na-ya
lavatory	туале́т ***m***	too-a-lyét
lavatory paper	туале́тная бума́га *f*	too-a-lyét-na-ya boo-ma-ga
law	зако́н ***m***	za-kon
laxative	слаби́тельное ***n*** (*decl as adj*)	sla-bee-tyél'-na-yé
lead (to)	вести́	vyés-tee
leaf	лист ***m***	leest
leak	уте́чка *f*	oo-tyéch-ka
learn	узнава́ть *impf*, узна́ть *pf*	oo-zna-vat', oo-znat'
leather	ко́жа *f*	ko-zha
leave (to) *abandon*	оставля́ть *impf*, оста́вить *pf*	a-stav-lyat', a-sta-veet'
leave (to) *by transport*	уезжа́ть *impf*, уе́хать *pf*	oo-yéz-zhat', oo-yé-hat'
leave (to) *go away*	уходи́ть *impf*, уйти́ *pf*	ooy-ha-deet', ooy-tee
left *adj*	ле́вый	lyé-viy
(on the) left	нале́во	na-lyé-va

left luggage	ка́мера *f* хране́ния	ka-myé-ra hra-nyé-nee-ya
leg	нога́ *f*	na-ga
lemon	лимо́н *m*	lee-mon
lemonade	лимона́д *m*	lee-ma-nat
lend (to)	дава́ть *impf*, дать *pf* взаймы́	da-vat', dat' vzay-mi
length	длина́ *f*	dlee-na
less	ме́ньше	myen'-she
lesson	уро́к *m*	oo-rok
let (to) *allow*	позволя́ть *impf*, позво́лить *pf*	paz-va-lyat', paz-vo-leet'
let (to) *rent*	сдава́ть *impf*, сдать *pf*	sda-vat', sdat'
letter	письмо́ *n*	pees'-mo
library	библиоте́ка *f*	bee-blee-a-tyé-ka
licence *driving*	води́тельские права́ *n pl*	va-dee-tyél'-skee-yé pra-va
life	жизнь *f*	zhizn'
lifebelt	спаса́тельный круг *m*	spa-sa-tyél'-niy krook
lifeboat	спаса́тельная шлю́пка *f*	spa-sa-tyél'-na-ya shlyoop-ka
lifeguard	спаса́тель *m*	spa-sa-tyél'
lift	лифт *m*	leeft
light	свет *m*	svyét
light *bulb*	ла́мпочка *f*	lam-pach-ka
light *colour*	све́тлый	svyét-liy
light *weight*	лёгкий	lyoh-keey
lighter fuel	бензи́н для зажига́лки	byén-zeen dlya za-zhi-gal-kee

lighthouse	маяк *m*	ma-yak
lightning	мóлния *f*	mol-nee-ya
like (as)	как	kak
(I) like	мне нрáвится	mnyé nra-veet-sa
line	лúния *f*	lee-nee-ya
linen	бельё *n*	byé-lyo
lingerie	жéнское бельё *n*	zhen-ska-yé byé-lyo
lip	губá *f*	goo-ba
lipstick	губнáя помáда *f*	goob-na-ya pa-ma-da
liqueur	ликёр *m*	lee-kyor
liquid *adj*	жúдкий	zhid-keey
liquid *noun*	жúдкость *f*	zhid-kast'
listen	слýшать *impf*, по ~ *pf*	sloo-shat', pa ~
litre	литр *m*	leetr
little *adj*	мáленький	ma-lyén'-keey
little *noun*	немнóго (+ *gen*)	nyé-mno-ga
live (to)	жить	zhit'
local	мéстный	myés-niy
lock	замóк *m*	za-mok
lock (to)	запирáть *impf*, заперéть *pf*	za-pee-rat', za-pyé-ryét'
long	длúнный	dleen-niy
look at (to)	смотрéть *impf*, по ~ *pf* (на + *acc*)	smat-ryet', pa ~ (na)
look for (to)	искáть *impf*, по ~ *pf*	ee-skat', pa ~
look like (to)	быть похóжим (на + *acc*)	bit' pa-ho-zhim (na)
loose	свобóдный	sva-bod-niy
lorry	грузовúк *m*	groo-za-veek

lose (to) *trans*	теря́ть *impf*, по ~ *pf*	tyé-ryat', pa ~
lost-property office	бюро́ (*indecl*) нахо́док	byoo-ro na-ho-dak
(a) lot	мно́го (+ *gen*)	mno-ga
loud	гро́мкий	grom-keey
love	любо́вь *f*	lyoo-bof'
love (to)	люби́ть	lyoo-beet'
lovely	прекра́сный	pryé-kras-niy
low	ни́зкий	neez-keey
luggage	бага́ж *m*	ba-gash
lunch	обе́д *m*	a-byéd

M

mad	сумасше́дший	soo-ma-shed-shiy
magazine	журна́л *m*	zhoor-nal
maid	го́рничная *f* (*decl as adj*)	gor-neech-na-ya
mail	по́чта *f*	poch-ta
main street	гла́вная у́лица *f*	glav-na-ya oo-lee-tsa
make (to)	де́лать *impf*, с ~ *pf*	dyé-lat', s ~
make love (to)	занима́ться *impf*, заня́ться *pf* любо́вью	za-nee-mat'-sa, za-nyat'-sa lyoo-bo-vyoo
make-up	косме́тика *f*	kas-myé-tee-ka
male *adj*	мужско́й	moozh-skoy
man *general*	челове́к *m*	che-la-vyék
man *male*	мужчи́на *m* (*decl as f*)	moozh-shee-na
man-made *fabrics*	синтети́ческий	seen-tyé-tee-chyés-keey
manager *hotel*	администра́тор *m*	ad-mee-nee-stra-tar
manicure	маникю́р *m*	ma-nee-kyoor

many	мно́го (+ *gen*)	**mno-ga**
map *country*	ка́рта *f*	**kar-ta**
map *town*	план	**plan**
marble *noun*	мра́мор *m*	**mra-mar**
March	март *m*	**mart**
market	ры́нок *m*	**ri-nak**
married *of a man*	жена́тый	**zhe-na-tiy**
married *of a woman*	за́мужем (*indecl*)	**za-moo-zhem**
Mass	ме́сса *f*	**myés-sa**
match *light*	спи́чка *f*	**speech-ka**
match *sport*	матч *m*	**mach**
material	ткань *f*	**tkan'**
matinée	дневно́й спекта́кль *m*	**dnyév-noy spyék-takl'**
mattress	матра́ц *m*	**ma-trats**
mausoleum	мавзоле́й *m*	**mav-za-lyéy**
May	май *m*	**may**
maybe	мо́жет быть	**mo-zhet bit'**
me	меня́	**me-nya**
meal	еда́ *f*	**yé-da**
mean (to) *of person*	хоте́ть сказа́ть	**ha-tyét' ska-zat'**
mean (to) *of word*	зна́чить	**zna-cheet'**
measurements	разме́ры *m pl*	**raz-myé-ri**
meat	мя́со	**mya-sa**
medicine	лека́рство *n*	**lyé-karst-va**
meet (to) *trans*	встреча́ть *impf*, встре́тить *pf*	**vstryé-chat', vstryé-teet'**
meet (to) *intrans*	встреча́ться *impf*, встре́титься *pf* (с + *instr*)	**vstryé-chat'-sa, vstryé-teet'-sa (s)**

mend (to)	чини́ть *impf*, по ~ *pf*	chee-neet', pa ~
menstruation	менструа́ция *f*	myén-stroo-a-tsi-ya
mess	беспоря́док *m*	byés-pa-rya-dak
message	запи́ска *f*	za-pees-ka
metal	мета́лл *m*	myé-tal
metro	метро́ (*indecl*)	myé-tro
midday	по́лдень *m*	pol-dyén'
middle	середи́на *f*	syé-ryé-dee-na
middle-aged	сре́дних лет (*indecl*)	sryéd-neeh lyét
middle class *noun*	буржуази́я *f*	boor-zhoo-a-zee-ya
midnight	по́лночь *f*	pol-nach'
mild	мя́гкий	myah-keey
milk	молоко́ *n*	ma-la-ko
mineral water	минера́льная вода́ *f*	mee-nyé-ral'-na-ya va-da
minute	мину́та *f*	mee-noo-ta
mirror	зе́ркало *n*	zyér-ka-la
miss (to) *train*	опа́здывать *impf*, опозда́ть *pf* (на + *acc*)	a-paz-di-vat', a-paz-dat' (na)
mistake	оши́бка *f*	a-ship-ka
mix (to)	сме́шивать *impf*, смеша́ть *pf*	smyé-shi-vat', smyé-shat'
mixed	сме́шанный	smyé-shan-niy
modern	совреме́нный	sa-vryé-myén-niy
moment	моме́нт *m*	ma-myént
monastery	монасты́рь *m*	ma-nas-tir'
Monday	понеде́льник *m*	pa-nyé-dyél'-neek
money	де́ньги *f pl*	dyén'-gee
monk	мона́х *m*	ma-nah
month	ме́сяц *m*	myé-syats

monument	па́мятник *m*	pa-myat-neek
moon	луна́ *f*	loo-na
more	бо́льше (+ *gen*)	bol'-she
morning	у́тро *n*	oo-tra
mosque	мече́ть *f*	myé-chyét'
mosquito	кома́р *m*	ka-mar
most	большинство́ *n* (+ *gen*)	bal'-shin-stvo
mother	мать *f*	mat'
motor	мото́р *m*, дви́гатель *m*	ma-tor, dvee-ga-tyél'
motor bike	мотоци́кл *m*	ma-ta-tsikl
motor boat	мото́рная ло́дка *f*	ma-tor-na-ya lot-ka
motorway	автостра́да *f*	av-ta-stra-da
mountain	гора́ *f*	ga-ra
mouth	рот *m*	rot
move (to) *intrans*	дви́гаться *impf*, дви́нуться *pf*	dvee-gat'-sa, dvee-noot'-sa
much	мно́го (+ *gen*)	mno-ga
museum	музе́й *m*	moo-zyéy
music	му́зыка *f*	moo-zi-ka
must *to have to*		
I must	я до́лжен *m*, должна́ *f*	ya dol-zhen, ya-dalzh-na
you must	вы должны́ (+ *inf*)	vi dalzh-ni
mutton	бара́нина *f*	ba-ra-nee-na
my	мой *m*, моя́ *f*, моё *n*, мои́ *pl*	moy, ma-ya, ma-yo, ma-ee
myself *emphatic*	сам *m*, сама́ *f*	sam, sa-ma
myself *object*	себя́	se-bya

N

nail *finger, toe*	нóготь *m*	no-gat'
nail file	пи́лка *f* для ногтéй	peel-ka dlya nak-tyéy
nail polish	лак *m* для ногтéй	lak dlya nak-tyéy
name *forename*	и́мя *n*	ee-mya
name *surname*	фами́лия *f*	fa-mee-lee-ya
napkin	салфéтка *f*	sal-fyét-ka
nappy	пелёнка *f*	pyé-lyon-ka
narrow	у́зкий	ooz-keey
natural	естéственный	yés-tyést-vyé-niy
near (*prep*)	óколо (+ *gen*)	o-ka-la
nearly	почти́	pach-tee
necessary	нýжный	noozh-niy
it is necessary	нýжно (+ *inf*)	noozh-na
neck	шéя *f*	she-ya
necklace	ожерéлье *n*	a-zhe-ryé-lyé
need (to)	нуждáться (в + *loc*)	noozh-dat'-sa (v)
needle	иглá *f*	ee-gla
nephew	племя́нник *m*	plyé-myan-neek
never	никогдá	nee-kag-da
new	нóвый	no-viy
news	нóвости *f pl*	no-vas-tee
newsagent *kiosk*	газéтный киóск *m*	ga-zyét-niy kee-osk
distribution chain	'Союзпечáть' *f*	sa-yooz-pyé-chat'
newspaper	газéта *f*	ga-zyé-ta
newsreel	киножурнáл *m*	kee-na-zhoor-nal
New Year's Day	Нóвый год *m*	no-viy got
New Zealand	Нóвая Зелáндия *f*	no-va-ya zyé-lan-dee-ya
next	слéдующий	slyé-doo-shiy
niece	племя́нница *f*	plyé-myan-nee-tsa

night	ночь *f*	noch'
night bar	ночно́й бар *m*	nach-noy bar
nightdress	ночна́я руба́шка *f*	nach-na-ya roo-bash-ka
no	нет	nyét
nobody	никто́	nee-kto
noisy	шу́мный	shoom-niy
non-alcoholic	безалкого́льный	byéz-al-ka-gol'-niy
none	ни оди́н *m*, одна *f* одно́ *n*	nee a-deen, ad-na, ad-no
normal	обы́чный	a-bish-niy
north	се́вер *m*	syé-vyér
nose	нос *m*	nos
not	не	nyé
notebook	записна́я кни́жка *f*	za-pees-na-ya kneezh-ka
notes *money*	бума́жные де́ньги *m pl*	boo-mash-ni-yé dyen-gee
nothing	ничто́	nee-shto
notice	объявле́ние *n*	ab-yav-lyé-nee-yé
notice (to)	замеча́ть *impf*, заме́тить *pf*	za-myé-chat', za-myé-teet'
novel	рома́н *m*	ra-man
November	ноя́брь *m*	na-yabr'
now	тепе́рь	tyé-pyér'
number	но́мер *m*	no-myér
nurse	медсестра́ *f*	myéd-syés-tra
nylon *adj*	нейло́новый	nyéy-lo-na-viy

O

obtain (to)	получа́ть *impf*, получи́ть *pf*	pa-loo-chat', pa-loo-cheet'

occupation *job*	профе́ссия *f*	pra-fyés-see-ya
occupied	за́нятый	za-nya-tiy
ocean	океа́н *m*	a-kyé-an
October	октя́брь *m*	ak-tyabr'
odd *opp. even*	нечётный	nyé-chyot-niy
odd *strange*	стра́нный	stran-niy
of course	коне́чно	ka-nyésh-na
offer	предложе́ние *n*	pryéd-la-zhe-nee-yé
offer (to)	предлага́ть *impf*, предложи́ть *pf*	pryéd-la-gat', pryéd-la-zhit'
often	ча́сто	chas-ta
oil	ма́сло *n*	mas-la
oily	жи́рный	zhir-niy
ointment	мазь *f*	maz'
OK	ла́дно	lad-na
old	ста́рый	sta-riy
on, on to	на (+ *loc*), на (+ *acc*)	na, na
once	раз	raz
on foot	пешко́м	pyésh-kom
only *adv*	то́лько	tol'-ка
on time	во́-время	vo-vryé-mya
open	откры́то	at-kri-ta
open (to)	открыва́ть *impf*, откры́ть *pf*	at-kri-vat', at-krit'
open-air	на откры́том во́здухе	na at-kri-tam voz-doo-hyé
opera	о́пера *f*	o-pyé-ra
opera glasses	бино́кль *m*	bee-nokl'
opportunity	возмо́жность *f*	vaz-mozh-nast'
opposite	противополо́жный	pra-tee-va-pa-lozh-niy

optician's	óптика *f*	**op-tee-ka**
or	и́ли	**ee-lee**
orange *adj colour*	ора́нжевый	**a-ran-zhe-viy**
orange *noun fruit*	апельси́н *m*	**a-pyél'-seen**
orchestra	орке́стр *m*	**ar-kyéstr**
order (to)	зака́зывать *impf*, заказа́ть *pf*	**za-ka-zi-vat', za-ka-zat'**
ordinary	обыкнове́нный	**a-bik-na-vyén-niy**
other	друго́й	**droo-goy**
otherwise	ина́че	**ee-na-chyé**
our	наш *m*, на́ша *f*, на́ше *n*, на́ши *pl*	**nash, na-sha, na-she, na-shi**
out	из	**eez**
out of order	не в поря́дке	**nyé fpa-ryat-kyé**
outside *on the street*	на у́лице	**na-oo-lee-tse**
over *prep*	над (+ *instr*)	**nad**
overcoat	пальто́ *n* (*indecl*)	**pal'-to**
owe (to)	быть до́лжным	**bit'-dolzh-nim**
I owe him ...	я до́лжен/должна́ *f* ему́ ...	**ya dol-zhen/dalzh-na yé-moo ...**
you owe me ...	вы должны́ мне ...	**vi dalzh-ni mnyé ...**
owner	владе́лец *m*	**vla-dyé-lyéts**

P

pack (to) *luggage*	скла́дывать *impf*, сложи́ть *pf* чемода́н	**skla-di-vat', sla-zhit' chyé-ma-dan**
packet	паке́т *m*	**pa-kyét**
packet *of cigarettes*	па́чка *f*	**pach-ka**
page	страни́ца *f*	**stra-nee-tsa**

paid	упла́ченный	oo-pla-chyén-niy
pain	боль *f*	bol'
painkiller	болеутоля́ющее *n*	bo-lyé-oo-ta-lya-yoo-shyé-yé
paint (to) *house*	кра́сить *impf*, по ~ *pf*	kra-seet', pa ~
paint (to) *painting*	писа́ть *impf*, на ~	pee-sat', na ~
painter	худо́жник *m*	hoo-dozh-neek
painting	карти́на *f*	kar-tee-na
pair	па́ра *f*	pa-ra
palace	дворе́ц *m*	dva-ryéts
pale	бле́дный	blyéd-niy
paper	бума́га *f*	boo-ma-ga
parcel *large postal*	посы́лка *f*	pa-sil-ka
parcel *small postal*	бандеро́ль *f*	ban-dyé-rol'
parents	роди́тели *m pl*	ra-dee-tyé-lee
park (to)	ста́вить, по ~ маши́ну	sta-veet', pa ~ ma-shi-noo
park	парк *m*	park
part *actor's*	роль *f*	rol'
part *of something*	часть *f*	chast'
party	вечери́нка *f*	vyé-chyé-reen-ka
pass (to)	передава́ть *impf*, переда́ть *pf*	pyé-ryé-da-vat', pyé-ryé-dat'
passenger	пассажи́р *m*	pas-sa-zhir
passion	страсть *f*	strast'
passport	па́спорт *m*	pas-part
past *adj*	про́шлый	prosh-liy
path	тропи́нка *f*	tra-peen-ka
pavement	тротуа́р *m*	tra-too-ar
pay (to)	плати́ть *impf*, за ~ *pf*	pla-teet', za ~

payment	опла́та *f*	**a-pla-ta**
peace	мир *m*	**meer**
peach	пе́рсик *m*	**pyér-seek**
pear	гру́ша *f*	**groo-sha**
pearl	жемчу́жина *f*	**zhem-choo-zhi-na**
pedal	педа́ль *f*	**pyé-dal'**
pedestrian	пешехо́д *m*	**pyé-she-hot**
pedestrian crossing	перехо́д *m*	**pyé-ryé-hod**
pedestrian precinct	пешехо́дная зо́на *f*	**pyé-shyé-hod-na-ya zo-na**
pen	ру́чка *f*	**rooch-ka**
pencil	каранда́ш *m*	**ka-ran-dash**
penknife	перочи́нный нож *m*	**pyé-ra-cheen-niy nosh**
pensioner	пенсионе́р *m*	**pyén-see-a-nyér**
people	лю́ди *pl*	**lyoo-dee**
perfect	соверше́нный	**sa-vyér-shen-niy**
performance *theatre*	представле́ние *n*	**prýed-sta-vlyé-nee-yé**
perfume	духи́ *m pl*	**doo-hee**
perhaps	мо́жет быть	**mo-zhet bit'**
permission	разреше́ние *n*	**raz-ryé-she-nee-yé**
permit *noun*	разреше́ние *n*	**raz-ryé-she-nee-yé**
permit (to)	разреша́ть *impf*, разреши́ть *pf*	**raz-ryé-shat', raz-ryé-shit'**
person	челове́к *m*	**che-la-vyék**
personal	ли́чный	**leech-niy**
petrol	бензи́н *m*	**byén-zeen**
petrol can	бидо́н *m* для бензи́на	**bee-don dlya byén-zee-na**
petrol station	бензоколо́нка *f*	**byén-za-ka-lon-ka**
petticoat	ни́жняя ю́бка *f*	**neezh-nya-ya yoop-ka**

photograph	фотосни́мок *m*	fo-ta-snee-mak
photograph (to)	фотографи́ровать *impf*, с ~ *pf*	fa-ta-gra-fee-ra-vat', s ~
photographer	фото́граф *m*	fa-to-graf
pick (to) *choose*	выбира́ть *impf*, вы́брать *pf*	vi-bee-rat', vi-brat'
pick (to) *gather*	собира́ть *impf*, собра́ть *pf*	sa-bee-rat', sa-brat'
picnic	пикни́к *m*	peek-neek
piece	кусо́к *m*	koo-sok
pill	табле́тка *f*	ta-blyét-ka
pillow	поду́шка *f*	pa-doosh-ka
pin	була́вка *f*	boo-laf-ka
(safety) pin	англи́йская була́вка *f*	an-gleey-ska-ya boo-laf-ka
ping-pong	пинг-по́нг *m*	peeng-pong
pink	ро́зовый	ro-za-viy
pipe	тру́бка *f*	troop-ka
pity (to)	жале́ть *impf*, по ~ *pf*	zha-lyét', pa ~
place	ме́сто *n*	myés-ta
plain	просто́й	pra-stoy
plan	план *m*	plan
plant	расте́ние *n*	ras-tyé-nee-yé
plaster *adhesive*	пла́стырь *m*	plas-tir'
plastic *adj*	пластма́ссовый	plas-mas-sa-viy
plate	таре́лка *f*	ta-ryél-ka
platform	платфо́рма *f*	plat-for-ma
play (to)	игра́ть *impf*, сыгра́ть *pf*	ee-grat', si-grat'
play *theatre*	пье́са *f*	pyé-sa

player *in a game*	игрóк *m*	ee-grok
please	пожáлуйста	pa-zha-loo-sta
pleased	довóлен *m*, довóльна *f* (+ *instr*)	da-vo-lyén, da-vol'-na
plenty	мнóго (+ *gen*)	mno-ga
pliers	плоскогýбцы *m pl*	pla-ska-goop-tsi
plug *electric*	штéпсельная вúлка *f*	shtep-syél'-na-ya veel-ka
plug *washbasin*	прóбка *f*	prop-ka
plum	слúва *f*	slee-va
pocket	кармáн *m*	kar-man
poisonous	ядовúтый	ya-da-vee-tiy
policeman *militiaman*	милиционéр *m*	mee-lee-tsi-a-nyér
police station	отделéние *n* милúции	at-dyé-lyé-nee-yé mee-lee-tsi-ee
political	политúческий	pa-lee-tee-chyés-keey
politician	полúтик *m*	pa-lee-teek
politics	полúтика *f*	pa-lee-tee-ka
pollution	загрязнéние *n* окружáющей среды́	za-gryaz-nyé-nee-yé a-kroo-zha-yoo-shey sryé-di
pond	пруд *m*	prood
poor	бéдный	byéd-niy
popular	популя́рный	pa-poo-lyar-niy
port	порт *m*	port
porter	носúльщик *m*	na-seel'-sheek
possible	возмóжный	vaz-mozh-niy
post (to)	посылáть *impf*, послáть *pf*	pa-si-lat', pa-slat'
post box	почтóвый я́щик *m*	pach-to-viy ya-sheek

postcard	откры́тка *f*	at-krit-ka
poster	плака́т *m*	pla-kat
postman	почтальо́н *m*	pach-tal'-on
post office	по́чта *f*	poch-ta
poste restante	до востре́бования	da-vas-tryé-ba-va-nee-ya
postpone (to)	откла́дывать *impf*, отложи́ть *pf*	at-kla-di-vat', at-la-zhit'
pound	фунт *m*	foont
powder	порошо́к *m*	pa-ra-shok
prefer (to)	предпочита́ть *impf*, предпоче́сть *pf*	pryéd-pa-chee-tat', pryéd-pa-chyést'
pregnant	бере́менная *f*	byé-ryé-myé-na-ya
prepare (to)	приготовля́ть *impf*, пригото́вить *pf*	pree-ga-ta-vlyat', pree-ga-to-veet'
prescription	реце́пт *m*	ryé-tsept
present *gift*	пода́рок *m*	pa-da-rak
president	президе́нт *m*	pryé-zee-dyént
press (to) *iron*	гла́дить *impf*, по~ *pf*	gla-deet', pa~
pretty	краси́вый	kra-see-viy
price	цена́ *f*	tse-na
priest	свяще́нник *m*	svya-shyén-neek
prime minister	премье́р-мини́стр *m*	pryé-myér mee-neestr
print *photo*	отпеча́ток *m*	at-pyé-cha-tak
print (to)	печа́тать *impf*, на~ *pf*	pyé-cha-tat', na~
private	ча́стный	chas-niy
problem	пробле́ма *f*	pra-blyé-ma
profession	профе́ссия *f*	pra-fyés-see-ya
programme	програ́мма *f*	pra-gram-ma
promise	обеща́ние *n*	a-byé-sha-nee-yé

promise (to)	обещáть	a-byé-shat'
promptly	немéдленно	nyé-myéd-lyén-na
Protestant	протестáнтский	pra-tyés-tant-skeey
provide (to)	давáть *impf*, дать *pf*	da-vat', dat'
public *adj*	публи́чный	poo-bleech-niy
public holiday	прáздник *m*	praz-neek
pull (to)	тянýть *impf*, по ~ *pf*	tya-noot', pa ~
pump	насóс *m*	na-sos
pure	чи́стый	chees-tiy
purse	кошелёк *m*	ka-she-lyok
push (to)	толкáть *impf*, толкнýть *pf*	tal-kat', talk-noot'
put (to)	класть *impf*, положи́ть *pf*	klast', pa-la-zhit'
pyjamas	пижáма *f*	pee-zha-ma

Q

quality	кáчество *n*	ka-chyést-va
quantity	коли́чество *n*	ka-lee-chyést-va
quarter	чётверть *f*	chet-vyért'
queen	королéва *f*	ka-ra-lyé-va
question	вопрóс *m*	va-pros
queue	óчередь *f*	o-chyé-ryét'
queue (to)	стоя́ть *impf*, по ~ *pf* в óчереди	sta-yat', pa ~ vo-chyé-ryé-dee
quick	бы́стрый	bis-triy
quickly	бы́стро	bis-tra
quiet	совсéм	sav-syém
quite	ти́хий	tee-heey

R

race *athletics*	бег *m*	byék
racecourse	ипподрóм *m*	eep-pa-drom
races *horse*	скáчки *m pl*	skach-kee
racket	ракéтка *f*	ra-kyét-ka
radiator	радиáтор *m*	ra-dee-a-tar
radio	рáдио *n* (*indecl*)	ra-dee-o
railway	желéзная дорóга *f*	zhe-lyéz-na-ya da-ro-ga
rain	дождь *m*	dosht'
it is raining	идёт дождь	ee-dyot dosht'
raincoat	плащ *m*	plash
rare	рéдкий	ryéd-keey
rash *noun*	сыпь *f*	sip'
rather *adv*	скорéе	ska-ryé-yé
raw	сырóй	si-roy
razor	бри́тва *f*	breet-va
razor blades	лéзвия *n pl*	lyéz-vee-ya
reach (to)	достигáть *impf*, дости́гнуть *pf* (+*gen*)	da-stee-gat', da-steeg-noot'
read (to)	читáть *impf*, про ~ *pf*	chee-tat', pra ~
ready	готóвый	ga-to-viy
real	настоя́щий	na-sta-ya-sheey
really	действи́тельно	dyéy-stvee-tyél'-na
reason	причи́на *f*	preé-chee-na
receipt	квитáнция *f*	kvee-tan-tsi-ya
receive (to)	получáть *impf*, получи́ть *pf*	pa-loo-chat', pa-loo-cheet'
recent	недáвний	nyé-dav-niy
recipe	рецéпт *m*	ryé-tsept

recognize (to)	узнава́ть *impf*, узна́ть *pf*	oo-zna-vat', oo-znat'
recommend (to)	рекомендова́ть	ryé-ka-myén-da-vat'
record *music*	пласти́нка *f*	pla-steen-ka
record *sport*	реко́рд *m*	ryé-kort
record player	прои́грыватель *m*	pra-ee-gri-va-tyél'
red	кра́сный	kras-niy
refrigerator	холоди́льник *m*	ha-la-deel'-neek
region	о́бласть *f*	o-blast'
register (to) *a letter*	посыла́ть *impf*, посла́ть *pf* заказны́м	pa-si-lat', pa-slat' za-kaz-nim
register (to) *luggage*	сдава́ть в бага́ж	sda-vat' fba-gazh
registered letter	заказно́е письмо́ *n*	za-kaz-no-yé pees'-mo
relatives	ро́дственники *m pl*	rod-stvyén-nee-kee
religion	рели́гия *f*	ryé-lee-gee-ya
remember (to)	по́мнить *impf*, вс~ *pf*	pom-neet', vs~
rent	кварти́рная пла́та *f*	kvar-teer-na-ya- pla-ta
rent (to)	нанима́ть *impf*, наня́ть *pf*	na-nee-mat', na-nyat'
repair (to)	ремонти́ровать, от~	ryé-man-tee-ra-vat', at~
repeat (to)	повторя́ть *impf*, повтори́ть *pf*	paf-ta-ryat', paf-ta-reet'
reply (to)	отвеча́ть *impf*, отве́тить *pf*	at-vyé-chat', at-vyé-teet'
repression	репре́ссия *f*	ryé-pryés-see-ya
reservation	зака́з *m*	za-kaz
reserve (to)	зака́зывать *impf*, заказа́ть *pf*	za-ka-zi-vat', za-ka-zat'

reserved	зáнято	za-nya-ta
restaurant	ресторáн *m*	ryes-ta-ran
restaurant car	вагóн-ресторáн *m*	va-gon ryes-ta-ran
result	результáт *m*	ryé-zool'-tat
return (to) *give back*	возвращáть *impf*, вернýть *pf*	vaz-vra-shat', vyer-noot'
return (to) *go back*	возвращáться *impf*, вернýться *pf*	vaz-vra-shat'-sa, vyér-noot'-sa
reward	нагрáда *f*	na-gra-da
ribbon	лéнта *f*	lyén-ta
rich	богáтый	ba-ga-tiy
ride	прогýлка *f*	pra-gool-ka
ride (to) *horse*	éхать *impf*, по ~ *pf* верхóм	yé-hat', pa ~ vyér-hom
right *adj*	прáвый	pra-viy
right *adv*	прáвильно	pra-veel'-na
(on the) right	напрáво	na-pra-va
ring	кольцó *n*	kal'-tso
ripe	спéлый	spyé-liy
rise (to)	поднимáться *impf*, поднятáься *pf*	pad-nee-mat'-sa, pad-nyat'-sa
river	рекá *f*	ryé-ka
road *between towns*	дорóга *f*	da-ro-ga
road *within towns*	ýлица *f*	oo-lee-tsa
road map	дорóжная кáрта *f*	da-rozh-na-ya kar-ta
road sign	дорóжный знак *m*	da-rozh-niy znak
road works	ремóнтные рабóты *f pl*	ryé-mont-ni-yé ra-bo-ti
rock	скалá *f*	ska-la
roll *bread*	бýлочка *f*	boo-lach-ka

roof	кры́ша *f*	kri-sha
room	ко́мната *f*	kom-na-ta
rope	верёвка *f*	vyé-ryof-ka
rotten	гнило́й	gnee-loy
rough	гру́бый	groo-biy
round *adj*	кру́глый	kroo-gliy
row	ряд *m*	ryat
rowing boat	ло́дка *f*	lot-ka
rubber *eraser*	рези́нка *f*	ryé-zeen-ka
rubbish	му́сор *m*	moo-sar
rucksack	рюкза́к *m*	ryook-zak
rude	невéжливый	nyé-vyézh-lee-viy
ruin	разва́лина *f*	raz-va-lee-na
run (to) *car*, *etc.*	éздить	yéz-deet'
run (to) *engine*, *etc.*	рабо́тать	ra-bo-tat'
run (to) *person*	бежа́ть *impf*, по ~ *pf*	byé-zhat', pa ~
Russia	Росси́я *f*	ras-see-ya
Russian	ру́сский *m*	roos-skeey

S

sad	гру́стный	groos-niy
safe *secure*	безопа́сный	byé-za-pas-niy
safe *unharmed*	в безопа́сности (*indecl*)	fbyé-za-pas-nas-tee
sailor	моря́к *m*	ma-ryak
salad	сала́т *m*	sa-lat
salary	зарпла́та *f*	zar-pla-ta
(for) sale	в прода́же (*indecl*)	fpra-da-zhe
salesgirl	продавщи́ца *f*	pra-daf-shee-tsa
salesman	продавéц *m*	pra-da-vyéts

salt	соль *f*	sol'
salty/salted	солёный	sa-lyo-niy
same	тот же *m*, та же *f*, то же *n*	tot zhe, ta zhe, to zhe
sand	песо́к *m*	pyé-sok
sandals	санда́лии *f pl*	san-da-lee-ee
sandwich	бутербро́д *m*	boo-ter-brot
sanitary towels	гигиени́ческие салфе́тки *f pl*	gee-gyé-nee-chyés-kee-yé sal-fyét-kee
satisfactory	удовлетвори́тельный	oo-da-vlyét-va-ree-tyél'-niy
Saturday	суббо́та *f*	soob-bo-ta
saucepan	кастрю́ля *f*	ka-stryoo-lya
saucer	блю́дце *n*	blyood-tse
save (to) *money*	эконо́мить	e-ka-no-meet
save (to) *rescue*	спаса́ть *impf*, спасти́ *pf*	spa-sat', spa-stee
say (to)	говори́ть *impf*, сказа́ть *pf*	ga-va-reet', ska-zat'
scald oneself (to)	обва́риватся *impf*, обвари́ться *pf*	ab-va-ree-vat'-sa, ab-va-reet'-sa
scarf *long*	шарф *m*	sharf
(head) scarf	плато́к *m*	pla-tok
scenery	пейза́ж *m*	pyéy-zash
scent	духи́ *m pl*	doo-hee
school	шко́ла *f*	shko-la
scissors	но́жницы *pl*	nosh-nee-tsi
score	счёт *m*	shyot
Scotland	Шотла́ндия *f*	shat-lan-dee-ya
Scottish	шотла́ндский	shat-land-skeey

scratch (to)	цара́пать *impf*, цара́пнуть *pf*	tsa-ra-pat', tsa-rap-noot'
screw	винт *m*	veent
sculpture	скульпту́ра *f*	skool'p-too-ra
sea	мо́ре *n*	mo-ryé
seasickness	морска́я боле́знь *f*	mar-ska-ya ba-lyézn'
season	вре́мя *n* го́да	vryé-mya go-da
seat	ме́сто *n*, сиде́нье *n*	myés-ta, see-dyé-nyé
seat belt	реме́нь *m*	ryé-myén
second	второ́й	fta-roy
second *time*	секу́нда *f*	syé-koon-da
second class	второ́й класс *m*	fta-roy klass
second-hand	поде́ржанный	pa-dyér-zha-niy
see (to)	ви́деть *impf*, у~ *pf*	vee-dyét', oo~
seem (to)	каза́ться *impf*, по~ *pf*	ka-zat'-sa, pa~
self-service	самообслу́живание *n*	sa-ma-ab-sloo-zhi-va-nee-yé
sell (to)	продава́ть *impf*, прода́ть *pf*	pra-da-vat', pra-dat'
send (to)	посыла́ть *impf*, посла́ть *pf*	pa-si-lat', pa-slat'
separately	отде́льно	at-dyél'-na
September	сентя́брь *m*	syén-tyabr'
serve (to)	обслу́живать *impf*, обслужи́ть *pf*	ab-sloo-zhi-vat', ab-sloo-zhit'
service	обслу́живание *n*	ab-sloo-zhi-va-nee-yé
service *church*	слу́жба *f*	sloozh-ba
several	не́сколько (+ *gen*)	nyé-skal'-ka
sew (to)	шить *impf*, с~ *pf*	shit', s~

shade *of sun*	тень *f*	tyén'
shallow	мéлкий	myél'-keey
shampoo	шампýнь *m*	sham-poon'
shape	фóрма *f*	for-ma
share	разделя́ть *impf*, разделúть *pf*	raz-dyé-lyat', raz-dyé-leet'
sharp	óстрый	o-striy
shave oneself (to)	брúться *impf*, по ~ *pf*	breet'-sa, pa ~
shaving brush	кúсточка *f* для бритья́	kees-tach-ka dlya bree-tya
shaving cream	крем *m* для бритья́	kryém dlya bree-tya
shawl	шаль *f*	shal'
she	онá	a-na
sheet	простыня́ *f*	pra-sti-nya
shell	рáковина *f*	ra-ka-vee-na
shelter	приют *m*	pree-yoot
shine (to)	блестéть *impf*, блеснýть *pf*	blyé-styét', blyés-noot'
shingle	гáлька *f*	gal'-ka
ship *motor*	теплохóд *m*	tyé-pla-hot
ship *steamer*	парохóд *m*	pa-ra-hot
shirt	рубáшка *f*	roo-bash-ka
shock	удáр *m*	oo-dar
shoes *woman's*	тýфли *f pl*	too-flee
shoes *man's*	ботúнки *m pl*	ba-teen-kee
shoelaces	шнуркú *m pl*	shnoor-kee
shoe polish	крем *m* для чúстки óбуви	kryém dlya cheest-kee-o-boo-vee
shoe shop	обувнóй магазúн *m*	a-boof-noy ma-ga-zeen
shop	магазúн *m*	ma-ga-zeen

shore	бéрег *m*	**byé-ryék**
short	корóткий	**ka-rot-keey**
shorts	шóрты *pl*	**shor-ti**
shoulder	плечó *n*	**plyé-cho**
show *theatre*	спектáкль *m*	**spyék-takl'**
show (to)	покáзывать *impf*, покáзáть *pf*	**pa-ka-zi-vat', pa-ka-zat'**
shower	душ *m*	**doosh**
shut (to)	закрывáть *impf*, закры́ть *pf*	**za-kri-vat', za-krit'**
shut *past participle*	закры́то	**za-kri-ta**
sick (to be) *ill*	болéть	**ba-lyét'**
side	сторонá *f*	**sta-ra-na**
sidewalk	тротуáр *m*	**tra-too-ar**
sights	достопримечáтельности *f pl*	**da-sta-pree-myé-cha-tyél'-nas-tee**
sightseeing	осмóтр *m* достопримечáтельностей	**a-smotr da-sta-pree-myé-cha-tyél'-na-styéy**
sign	знак *m*	**znak**
sign (to)	подпи́сывать *impf*, подписáть *pf*	**pad-pee-si-vat', pad-pee-sat'**
signpost	указáтель *m*	**oo-ka-za-tyél'**
silver	серебрó *n*	**syé-ryé-bro**
simple	простóй	**pra-stoy**
since	с (+ *gen*)	**s**
sing (to)	петь *impf*, спеть *pf*	**pyét', spyét'**
single	одинóкий	**a-dee-no-keey**
sister	сестрá *f*	**syés-tra**
sit (to)	сидéть	**see-dyét'**

sit down (to)	сади́ться *impf*, сесть *pf*	sa-deet'-sa, syést'
size	разме́р *m*	raz-myér
skate (to)	ката́ться *impf*, по ~ *pf* на конька́х	ka-tat'-sa, pa ~ na kan'-kah
skates	коньки́ *m pl*	kan'-kee
skating rink	като́к *m*	ka-tok
ski (to)	ката́ться на лы́жах	ka-tat'-sa na li-zhah
skid (to)	заноси́ть *impf*, занести́ *pf*	za-na-seet', za-nyés-tee
skirt	ю́бка *f*	yoop-ka
skis	лы́жи *m pl*	li-zhi
sky	не́бо *n*	nyé-ba
sleep (to)	спать	spat'
sleeper	спа́льный ваго́н *m*	spal'-niy va-gon
sleeping bag	спа́льный мешо́к *m*	spal'-niy myé-shok
sleeve	рука́в *m*	roo-kaf
slice	кусо́к *m*	koo-sok
slip	комбина́ция *f*	kam-bee-na-tsi-ya
slippers	та́почки *f pl*	ta-pach-kee
slow	ме́дленный	myé-dlyén-niy
small	ма́ленький	ma-lyén'-keey
smart	наря́дный	na-ryad-niy
smell	за́пах *m*	za-pah
smell (to) *intrans*	па́хнуть	pah-noot'
smell (to) *trans*	ню́хать *impf*, по ~ *pf*	nyoo-hat', pa ~
smile (to)	улыба́ться *impf*, улыбну́ться *pf*	oo-li-bat'-sa, oo-lib-noot'-sa
smoke (to)	кури́ть *impf*, по ~ *pf*	koo-reet', pa ~
no smoking	не кури́ть	nyé koo-reet'

snack	заку́ска *f*	za-koos-ka
snack bar	буфе́т *m*	boo-fyét
snow	снег *m*	snyék
it is snowing	идёт снег	ee-dyot snyék
so	так	tak
soap	мы́ло *n*	mi-la
sober	тре́звый	tryéz-viy
socialism	социали́зм *m*	sa-tsi-a-leezm
socket	розе́тка *f*	ra-zyét-ka
socks	носки́ *m pl*	nas-kee
soda *water*	газиро́ванная вода́ *f*	ga-zee-ro-van-na-ya va-da
soft	мя́гкий	myah-keey
sold	про́дано	pro-da-na
sole *shoe*	подо́шва *f*	pa-dosh-va
solid	про́чный	proch-niy
some	не́сколько (+ *gen*)	nyé-skal'-ka
somebody	кто́-то	kto-ta
something	что́-то	shto-ta
sometimes	иногда́	ee-nag-da
somewhere	где́-то	gdyé-ta
son	сын *m*	sin
song	пе́сня *f*	pyés-nya
soon	ско́ро	sko-ra
sore throat	анги́на *f*	an-gee-na
sorry	винова́т	vee-na-vat
sort	сорт *m*	sort
sound	звук *m*	zvook
sour	ки́слый	kees-liy
south	юг *m*	yook

souvenir	сувени́р *m*	soo-vyé-neer
Soviet	сове́тский	sa-vyét-skeey
Soviet Union	Сове́тский Сою́з *m*	sa-vyét-skeey sa-yooz
space	простра́нство *n*	pra-stran-stva
spare *adj*	запа́сный	za-pas-niy
speak (to)	говори́ть	ga-va-reet'
speciality	специа́льность *f*	spyé-tsi-al'-nast'
spectacles	очки́ *m pl*	ach-kee
speed	ско́рость *f*	sko-rast'
speed limit	ограниче́ние *n* ско́рости	a-gra-nee-chyé-nee-yé sko-ras-tee
spend (to) *money*	тра́тить *impf*, ис~ *pf*	tra-teet', ees~
spend (to) *time*	проводи́ть *impf*, провести́ *pf*	pra-va-deet', pra-vyés-tee
spice	спе́ция *f*	spyé-tsi-ya
spine	спина́ *f*	spee-na
spoon	ло́жка *f*	losh-ka
sport	спорт *m*	sport
sportsman	спортсме́н *m*	sparts-myén
sprain (to)	растяну́ть *pf*	ras-tya-noot'
spring	весна́ *f*	vyés-na
square *adj*	квадра́тный	kva-drat-niy
square *in town*	пло́щадь *f*	plo-shat'
stadium	стадио́н *m*	sta-dee-on
stage	сце́на *f*	stse-na
stain	пятно́ *n*	pyat-no
stained	испа́чканный	ees-pach-kan-niy
stairs	ле́стница *f*	lyést-nee-tsa
stale	несве́жий	nye-svyé-zhiy
stale *bread*	чёрствый	chyorst-viy

stalls	парте́р *m*	par-ter
stamp	ма́рка *f*	mar-ka
stand (to)	стоя́ть	sta-yat'
start (to)	начинать *impf*, нача́ть *pf*	na-chee-nat', na-chat'
state *adj*	госуда́рственный	ga-soo-dar-stvyén-niy
state *noun*	госуда́рство *n*	ga-soo-dar-stva
station	ста́нция *f*	stan-tsi-ya
station *terminal*	вокза́л *m*	vag-zal
stationer's	магази́н *m* канцеля́рских това́ров	ma-ga-zeen kan-tse-lyar-skeeh ta-va-raf
statue	ста́туя *f*	sta-too-ya
stay (to)	остана́вливаться *impf*, останови́ться *pf*	a-sta-na-vlee-vat'-sa, a-sta-na-veet'-sa
step	шаг *m*	shak
steward	стю́ард *m*	styoo-ard
stewardess	стюарде́сса *f*	styoo-ar-des-sa
stick	па́лка *f*	pal-ka
stiff	жёсткий	zhost-keey
still *adj*	неподви́жный	nyé-pad-veezh-niy
still *adv*	ещё	yé-sho
sting	уку́с *m*	oo-koos
stockings	чулки́ *m pl*	chool-kee
stolen	укра́денный	oo-kra-dyén-niy
stomach	желу́док *m*	zhe-loo-dak
stomach-ache	боль *f* в желу́дке	bol' vzhe-lood-kyé
stone	ка́мень *m*	ka-myén'
stool	табуре́тка *f*	ta-boo-ryét-ka

stop *bus, etc.*	остано́вка *f*	a-sta-nof-ka
stop (to)	остана́вливаться *impf*, остановиться *pf*	a-sta-na-vlee-vat'-sa, a-sta-na-veet'-sa
store	магази́н *m*	ma-ga-zeen
storm	гроза́ *f*	gra-za
stove	плита́ *f*	plee-ta
straight	прямо́й	prya-moy
straight on	пря́мо	prya-ma
strange	стра́нный	stran-niy
strap	ремешо́к *m*	ryé-myé-shok
stream	руче́й *m*	roo-chyéy
street	у́лица *f*	oo-lee-tsa
street map	план *m* го́рода	plan go-ra-da
string	верёвка *f*	vyé-ryof-ka
strong *person*	си́льный	seel'-niy
strong *thing*	про́чный	proch-niy
student	студе́нт *m*, ~ка *f*	stoo-dyént, ~ka
study (to) *intrans*	учи́ться	oo-cheet'-sa
study (to) *trans*	изуча́ть	ee-zoo-chat'
style	стиль *m*	steel'
subject	те́ма *f*	tyé-ma
suburb	при́город *m*	pree-ga-rat
subway	подзе́мный перехо́д *m*	pad-zyém-niy pyé-ryé-hot
such	тако́й	ta-koy
suddenly	вдруг	fdroog
sugar	са́хар *m*	sa-har
suggestion	предложе́ние *n*	pryéd-la-zhe-nee-yé
suit	костю́м *m*	ka-styoom

suitcase	чемода́н *m*	chyé-ma-**dan**
summer	ле́то *n*	**lyé**-ta
sun	со́лнце *n*	**son**-tse
sunbathe (to)	принима́ть со́лнечную ва́нну	pree-nee-**mat'** sol-**nyéch**-noo-yoo **van**-noo
sunburn	зага́р *m*	za-**gar**
Sunday	воскресе́нье *n*	vas-krye-**syé**-nyé
sun-glasses	тёмные очки́ *pl*	**tyom**-ni-yé ach-**kee**
sunhat	пана́ма *f*	pa-**na**-ma
sunny	со́лнечный	**sol**-nyéch-niy
sunshade	зо́нтик *m*/тент *m*	**zon**-teek/**tyént**
sun-tan cream	крем *m* для зага́ра	**kryém** dlya za-**ga**-ra
supper	у́жин *m*	**oo**-zhin
sure	уве́ренный	oo-**vyé**-ryén-niy
surface mail	обы́чная по́чта *f*	a-**bish**-na-ya **poch**-ta
surgery	приёмная врача́	pree-**yom**-na-ya vra-**cha**
surgery hours	часы́ *m pl* приёма	cha-**si** pree-**yo**-ma
surprise (to)	удивля́ть *impf*, удиви́ть *pf*	oo-deev-**lyat'**, oo-dee-**veet'**
surroundings	окре́стности *f pl*	a-**kryést**-nas-tee
suspender belt	по́яс *m*	**po**-yas
sweat	пот *m*	**pot**
sweater	сви́тер *m*	**svee**-ter
sweet *adj*	сла́дкий	**slat**-keey
sweet *noun*	конфе́та *f*	kan-**fyé**-ta
swings	каче́ли *pl*	ka-**chyé**-lee
swim (to)	пла́вать	**pla**-vat'
swimming pool	пла́вательный бассе́йн *m*	**pla**-va-tyél'-niy bas-**syéyn**
switch *noun light*	выключа́тель *m*	vi-klyoo-**cha**-tyél'

swollen	опу́хший	a-pooh-shiy
synagogue	синаго́га *f*	see-na-go-ga

T

table	стол *m*	stol
tablecloth	ска́терть *f*	ska-tyért'
tablet	табле́тка *f*	ta-blyét-ka
table-tennis	насто́льный те́ннис *m*	na-stol'-niy tyén-nees
tailor	портно́й *m* (*decl as adj*)	part-noy
take (to)	брать *impf*, взять *pf*	brat', vzyat'
take (to) *medicine*	принима́ть *impf*, приня́ть *pf*	pree-nee-mat', pree-nyat'
talk (to)	разгова́ривать (с + *instr*)	raz-ga-va-ree-vat' (s)
tall	высо́кий	vi-so-keey
tampon	тампо́н *m*	tam-pon
tank	бак *m*	bak
tanned	загоре́лый	za-ga-ryé-liy
tap	кран *m*	kran
taste	вкус *m*	vkoos
taste (to)	про́бовать *impf*, по ~ *pf*	pro-ba-vat', pa ~
tax	нало́г *m*	na-lok
taxi	такси́ *n* (*indecl*)	tak-see
taxi rank	стоя́нка *f* такси́	sta-yan-ka tak-see
tea	чай *m*	chay
teach (to)	препodава́ть	pryé-pa-da-vat'
team	кома́нда *f*	ka-man-da
tear *rent*	проре́з *m*	pra-ryéz

tear (to)	рвáть *impf*, по~ *pf*	rvat', pa~
telegram	телегрáмма *f*	tyé-lyé-gram-ma
telephone	телефóн *m*	tyé-lyé-fon
telephone (to)	звонúть *impf*, по~ *pf* по телефóну	zva-neet', pa~ pa-tyé-lyé-fo-noo
telephone box	телефóн-автомáт *m*	tyé-lyé-fon af-ta-mat
telephone call	телефóнный звонóк *m*	tyé-lyé-fon-niy zva-nok
telephone directory	телефóнный спрáвочник *n*	tyé-lyé-fon-niy spra-vach-neek
telephone number	нóмер *m* телефóна	no-myér tyé-lyé-fo-na
telephone operator	телефонúстка *f*	tyé-lyé-fa-neest-ka
television set	телевúзор *m*	tyé-lyé-vee-zar
telex	телéкс *m*	tyé-lyéks
tell (to)	сказáть *pf*	ska-zat'
temperature	температýра *f*	tyém-pyé-ra-too-ra
temporary	врéменный	vryé-myén-niy
tennis	тéннис *m*	tyén-nees
tent	палáтка *f*	pa-lat-ka
tent peg	палáточный прикóлыш *m*	pa-la-tach-niy pree-ko-lish
terrace	террáса *f*	tyé-ras-sa
than	чем	chyém
thank you	спасúбо	spa-see-ba
that	тот *m*, та *f*, то *n*	tot, ta, to
theatre	теáтр *m*	tyé-atr
their	их	eeh
then	тогдá	tag-da
there	там	tam
there is/are	есть	yést'

thermometer	гра́дусник *m*	gra-doos-neek
these	э́ти	e-tee
they	они́	a-nee
thick	то́лстый	tol-stiy
thief	вор *m*	vor
thin	то́нкий	ton-keey
thing	вещь *f*	vyésh'
think (to)	ду́мать *impf*, по ~ *pf*	doo-mat', pa ~
thirsty (to be)	хоте́ть пить	ha-tyet' peet'
I am thirsty	я хочу́ пить	ya ha-choo peet'
this	э́тот *m*, э́та *f*, э́то *n*	e-tat, e-ta, e-ta
those	те	tyé
though	хотя́	ha-tya
thread	ни́тка *f*	neet-ka
throat	го́рло *n*	gor-la
through	че́рез (+ *acc*)	che-ryez
throw (to)	броса́ть *impf*, бро́сить *pf*	bra-sat', bro-seet'
thumb	большо́й па́лец *m*	bal'-shoy pa-lyéts
thunder	гром *m*	grom
Thursday	четве́рг *m*	chet-vyérg
ticket	биле́т *m*	bee-lyét
ticket office	ка́сса *f*	kas-sa
tide *high*	прили́в *m*	pree-leef
tide *low*	отли́в *m*	at-leef
tie	га́лстук *m*	gal-stook
tie *sport*	ра́вный счёт *m*	rav-niy shyot
tight	у́зкий	ooz-keey
tights	колго́тки *f pl*	kal-got-kee
time	вре́мя *n*	vryé-mya

timetable	расписа́ние *n*	ras-pee-sa-nee-yé
tin	консе́рвная ба́нка *f*	kan-syérv-na-ya ban-ka
tin opener	открыва́лка *f*	at-kri-val-ka
tip *for service*	чаевы́е *pl* (*decl as adj*)	cha-yé-vi-yé
tip (to)	дава́ть *impf*, дать *pf* на чай	da-vat', dat' na chay
tired (to be)	быть уста́лым	bit' oo-sta-lim
to	к (+ *dat*), в (+ *acc*), на (+ *acc*)	k, v, na
toast	тост	tost
tobacco	таба́к *m*	ta-bak
today	сего́дня	syé-vod-nya
toe	па́лец *m* ноги́	pa-lyéts na-gee
together	вме́сте	fmyés-tyé
toilet	туале́т *m*	too-a-lyét
toilet paper	туале́тная бума́га *f*	too-a-lyét-na-ya boo-ma-ga
tomorrow	за́втра	zav-tra
tongue	язы́к *m*	ya-zik
tonight	сего́дня ве́чером	syé-vod-nya vyé-che-ram
too *also*	та́кже	tak-zhe
too *exceedingly*	сли́шком	sleesh-kam
too much, many	сли́шком мно́го (+ *gen*)	sleesh-kam mno-ga
tooth	зуб *m*	zoop
toothache	зубна́я боль *f*	zoob-na-ya bol'
toothbrush	зубна́я щётка *f*	zoob-na-ya shyot-ka
toothpaste	зубная па́ста *f*	zoob-na-ya pas-ta
toothpick	зубочи́стка *f*	zoo-ba-cheest-ka

top	верх *m*	vyérh
torch	электри́ческий фона́рик *m*	e-lyék-tree-chyés-keey fa-na-reek
torn	по́рванный	por-van-niy
touch (to)	тро́гать *impf*, тро́нуть *pf*	tro-gat', tro-noot'
tour	экску́рсия *f*	ek-skoor-see-ya
tourist	тури́ст *m*, тури́стка *f*	too-reest, too-reest-ka
tourist office	бюро́ *n* тури́зма	byoo-ro too-reez-ma
towel	полоте́нце *n*	pa-la-tyén-tse
tower	ба́шня *f*	bash-nya
town	го́род *m*	go-rat
toy	игру́шка *f*	ee-groosh-ka
traffic	у́личное движе́ние *n*	oo-leech-na-yé dvee-zhe-nee-yé
traffic jam	про́бка *f*	prob-ka
traffic lights	светофо́р *m*	svyé-ta-for
tragedy	траге́дия *f*	tra-gyé-dee-ya
trailer	прице́п *m*	pree-tsep
train	по́езд *m*	po-yézt
tram	трамвай *m*	tram-vay
transfer (to)	де́лать *impf*, с~ *pf* переса́дку (на + асс)	dyé-lat', z~ pyé-ryé-sat-koo (na)
transit	транзи́т *m*	tran-zeet
translate (to)	переводи́ть *impf*, перевести́ *pf*	pyé-ryé-va-deet', pyé-ryé-vyés-tee
translation	перево́д *m*	pyé-ryé-vot
travel (to)	е́хать *impf*, по~ *pf*	yé-hat', pa~
traveller	путеше́ственник *m*	poo-tyé-shest-vyén-neek

traveller's cheque	доро́жный чек *m*	**da-rozh-niy chyék**
treat (to)	лечи́ть	**lyé-cheet'**
treatment	лече́ние *n*	**lyé-chyé-nee-yé**
tree	де́рево *n*	**dyé-ryé-va**
trim (to)	подстрига́ть *impf*, подстри́чь *pf*	**pad-stree-gat', pad-streech'**
trip	пое́здка *f*	**pa-yézd-ka**
trolleybus	тролле́йбус *m*	**tra-lyéy-boos**
trouble	неприя́тности *f pl*	**nyé-pree-yat-nas-tee**
trousers	брю́ки *pl*	**bryoo-kee**
true	пра́вильный	**pra-veel'-niy**
trunk *luggage*	сунду́к *m*	**soon-dook**
trunks *swimming*	пла́вки *m pl*	**plaf-kee**
trunks *underwear*	трусы́ *m pl*	**troo-si**
truth	пра́вда *f*	**prav-da**
try (to)	про́бовать *impf*, по~ *pf*	**pro-ba-vat', pa~**
try on (to)	примеря́ть *impf*, приме́рить *pf*	**pree-myé-ryat', pree-myé-reet'**
Tuesday	вто́рник *m*	**ftor-neek**
tunnel	тунне́ль *m*	**toon-nel'**
turn (to)	повора́чивать *impf*, поверну́ть *pf*	**pa-va-ra-chee-vat', pa-vyér-noot'**
turning	поворо́т *m*	**pa-va-rot**
tweezers	щи́пчики *m pl*	**sheep-chee-kee**
twisted	искривлённый	**ees-kree-vlyon-niy**
typewriter	пи́шущая маши́нка *f*	**pee-shoo-sha-ya ma-shin-ka**
typist	машини́стка *f*	**ma-shi-neest-ka**

U

ugly	некраси́вый	nyé-kra-**see**-viy
umbrella	зо́нтик *m*	**zon**-teek
uncle	дя́дя *m* (*decl as f*)	**dya**-dya
uncomfortable	неудо́бный	nyé-oo-**dob**-niy
unconscious	потеря́вший созна́ние	pa-tyé-**ryaf**-shiy saz-**na**-ni-yé
under	под (+ *instr*)	**pod**
underground *railway*	метро́ (*indecl*)	myé-**tro**
understand (to)	понима́ть *impf*, поня́ть *pf*	pa-nee-**mat'**, pa-**nyat'**
underwear	ни́жнее бельё *n*	**neezh**-nyé-yé byé-**lyo**
United States (U.S.A.)	Соединённые Шта́ты *pl* (США)	sa-yé-dee-**nyon**-ni-yé **shta**-ti (s-**sha**)
university	университе́т *m*	oo-nee-vyér-see-**tyét**
until	до (+ *gen*)	**do**
unusual	необы́чный	nyé-a-**bich**-niy
up	вверх	**vvyérh**
upstairs *rest*	наверху́	na-vyér-**hoo**
urgent	сро́чный	**sroch**-niy
us	нас	**nas**
use (to)	употребля́ть *impf*, употреби́ть *pf*	oo-pa-tryé-**blyat'**, oo-pa-tryé-**beet'**
useful	поле́зный	pa-**lyéz**-niy
useless	бесполе́зный	byés-pa-**lyéz**-niy
U.S.S.R.	СССР	es-es-es-**er**
usual	обы́чный	a-**bich**-niy

V

vacant	свобо́дный	sva-**bod**-niy
vacation	кани́кулы *pl*	ka-**nee**-koo-li

valid	действи́тельный	dyéy-stvee-tyél'-niy
valley	доли́на *f*	da-lee-na
valuable	це́нный	tsen-niy
value	це́нность *f*	tsen-nast'
variety show	варьете́ (*indecl*)	va-ryé-te
vase	ва́за *f*	va-za
veal	теля́тина *f*	tyé-lya-tee-na
vegetarian	вегетариа́нский	vyé-gyé-ta-ryan-skeey
vein	ве́на *f*	vyé-na
very	о́чень	o-chyén'
very little	о́чень немно́го (+ *gen*)	o-chyén' nyé-mno-ga
very much	о́чень мно́го (+ *gen*)	o-chyén' mno-ga
vest	ма́йка *f*	may-ka
view	вид *m*	veed
village	село́ *n*	syé-lo
violin	скри́пка *f*	skreep-ka
visa	ви́за *f*	vee-za
visibility	ви́димость *f*	vee-dee-mast'
visit (to)	посеща́ть *impf*, посети́ть *pf*	pa-syé-shat', pa-syé-teet'
voice	го́лос *m*	go-las
voltage	напряже́ние *n*	na-prya-zhe-nee-yé
voyage	путеше́ствие *n*	poo-tyé-shest-vee-yé

W

wait (to)	ждать *impf*, подожда́ть *pf*	zhdat', pa-dazh-dat'
waiter	официа́нт *m*	a-fee-tsi-ant
waiting room	зал *m* ожида́ния	zal a-zhi-da-nee-ya

waitress	официа́нтка *f*	a-fee-tsi-**ant**-ka
wake (to) *trans*	буди́ть *impf*, раз ~ *pf*	boo-**deet'**, raz ~
Wales	Уэ́льс *m*	oo-**el's**
walk	прогу́лка *f* пешко́м	pra-**gool**-ka pyésh-**kom**
walk (to)	идти́ *impf*, пойти́ *pf*	eet-**tee**, pay-**tee**
wall	стена́ *f*	styé-**na**
wall plug	розе́тка *f*	ra-**zyét**-ka
wallet	бума́жник *m*	boo-**mash**-neek
want (to)	хоте́ть	ha-**tyét'**
wardrobe	шкаф *m*	shkaf
warm	тёплый	**tyo**-pliy
wash (to) *clothes*	стира́ть *impf*, по ~ *pf*	stee-**rat'**, pa ~
wash (to) *oneself*	мы́ться *impf*, по ~ *pf*	**mit'**-sa, pa ~
washbasin	умыва́льник *m*	oo-mi-**val'**-neek
washing powder	стира́льный порошо́к *m*	stee-**ral'**-niy pa-ra-**shok**
watch	часы́ *m pl*	cha-**si**
water	вода́ *f*	va-**da**
waterfall	водопа́д *m*	va-da-**pad**
we	мы	mi
wear (to)	носи́ть	na-**seet'**
weather	пого́да *f*	pa-**go**-da
weather forecast	прогно́з *m* пого́ды	pra-**gnoz** pa-**go**-di
wedding ring	сва́дебное кольцо́ *n*	**sva**-dyéb-na-yé kal'-**tso**
Wednesday	среда́ *f*	sryé-**da**
week	неде́ля *f*	nyé-**dyé**-lya
weigh (to) *intrans*	ве́сить	**vyé**-seet'
Welsh	уэ́льский	oo-**el'**-skeey
west	за́пад *m*	**za**-pad
wet	мо́крый	**mo**-kriy

what?	что?	shto
wheel	колесó *n*	ka-lyé-so
wheelchair	инвали́дное крéсло *n*	een-va-leed-na-yé kryés-la
when?	когдá?	kag-da
where?	где?	gdyé
which	котóрый	ka-to-riy
which?	какóй? (*decl as adj*)	ka-koy
while	покá	pa-ka
white	бéлый	byé-liy
who?	кто?	kto
whole	цéлый	tse-liy
whose?	чей? *m*, чья? *f*, чьё? *n*, чьи? *pl*	chyéy. chya. chyo. chee
why?	почемý?	pa-chyé-moo
wide	ширóкий	shi-ro-keey
widow	вдовá *f*	vda-va
widower	вдовéц *m*	vda-vyéts
wife	женá *f*	zhe-na
wild	ди́кий	dee-keey
win (to)	выи́грывать *impf*, вы́играть *pf*	vi-ee-gri-vat', vi-ee-grat'
wind	вéтер *m*	vyé-tyér
window	oкнó *n*	ak-no
wine	винó *n*	vee-no
winter	зимá *f*	zee-ma
wish (to)	желáть *impf*, по ~ *pf*	zhe-lat', pa ~
with	с (+ *instr*)	s
without	без (+ *gen*)	byéz
woman	жéнщина *f*	zhen-shee-na

wonderful	чуде́сный	choo-dyés-niy
wood	лес *m*	lyés
wool	шерсть *f*	sherst'
word	сло́во *n*	slo-va
work	рабо́та *f*	ra-bo-ta
work (to)	рабо́тать	ra-bo-tat'
worry (to)	волнова́ться *impf*, вз ~ *pf*	val-na-vat'-sa, vz ~
worse	ху́же	hoo-zhe
worth (to be)	сто́ить	sto-eet'
wrap (to)	завёртывать *impf*, заверну́ть *pf*	za-vyor-ti-vat', za-vyer-noot'
wrist	запя́стье *n*	za-pyas-tyé
write (to)	писа́ть *impf*, на ~ *pf*	pee-sat', na ~
writing paper	почто́вая бума́га *f*	pach-to-va-ya boo-ma-ga
wrong	непра́вильный	nyé-pra-veel'-niy
it is wrong	непра́вильно	nyé-pra-veel'-na

Y

yacht	я́хта *f*	yah-ta
yard	двор *m*	dvor
year	год *m*	god
yellow	жёлтый	zhol-tiy
yes	да	da
yesterday	вчера́	fchyé-ra
yoghurt	простоква́ша *f*	pra-sta-kva-sha
you *sing/familiar*	ты	ti
you *pl/formal*	вы	vi
young	молодо́й	ma-la-doy

your *sing/familiar*	твой *m*, твоя́ *f*, твоё *n*, твои́ *pl*	tvoy, tva-ya, tva-yo, tva-ee
your *pl/formal*	ваш *m*, ва́ша *f*, ва́ше *n*, ва́ши *pl*	vash, va-sha, va-she, va-shi

Z

zoo	зоопа́рк *m*	zoo-park

NOTES